DESPERATE BARGAIN

OTHER BOOKS BY THE AUTHOR

Labor U.S.A.
Count Down In The Holyland

DESPERATE BARGAIN

Why Jimmy Hoffa Had to Die

Lester Velie

READER'S DIGEST PRESS

Distributed by
Thomas Y. Crowell Company
New York, 1977

Manufactured in the United States of America

LIBRARY OF CONGRESS CATALOGING IN PUBLICATION DATA
Velie, Lester.
  Desperate bargain.
  Includes index.
  1. Hoffa, James Riddle, 1913–   2. Organized
crime—United States. 3. Trade-unions—United States—
Officials and employees—Biography. I. Title.
HD6509.H6V44 1977   331.88'11'3883240924 [B]   77-12084
ISBN 0-88349-156-7

10   9   8   7   6   5   4   3   2   1

To those brave men and women
in the Teamsters who
are fighting for decent unionism
and so for all of us

CONTENTS

INTRODUCTION

THIS BOOK GREW out of a search for another man's identity—that of James R. Hoffa, the late president of the Teamsters—and much else, besides. The search began when I first met Hoffa in 1955. He was a ninth vice-president of the International Brotherhood of Teamsters at the time and little known outside his home base of Detroit.

As a magazine writer interested in Hoffa's rising star in the country's biggest and most powerful union, I had come to Chicago at Hoffa's invitation. He had let me watch him up close doing his job as a labor leader—settling members' grievances with employers, barking orders to subordinates over the telephone. We had talked on and off for several hours.

It was clear from the two days spent with Hoffa, then forty-three, that I was in the presence of a giant—in intellect, in energy, in will. But I was in the presence, too, of something else that wasn't as clear as his union role. For shadowing Hoffa—waiting for him outside meeting rooms, sitting beside him at meals, carrying his bag to the airport—was a Capone gang associate whom I had described in a prior article as a labor racketeer and looter of union welfare funds. What was this mobster to Hoffa? And what was Hoffa to the mobster and to the Chicago Capone gang?

Back home in New York to write the article, I tossed sleeplessly over the question: Who was Hoffa? Was he a labor leader? Or was he an underworld fox who had gotten in among the labor union chickens? Hoffa's full name was James Riddle Hoffa. My dilemma was reflected in the title of the article: ''The Riddle in the Middle of America's Most Powerful Union.''

Although I became a Hoffa watcher and wrote seventeen magazine articles about him over the next twenty years, a precise definition of who Hoffa was in the American scheme of things eluded me. One could depict Hoffa's many roles without synthesizing them into one overall key role.

Hoffa could be depicted as a man of violence surrounded by violence. He once told an interviewer that he had limited his family to two children because he feared an early, violent death. Awakened from a sound sleep, he would roll out of bed brandishing a revolver in one continuous motion of waking and preparing for invaders.

Hoffa was a man, too, with larger-than-life visions of power.

As a labor leader, he was not content to boss the country's biggest union—1,500,000 strong in his day—but saw himself as another John L. Lewis welding a labor federation of many millions. Booted out of the AFL-CIO, Hoffa allied himself with two major national unions to form an embryo rival federation. One of his allies, oddly enough, was the Mr. Clean of the labor movement, the late Walter Reuther, then head of the United Auto Workers. Only Hoffa's involvement in federal investigations and the courts prevented him from going on from there.

As a banker, Hoffa was not content to command millions of lendable funds in the Teamsters' biggest pension fund, but dreamed of using these funds to buy into and control major banks.

As a politician, Hoffa was not satisfied to elect judges and prosecutors in Detroit, but formed a national political organization to apply pressure on Washington's Capitol Hill.

When Hoffa disappeared in July 1975, I set out to discover the reasons behind the apparent gangland abduction and murder. For if I learned why it was necessary for the underworld to kill Hoffa, I might also learn who Hoffa really was. Seeking this answer, I went on to explore some little-known facts of underworld and upper-world life.

One of these facts is that the upper world uses the underworld to satisfy needs and provide services banned by its own upper-world laws. These range from mob-controlled bookies who permit the straight world to put down a bet on a horse, to dope pushers who sell cocaine to chic consumers on Manhattan's Upper East Side, to gangsters with union connections who arrange ''sweetheart'' deals for employers who want to chisel on their employees.

In turn, the underworld depends for its very existence on a host of upper-world intermediaries—lawyers and others who hide clandestine investments, bankers who launder hot money, labor leaders who sell union power. These go-betweens, not of the mobs but serving both worlds, form a "supermob."

Jim Hoffa turned out to be a major figure in this Supermob. As Teamster president, he had two constituencies: his members—and the gangsters whose muscle had helped him up the union ladder. Hoffa served his gangster constituency by wiring them into Teamster union power and Teamster union pension-fund cash. In his Supermob role, Hoffa probably did more to expand the affluence of the gangs and knit them into the fabric of American life than any gangster since Al Capone.

When Hoffa lost his Teamster presidency, he lost his role as Supermob's biggest figure. Of no further use to the mobs, Hoffa lived on borrowed time from the moment he left prison. Instead of a conduit to the upper world, he had become a menace. He could blow the whistle.

Lester Velie
New York, April 15, 1977

PART I

WHO KILLED JIMMY HOFFA?

Chapter One

DESPERATE BARGAIN

IN THE EARLY THIRTIES, precise date unknown, the Detroit Mafia put two youths, barely out of their teens, on trial for their lives. One was a chunky and cheeky kid by the name of Jimmy Hoffa, then starting his union career by organizing warehouse workers and truck drivers. The other was his close pal and companion-in-arms, Owen Bert Brennan.

Young Hoffa and his friend were interfering with Mafia business—the lucrative business, generously financed by trucking employers, of cracking skulls to prevent troublemakers from organizing a union to win a living wage.

Hoffa, as broad almost as he was tall, had used his own muscle and that of fellow organizers to break skulls right back. Hoffa had also turned to the Mafia's then Detroit rival, the Purple Gang, for additional muscle. In the street wars that followed, several Mafia "soldiers" had been killed.

Hoffa's Mafia judges, as he revealed to an intimate later, were "three old Italian men." The "court" was an office in a building that still houses vending-machine enterprises run by Detroit mobsters.

The charge was that Hoffa and his friend had spilled Mafia blood.

The penalty was death.

Did young Hoffa have anything to say?

He did. With the personal force and negotiating skill that were to take him far, Jim Hoffa convinced his Mafia judges that he was worth more to them alive than dead. For, alive, he could put union power at their disposal.

"Let live," young Hoffa argued in effect, "and we'll both live better." Impressed, the Mafia court let young Hoffa and his pal, Brennan, walk out—neither bloodied nor bowed.

Mafia trials leave no transcripts behind them, so it is not known precisely what was said or undertaken on either side. But it is clear from what followed that a bargain was struck and a commitment made. In return for future services, Hoffa would have both his life and new and powerful friends to help him on his way.

The promise of one's soul or life to an evil power in return for the satisfaction of an urgent need is so common to folklore that scholars have given it a name: "the desperate bargain."[1] Faust, the most famous of the desperate bargainers, signed away his soul to Mephistopheles in return for his lost youth and sexual powers. Hoffa made his desperate bargain just for power.

To James Riddle Hoffa, the mobs turned over the Teamster locals they controlled, so giving him his first push up the Teamster ladder. Ultimately, they provided a shortcut to the Teamster presidency.

From Hoffa, the mobs obtained golden union favors: Teamster power to police lucrative monopoly rackets; millions in commissions from the control of Teamster health and wel-

1. Alan R. Velie, *Shakespeare's Repentance Plays* (Rutherford, N.J.: Fairleigh Dickinson University Press, 1972).

fare insurance; even more millions in loans from the Teamsters' biggest pension fund.

In the summer of 1975, some four decades after his first Mafia trial, one or more Mafia judges seemingly tried Hoffa for a second time. Although this time Hoffa was not present, there were similarities between the two "trials" for, once again, Hoffa was without power and, once again, he was a man in the way. Now he was a threat to a vast and lucrative industry that sells union favors. In return for a payoff to a crooked union dealer, underworld fixers had been, for some time, arranging deals—sweetheart contracts—with employers who, thus, chiseled on Teamsters' wages and benefits. These even had their own special Teamster name: the "under-the-bonnet" deal from the British word *bonnet* for the hood of a car or trunk. To Hoffa, the sweetheart deal once had been one method of repaying gangsters for helping him up the union ladder. With Hoffa as a friend, gangsters or those associated with them had arranged deals, sold "labor peace," blocked and called off strikes—and prevented unionization altogether. During Hoffa's years as president of the Teamsters, gangsters with a pipeline to him had achieved new wealth and influence in their communities. Thanks to Hoffa, for instance, one lawyer, starting as an errand boy for gangsters, had gone on to become a nationally important labor-influence peddler. When I first met this young Chicago lawyer, Sydney Korshak, in 1948, he was carrying messages from the Chicago Capone gang to Willie Bioff, an imprisoned panderer-extortionist.

"Any message he [Korshak] might deliver to you is a message from us," Chicago Capone gangster "Cherry Nose" Gioe told Willie Bioff—so Bioff testified in the Hollywood extortion trial that sent seven Capone gangsters to jail.

When I ran into Korshak several years later, he was arranging deals with Hoffa that forced women mattress-factory workers to accept sweatshop wages—some 33 percent below the going factory wage at the time. And when *New York Times* reporter Seymour Hersh investigated Korshak in 1976, he found him serving some of the country's biggest corporations with "labor advice," enjoying a million-dollar yearly income and wealth beyond the dreams of avarice. In Korshak's Beverly Hills garage were eight family cars, among them two Cadillacs and two Mercedes Benzes.

Mysteriously, the McClellan Senate Rackets Committee of the late 1950s never fully explored Hoffa's relationship with Korshak. However, the Senate Rackets Committee did reveal widespread payoffs under Hoffa.

Fresh out of prison in 1971 and with Frank E. Fitzsimmons firmly in power as Teamster president, Hoffa was much like a politician out of office: a platform was needed to keep him in the public eye until he could run again. So Hoffa undertook to finance a prison-reform organization known as the National Association of Justice. He footed the outfit's $5,000-a-month expenses and served as its lecture star and television attraction. Ostensibly, Hoffa made the rounds of universities and other forums to preach prison reform. Actually, he met quietly with Teamster rank and filers, with local leaders and trucking employers whose eyes and ears kept Hoffa intimately in touch with the vast union's doings.

While traveling the country, Hoffa learned of the mammoth growth of the sweetheart-contract industry, finding that it had blossomed like an ugly weed.

Hoffa knew the anatomy of the under-the-bonnet deal as he knew the inside of his hand.

It had its outside men. These were respectable labor-relations lawyers, some of them former examiners for the National Labor Relations Board. Approached by a crooked employer seeking a deal, the lawyer—as Teamster jargon put it—"knew the hot buttons to push" to reach the industry's inside men. These were the fixers with lines both to the underworld and to the Teamsters. Where the trucking employer was big enough, he could make his own direct deal, usually with a Teamster higher-up.

Hoffa knew the geography of the sweetheart deal industry, too—where it flourished most. In the northern New Jersey union-and-racket fiefdom of Anthony "Tony Pro" Provenzano, truckers who were losing business to crooked competitors told Hoffa that fully 65 percent of all truckers were operating under soft deals. In the New Jersey–New York City area as a whole, it was estimated that 50 percent of all truck drivers were non-union or were working under subcontract conditions, as Teamster leaders turned their backs. In the Detroit area—where Anthony "Tony Jack" Giacalone was the man to see for a Teamster fix—in St. Louis, in Chicago, Atlanta, Miami, Hoffa learned that under-the-bonnet deals had reached forest-fire proportions. And rank and filers were being scorched.

Consider the case of Pat Corcoran (a pseudonym), an over-the-road driver for Terminal Transport Company, based in Atlanta. Pat paid full union dues, which, in 1977, came to $16 monthly. But Pat's employer did not provide him with the $100-odd weekly fringe benefits required by the standard contract. He was not protected by a pension, received none of the ten paid holidays, no sick leave and vacation, and no medical coverage.

Why?

Because Pat's local, No. 728, permitted Pat's boss to classify him as a "casual" worker. Since Pat had worked steadily for more than a year and since the standard Teamster contract stipulates that a casual worker becomes a permanent employee after thirty days, how could Pat be classified as a casual?

Easy. Terminal worked Pat (and other drivers) for twenty-seven or twenty-eight days, then fired and rehired him several days later. Once Pat compared notes with eleven other drivers for Terminal. All, he discovered, had been fired on the same day—a day in which the company was also busy hiring other drivers.

Who was the local Teamster leader who practiced this benign neglect of employer chiseling? It was no less than the executive assistant to Teamster president Frank Fitzsimmons— Weldon Mathis. He was simultaneously president of Pat Corcoran's Local 728 and an international vice-president.[2]

The use of casuals is but one of many ways to skin the Teamster driver. The simplest is to pay less than the standard hourly wage.

Simple arithmetic hints at the volume of cash that flowed into the industry from the deals arranged. Permitted to pay $1 an hour less than the standard Teamster contract, an employer with 100 drivers could reduce his payroll by $4,000 per week—$200,000 per year! So, for the lawyer-steerer there was a fat legal fee. For the crooked union man there was a bribe. And for the underworld fixer, there was a generous commission. One such fixer in Florida charged truckers 10 percent of their payroll to "handle their labor relations"—i.e., arrange a deal.

All this changed dramatically a decade after the McClellan hearings. Hoffa, the onetime purveyor of soft deals, became a tireless crusader against them. This turnaround had its roots in Hoffa's unending pursuit of greater and greater power.

In 1961, Hoffa had amended the Teamster constitution to pave the way for economic power that no other labor leader and, indeed, few other Americans could match. This was the power to cripple the country's economy by halting the country's wheels. Hoffa won this power by amending the Teamster constitution to permit him to replace the old local and regional

---

2. Although headquartered in Washington, D.C., and rarely in Atlanta, Mathis drew $20,800 as Local 728 president in 1975, plus another $61,000 from his other two jobs—a total of $81,800.

bargaining with national contract negotiations. As president, Hoffa had met with employer representatives of two hundred trucking associations from coast to coast. Out of their negotiations had evolved the Master Freight Agreement, which set wages for all Teamster truck drivers everywhere.

To Hoffa, the Master Freight Agreement was the achievement of his life, his masterpiece. It transformed him not only into an economic giant, but into a union giant as well. From a figurehead at Teamster headquarters who collected per capita dues from locals controlled by others, Hoffa became an awesome union figure who controlled all of his drivers' wages, pensions, and other benefits. The national contract bound rank-and-file drivers to "Jimmy" with a fierce loyalty, for it brought high wages to Teamsters in low-pay areas such as Mississippi and elsewhere as well as in high-pay areas like New York and California. The national agreement also permitted the mob-connected Hoffa to pose as a labor statesman of historic proportions.

In power, Hoffa had policed and protected the national agreement as a father would protect his own child—which, in Hoffa's case, it was. Under-the-bonnet deals that permitted an employer to chisel on the standard national contract had been out.

Employers recall that they could call Hoffa at any time of day or night to complain about a competitor who had bribed his way to a favored deal that violated the master agreement. Hoffa would call the regional Teamster vice-president and order him to "get on the ball." Rank and filers who were shortchanged by sweetheart deals could call Hoffa, too. He would interrupt meetings to take such calls, many of them collect. Indeed, Hoffa exerted so much time and energy enforcing the standard national agreement that accusations of sweetheart deals upset him as no other charge could. Once, while answering questions from economics students at the

Massachusetts Institute of Technology, Hoffa burst from the room, obviously in distress. A professor found Hoffa in the hall sobbing.

"They're accusing me of dealing in sweetheart contracts," Hoffa blurted.

True, special friends among employers—particularly among the giant trucking lines—had still been able to get favors from Hoffa. So had some underworld pals. But the under-the-bonnet deals that Hoffa had permitted were on a selective basis. As one New Jersey trucker estimated, such deals had not exceeded 5 percent of truckers' contracts.

How did Hoffa get away with this war against a major source of underworld income? Why didn't the gangsters to whom Hoffa owed his swift union rise eliminate him in the 1960s?

This, in fact, had been seriously considered.

"Let's grab that Jimmy Hoffa," Detroit Mafia boss Anthony "Tony Z" Zerilli had proposed to enforcer Tony Jack Giacalone in 1963.[3]

But the mob didn't "grab that Jimmy Hoffa" then. As Tony Giacalone had argued successfully, Hoffa was "our connection" with the Teamsters' biggest pension fund. So there were other important uses for him. He could pour millions of dollars in loans and finders' fees to gangsters. Hoffa could fulfill his obligations to both of his constituencies: to his members and his hoodlums.

Ten years later, as Hoffa fought to return to power after four years in prison, he could no longer offer the underworld an equally lucrative substitute for the sweetheart deal racket. A pension-reform law, policed by the Labor and Justice departments, was ending the wild and unwatched pension-fund lending of the past.

3. From FBI tapes of conversations between Tony Giacalone and his brother, Vito, in a Giacalone business office. Detroit *News,* Aug. 1, 1976.

This doomed Hoffa. During the last months of his life, he had to choose between the Teamster rank and file and the mobs. To keep his bargain with the underworld he would have to stand aside as his members were victimized. He would have to stand aside, too, as his masterpiece—the national Master Freight Agreement—was destroyed.

As Hoffa gathered evidence of crooked deals, it was clear that, if he were in power, Hoffa would not stand aside. And in his effort to return to power, he might even blow the whistle on the sweetheart contract racket. Thus Hoffa, who had served the underworld loyally for most of his adult life, was now a threat to it. He wanted out from his desperate bargain. But from this kind of bargain, as Hoffa found one fateful day in July 1975, there is but one exit—death.

Chapter Two

THE
LAST DAY

ON THE NIGHT of July 29, 1975, Jim Hoffa telephoned from his Lake Orion home to Las Vegas to talk to the man he trusted most, Morris Shenker. As a criminal lawyer who had defended the biggest names in mobdom, Shenker knew how to keep a secret. Four years before, Hoffa had entrusted Shenker with the drive to spring him from jail—a campaign that had some secrets of its own: the use of underworld millions, for instance, to win political clout for that effort.

Hoffa had also entrusted Shenker with more Teamster pension-fund loans than any other borrower, a whopping $160,000,000. With part of it, Shenker had acquired the Dunes, a gambling hotel. He had become one of Las Vegas' biggest figures and was suspected of knowing many Las Vegas secrets, including Hoffa's hidden ownership of hotels there.

For his part, Shenker described Hoffa as a "straight shoot-er," and liked to say he "knew Jimmy better than anyone else did."

Among the things that Shenker knew about Hoffa was that he didn't use the telephone frivolously. On the telephone he talked business. Tersely.

But now, "the Jimmy on the line wasn't the Jimmy I knew," Shenker recalled later. "He rambled. He made conversation. He wanted to know about a room in Las Vegas in case he came out. As if Jimmy had to worry about a room anywhere in Las Vegas!

"I sensed he had something on his mind," Shenker recalled. "He seemed on the verge of telling me something. Perhaps he didn't trust the telephone."

The something that Hoffa couldn't trust to the telephone was his expected rendezvous the next day with Tony Pro Provenzano and Tony Jack Giacalone. Hoffa daily awaited an appeals court decision that he hoped would rid him of the restraints against union activity that his conditional pardon had imposed on him. The meeting with Giacalone and Provenzano could be a peace parley to work out a compromise through which Hoffa could resume some union activity. But it could also be a trap. Seemingly, Hoffa sensed danger. He wanted to talk to his old trusted counselor about it.

Hoffa had lived in the shadow of death most of his working life. He once told two authors at work on a book about him that he had limited his family to two children because he feared an early, violent death.[1] Hoffa had almost lost his life when the Mafia tried him in the 1930s. In 1964, when Hoffa was fifty-two, gangsters had again considered eliminating him, this time because of apparent dissatisfaction with his services to them.

Now, some nine years later, Hoffa apparently had been tried by Mafia judges a third time. Triple jeopardy.

The next morning Hoffa was as troubled as he had been on the telephone with Shenker the night before. He liked to fix his grandchildren's toys at a workbench in his two-and-a-half-story summer home, situated on Big Square Lake in Michigan

---

1. Ralph C. and Estelle James, *Hoffa and the Teamsters* (New York: Van Nostrand, 1965).

(with the post office address of Lake Orion). Here he kept things shipshape: each tool had its place and, at day's end, the bench was as neat as at the day's beginning. But on this Wednesday, July 30, Hoffa left tools and parts of toys scattered all over the workbench.

Usually an untroubled sleeper, Hoffa had slept fitfully during the night. Although he was an early riser who was sometimes seen mowing his lawn as early as 6 A.M., this day he lingered in bed. On rising, he did his customary thirty pushups and downed a breakfast that rarely changed: a half grapefruit, two soft-boiled eggs, and tea—no coffee.

At 8 A.M., Hoffa called around to Teamster friends, getting information, keeping abreast of union events. For the next several hours he did as he always did when he was at his summer place—he worked with his hands and back. Hoffa had been his own carpenter in adding a kitchen wing to his summer place. The home was surrounded by an aluminum picket fence and lay on some seven acres of grounds dotted by stone statuary of deer, squirrels, and other fauna. Here Hoffa mowed the lawn, chopped wood, and drained water when Big Square Lake overflowed in the spring; or repaired the slides and swings he had put up for his three grandchildren: young Jim's Geoffrey and David and daughter Barbara Crancer's Barbara Jo.

Near noon, Hoffa changed into blue slacks and a blue pull-over knit shirt. He told his wife, Josephine, that he was going out to meet with "Tony Jack and a couple of other guys."

To Josephine Hoffa, this news was no cause for concern. Giacalone had been over to see Hoffa the week before to discuss Giacalone's forthcoming tax-evasion trial. The men had parted amicably.

Hoffa climbed into his green 1974 Pontiac two-door hardtop, drove past a mailbox bearing a decal of a horse and coach—but no name—and down the private road that led away from his home. He headed south for his rendezvous at the Machus Red Fox Restaurant, some four miles from Detroit's city limits and nineteen miles from his summer place.

On his way, Hoffa stopped off at the Pontiac offices of an airport limousine service in which he was a secret partner. Here, he asked for his partner, Louis Linteau, an old friend and a companion-in-arms. While heading a Pontiac Teamster local, Linteau had gone to prison for extorting a bribe from an employer. When Linteau emerged, Hoffa had used muscle to reinstate him, according to Senate testimony, and to keep him in office over the objections of the local's members.

It was Linteau who had served as an intermediary in setting up the rendezvous with Giacalone and Provenzano. Giacalone had telephoned Linteau a week before and asked him to arrange the meeting. Linteau had done so. Now, apparently, Hoffa had some last-minute questions about it.

Louis Linteau was out when Hoffa arrived. Hoffa told several employees at the limousine service where he was going and whom he was going to meet. Under hypnosis later, they remembered the names Hoffa had mentioned: Tony Provenzano, Anthony "Tony Jack" Giacalone, and a man named Lenny. This was probably Lenny Schultz, a labor consultant who had served time for extortion.

At 2:30 P.M., an exasperated Hoffa called home to ask his wife whether Tony Jack had phoned. He had not.

About an hour later still, Hoffa called his partner, Linteau, and this time found him in.

"Where the hell's Giacalone," Hoffa said. "He stood me up." That was the last time Linteau—or any of Hoffa's family or friends—ever heard from Jimmy Hoffa.

Who killed Jimmy Hoffa?

How?

And where did the body of that restive little giant come to rest?

Chapter Three

CHUCKIE O'BRIEN

FOR CHUCKIE O'BRIEN, Wednesday, July 30, 1975, began with a problem. He needed a car. A secretary at Hoffa's old home local, No. 299, had called to say that an iced twenty-four-pound salmon had arrived by mail. Would Chuckie deliver it to the man to whom it was addressed—regional Teamster vice-president Bobby Holmes?

Although Chuckie wore two hats, that of business agent for Detroit Local 299 and that of general organizer for the Teamsters International, no car seemed to be available to him at the union hall. His own had been left behind at Hallandale, Florida, where Chuckie regularly had his headquarters. Chuckie couldn't rent one, because his credit cards had been lifted by the Teamsters' Washington headquarters.

Chuckie called his boyhood pal, Joey Giacalone, son of Tony Jack, the Detroit Mafia's enforcer. It seemed a natural enough thing to do: Chuckie was as close to the Giacalones as he was to the Hoffas. He called Tony Jack "Uncle Tony," and was at the Giacalone home a good deal. Chuckie's mother, Sylvia O'Brien Paris, provided another link to the Giacalones.

She had met Tony Giacalone through the Hoffas. When her second husband, John Paris, died, Chuckie's mother sought solace from Tony Jack. As an FBI electronic bug planted in a Giacalone business office later revealed, Sylvia Paris became Tony Giacalone's mistress. He set her up in an apartment and, until her death in 1970, was an almost daily visitor there.

Chuckie used Joey Giacalone's maroon Mercury to deliver the salmon. What else he did with the car that day, or what others did with it, became a matter of deep interest to local and federal investigators. And so did Chuckie.

Hoffa had known and cared for Chuckie O'Brien ever since Sylvia O'Brien Paris, the widow of a Kansas City underworld figure, had brought Chuckie to Detroit at about the age of nine. She met the Hoffas through her second husband, a union leader. Sylvia Paris and Josephine Hoffa became inseparable.

Hoffa, in turn, took a shine to young Chuckie, who seemed to remind Hoffa of himself as a kid. Chuckie was small but sturdy, fast with his tongue and fast with his fists.

Chuckie and his mother became a part of the Hoffa's family life. Chuckie played on the streets of Detroit's west side with Hoffa's son, "little Jim." Chuckie took to calling Hoffa "Dad." When Hoffa became Teamster president in 1957 and left for Washington, Chuckie and his mother moved into the Hoffa family's west side home. And when Hoffa traveled on his rounds to locals around the country, he liked to take Chuckie along, school sessions permitting.

At seventeen, when Chuckie could no longer abide school, Hoffa named him a business agent for Local 299. Thereafter, Chuckie—now a barrel-chested youth of five feet eight—was constantly at Hoffa's side, serving him as a bodyguard, companion, and disciple. He stood guard before hotel room doors as Hoffa conferred inside. Often, it was Chuckie alone who accompanied Hoffa on trouble-shooting flights. During Hoffa's three criminal trials, Chuckie was never far from him.

Once, when a demented youth peppered Hoffa with a pellet gun, Chuckie leaped on the youth and pummeled him—after Hoffa knocked him down.

Chuckie liked to tell friends that he was the union-leader son Hoffa had always wanted but didn't have in his own son, James P. Hoffa. Indeed, Hoffa showed Chuckie such affection and concern that veteran Teamsters around Detroit began to speculate whether Chuckie wasn't Hoffa's bastard son. One of Hoffa's last chores, for instance, before going off to prison was to call in Chuckie for a special good-bye.

"I want to make sure you'll be cared for for the rest of your life," Hoffa told Chuckie. Hoffa named him a "general organizer"—an International payroll job whose chief function seems to be to serve the political purposes of the Teamster president. With this job went a $20,000 salary, plus unlimited expenses. With it, too, went participation in a generous pension program for employees of the International—the same program that was later to yield Hoffa a $1,700,000 cash settlement. Since Chuckie was already a Local 299 business agent at $8,400 a year, he was now well-off indeed. To make sure that he would stay that way, Hoffa put him on a special list of twenty-six names, with orders to caretaker president Fitzsimmons that these must not be touched—i.e., fired— under any circumstances. And, as Chuckie O'Brien told fellow Teamsters, Hoffa had also turned over to him, as a gift, a shirt factory in Jamaica.

With Hoffa in prison, it was Chuckie rather than Hoffa's son, Jim, who usually drove Josephine Hoffa to Lewisburg for visits with her husband. These visits sometimes proved an ordeal for Chuckie as well as Hoffa. Josephine, whose tolerance for alcohol was low, had developed a drinking problem, and once, during a visit to Lewisburg, she fell and bruised herself. As a nonrelative, Chuckie was barred from visiting Hoffa, but he managed to get in several times by signing himself in as Hoffa's adopted son. These visits were cut off when prison officials checked up on Chuckie and found that there had been no adoption.

It was Chuckie, too, who had undertaken a major mission for Hoffa. A Louisiana Teamster leader, Edward Grady Partin, had provided the key testimony that had convicted Hoffa on a jury-tampering charge. Hoffa entrusted Chuckie with the job of spreading around more than $1,000,000 in bribes to prosecutors, judges, and other officeholders in Louisiana to pressure Partin into changing his story (he didn't). As Chuckie boasted later, Hoffa would not allow anyone else to carry the bag.

At the time of Hoffa's disappearance, Chuckie had grown up into a boy-man of forty-two. He was of medium height, with a barrel chest and a thick neck. His belly poured out over his belt buckle, bearing evidence of lavish credit-card living and the consequent onrush of middle age. Chuckie affected tooled-leather cowboy boots and short-sleeved sport shirts. He told romantic stories. His father, known as "Bing" O'Brien although his name was Sam Scaradino, had been a chauffeur for a Kansas City gangster. He had also been an alcoholic who had taken his life by hanging. But Chuckie liked to say that his father was a labor leader who died in a shootout with employers' goons. Chuckie indulged himself in Walter Mitty fantasies that he would someday be another maximum labor leader like Jim Hoffa. He also indulged himself in easygoing money habits.

When Hoffa gave Chuckie money to buy hardware for the new kitchen he was adding to his Lake Orion place, Chuckie pocketed the money and returned empty-handed. Once, in an expansive mood, Chuckie invited the entire Detroit Red Wings hockey team to steak dinners at a fashionable restaurant and grandly signed the $1,000-odd tab to be paid by Local 299 of Detroit. When the local's treasurer sent the tab back unpaid to the restaurant, Hoffa footed the bill. Hoffa footed the bill again when Chuckie gave some $600 in worthless checks to a druggist, who threatened to call in the police; and then, again, when Chuckie fell behind in the alimony and support payments to his divorced wife and two children and spent several nights in jail.

Now, investigators speculated, if there were a second rendezvous, away from the Machus Red Fox Restaurant, on Hoffa's last day, Chuckie O'Brien would be one of the few men Hoffa would trust to escort him there.

Since Tony Giacalone was a suspect in the Hoffa disappearance from the beginning, investigators had made a beeline for his cars even before Chuckie's movements were known.

On the front seat of a maroon Mercury were small puddles of blood. Great excitement! Then a great letdown. The blood, as laboratory tests showed, was that of a fish. Just as Chuckie stated, when the car's use that day was traced to him.

But soon after, the FBI found evidence that was persuasive enough to a federal court to order the Giacalone car impounded. FBI specialist Thomas McGinn flew up from Philadelphia. With him, occupying two first-class airplane seats, were two male German shepherd dogs. Trained to identify a human scent and communicate their findings to their trainer, the dogs first sniffed some unlaundered underwear of Jim Hoffa's. Turned loose in the interior of young Giacalone's maroon Mercury, one dog sniffed about until he reached a rear seat. Then he sat up on his haunches. According to the trainer, this meant he had identified Jim Hoffa's scent. The other dog sniffed the interior of the car's rear luggage compartment, then turned over and lay on his side. That was *his* way of telling his master he had smelled the scent of Jim Hoffa.

McGinn, the dogs' master, later said: "If the dogs pick up the scent of a person someplace, you can be damned sure that person was there." The dogs were veterans of hundreds of investigations, among them the search for Patty Hearst. "They just don't make mistakes," the trainer averred.

Still, there was a problem.

"We really don't know how long the scent was in the car," an FBI source said.

Later, a suburban businessman came forward to say that he had seen Hoffa in the car on the day of his disappearance. While driving past the Machus Red Fox Restaurant, the witness said, he recognized Hoffa as one of four men in a maroon car leaving the restaurant parking lot. Hoffa's hands appeared to be bound behind him. He was leaning forward and apparently shouting at the driver, a swarthy man who, the witness said, looked like photographs of Chuckie O'Brien.

Investigators felt reasonably certain that the witness had accurately identified Hoffa. "After all, he is a famous man," the witness said. About Chuckie O'Brien, investigators were not so sure. The witness identified O'Brien only after he was linked to the Hoffa disappearance and his picture had been published.

Meanwhile, on the day Hoffa disappeared, O'Brien was oblivious of the suspicion that was falling on him. For several days thereafter he played the role of old family friend to the two families that were as kin to him—and were both affected by the Hoffa disappearance: that of Jim Hoffa, apparent mob victim, and that of Tony Jack Giacalone, mob enforcer.

First, Chuckie O'Brien offered his services to the Hoffas. Jim Hoffa had disappeared on a Wednesday. On Thursday, O'Brien showed up at the home of Hoffa's son, and offered to sit for young Hoffa's children so that Jim could join his mother at Lake Orion. O'Brien's services were not accepted. Undaunted, he showed up again the next day, Friday, at Lake Orion to offer his help again.

Young Hoffa did not take kindly to O'Brien's solace or the proffered friendly services. He had confided to friends that his father, toward the end, had begun to fear his old friend Tony Jack Giacalone, so Chuckie O'Brien's continuing friendship with the Giacalones irked him. Also, although young Hoffa and O'Brien had grown up together, they didn't seem to approve of each other. Chuckie had regarded young Hoffa as a penny pincher who didn't dress as befitted the son of a Teamster president. Chuckie had been particularly upset when young Hoffa, on graduating from college and being offered a gift, had asked for a small car. Chuckie had argued that a Teamster president's son should have flashier transportation. For his part, young Hoffa regarded O'Brien as irresponsible. He resented the relationship between the elder Hoffa and Chuckie and tried to minimize it. He told reporters that Chuckie had not arrived in Detroit until he was married, when, in fact, Chuckie had been in Detroit since an early age. Young Hoffa also had recent reasons for seeking to dissociate himself from O'Brien. Chuckie had abandoned the elder Hoffa's comeback attempt and had gone over to Hoffa's successor, Fitzsimmons.

Under the stress of the Hoffa disappearance, the antagonisms between young Hoffa and O'Brien ignited a violent argument. O'Brien left Lake Orion and, spurned by the Hoffas, offered his help indirectly to the man he called "Uncle"—Anthony Giacalone.

On the third night after Hoffa's disappearance, Chuckie O'Brien showed up, unannounced, at the home of Detroit *Free Press* reporter Jo Thomas.

"Jo is the kind of a girl who takes in strays," a fellow reporter said of her. "She had dated Chuckie several times before he remarried, and he seemed to fascinate her."

This time, however, Jo Thomas found little to be fascinated about. She knew O'Brien was wanted for questioning in the Hoffa disappearance. She was scared.

Overcoming her fears, Jo let Chuckie in.

He had just had dinner with the Giacalones, O'Brien informed her: with Tony Jack and his wife, and with their son, Joey. In his rapid-fire way, Chuckie then came to the point of his nocturnal visit.

"Poor Tony Jack," said Chuckie. "He is being unfairly accused." Tony had had nothing to do with the Hoffa disappearance, Chuckie vowed. "Uncle Tony," said Chuckie, "was one of the best friends that Dad [Jim Hoffa] had."

Pausing to catch his breath, Chuckie went on to relate that he had spent Wednesday afternoon (the approximate time when Hoffa is believed to have been abducted) with Tony Jack at the Southfield Athletic Club—a statement he later recanted. He then reviewed Giacalone's activities on the day Hoffa disappeared almost hour by hour, reporting appointments with barbers, masseurs, lawyers.

Realizing that Chuckie was trying to plant an alibi for "Uncle Tony," Jo Thomas insisted that Chuckie call her fellow labor reporter, Ralph Orr. It was 12:30 A.M., and Orr was not pleased at being aroused from a deep sleep, but as Chuckie O'Brien repeated his Giacalone story verbatim, and Orr, too, realized what O'Brien was up to, he came wide awake. He became even wider awake when Chuckie O'Brien offered to produce Tony Jack for an interview that day. This would be a major beat, for Tony Jack had never submitted to an interview.

All of that day, a Saturday, reporter Orr sat glued to his telephone, waiting for a call from Tony Jack. Occasionally, Chuckie O'Brien would call to say that Giacalone would telephone any minute to reveal the time and place. But the call never came.

Chuckie's next move, several days later, was just as puzzling. Although he was wanted for questioning, he flew off to Washington. There, at the Teamsters' headquarters, Chuckie announced himself to a much surprised Teamster president, Fitzsimmons. Facing possible questioning himself, Fitzsimmons was embarrassed and angered.

"Get your ass out of here, and get back to Detroit and give yourself up," Fitzsimmons shouted at Chuckie. Soon after, several aides escorted O'Brien to a taxi and headed him for the airport.

What O'Brien had had in mind in visiting Fitzsimmons or what he said to him is not known. O'Brien remained silent before a federal grand jury later, invoking the Fifth Amendment against self-incrimination. What Fitzsimmons said, other than ordering Chuckie out, is not known either. Fitzsimmons was able to avoid a grand jury appearance.

At least part of O'Brien's visit to Fitzsimmons had to do with money. He was broke. And before being escorted out of the Teamster headquarters, he stayed long enough to get his credit cards back.

Chuckie's effort to plant an alibi for Tony Giacalone—apparently with Giacalone's knowledge—showed that Giacalone was a worried man. Giacalone knew the FBI had in its hands taped conversations that revealed the Detroit Mafia had plotted as far back as 1963 to "grab Jimmy Hoffa." He had somehow learned of the existence of the telltale tapes, for when he was convicted of tax evasion in 1976, Giacalone's lawyers asked the judge whether the FBI tapes would weigh in the sentencing. The judge would not say, but the sentence was a severe one, ten years.

Along with its knowledge of prior underworld plotting against Hoffa, the FBI had a local police report that raised further questions about Giacalone's possible involvement in the Hoffa disappearance. Several months before that disappearance, Giacalone had flown up from his Hallandale, Florida, retreat and had put up at the Grosse Point home of his younger brother, Vito. Local police intelligence officers, alerted to Giacalone's arrival at the airport, had put him under twenty-four-hour surveillance and had come up with some mysterious doings—which assumed significance after Hoffa disappeared.

In the late afternoon of February 19, 1975, Giacalone and his brother were observed meeting clandestinely with two Mafia labor racketeers, "Jimmy Q" Quasarano and Pete Vitale. Since Tony Jack was known to shy away from face-to-face meetings with fellow gangsters, the police believed the meeting had more than ordinary significance. This belief was strengthened that evening when another meeting took place at Vito Giacalone's home. Parked outside was a 1973 Lincoln limousine whose license plate identified it as registered in the name of Joseph Zerilli, the don of Detroit's Mafia.

"The old man [Zerilli] is a careful man," a police source told the Detroit *News*. "It's not his style to meet Tony Jack like that. Something heavy must have gone down."

To the FBI tapes and the February 19 police report was added another item that aroused police interest in Giacalone. This was the telltale note Hoffa had left behind him when he left his Lake Orion home to keep his fatal rendezvous. It read:

"T.J. 2 P.M."

Chapter Four

"TONY JACK"

THE TELLTALE NOTE that Hoffa left behind him coupled with Chuckie O'Brien's use of a Giacalone family car on the day Hoffa disappeared turned Tony Giacalone into a prime suspect. But a suspect must have a motive. Giacalone's motive, federal investigators believed, was the profit motive.

Let's take a closer look at Tony Giacalone.

During the Teamster convention at Miami in 1966, newspaper reporters from Detroit spotted a familiar, but unexpected, face. It belonged to Anthony "Tony Jack" Giacalone, who, only three years before, had been described in Senate Rackets Committee testimony as one of the heirs apparent to Detroit Mafia leadership. Because Giacalone was in charge of the mob's street action—numbers and loansharking—he was known as "king of the streets."

Giacalone was also the Detroit Mafia's enforcer of mob territory. The year prior to the Teamster convention, a gambling figure had come down from Pontiac to Detroit to get Giacalone's O.K. to operate a gambling joint there.

"If I hadn't gotten the O.K.," the gambling operator later testified, "I would be in the Detroit River now."

This statement was made when Giacalone was tried on gambling and bribery charges in 1969. He was acquitted and his police record remained at fifteen arrests—on charges of gambling, rape, felonious assault, loansharking, and armed robbery—with only one conviction: for bribing a police officer.

Giacalone's last known employment was in 1948, when he tended bar. Yet here was Tony Jack at this convention of honest toilers, in earnest confab with delegates. Naturally, reporters asked Jimmy Hoffa, then president of the Teamsters, what Giacalone was doing there.

"Mr. Giacalone is a guest here at the convention, who is showing respect to a responsible union," Hoffa explained.

Mr. Giacalone was "a guest" again at the next Teamster convention in 1971. Some of what guest Giacalone was doing there was uncovered by Michigan's organized crime unit, and surfaced both in the Detroit *News* and in a subsequent federal fraud indictment against Giacalone. The indictment provided the first official glimpse of who Giacalone really was and why he was a guest at Teamster conventions.

The story, as fleshed out by our own investigation, was this:

A Detroit surgeon, Dr. Raymond Stoller, conceived the idea of a hospital insurance plan for union members. The Teamsters, he thought, would be logical customers.

But how does one get to the Teamsters?

Via the Mafia, he learned from a lawyer; more specifically, through Tony Jack Giacalone. But, before Giacalone approached the Teamsters, Dr. Stoller was given to understand that certain arrangements had to be made. Dr. Stoller had formed the Integrated Medical Services Corporation to sell and service the hospital plan. The first Giacalone condition was that a lawyer for Giacalone's son, Kenneth G. Bernard, then

thirty, be made president of Dr. Stoller's corporation at
$30,000 a year. Duly installed as president, young Bernard
would then award Giacalone a contract. Of the $5 manage-
ment fee per Teamster per hospital day that would go to Integrated Medical Services, 20 percent or $1 per Teamster per
hospital day would go to Giacalone.

What for?

"For introductions and contacts with Teamster officials
which helped sell the plan to the Michigan Conference of
Teamsters," Kenneth Bernard explained.

Once invited in to give a helping hand, Tony Jack paid
himself and associates so generous a piece of the action that
Dr. Stoller's hospital plan had trouble surviving. Seven
months after it was launched, the plan foundered. Bernard left
as the $30,000-a-year president, and Giacalone's contract was
terminated. But not before he had received a $12,000 settle-
ment, plus another $12,000 for his brother, Vito, an ex-felon
whose services to the medical plan were not explained.

Tony Jack was subsequently acquitted on the fraud charge,
but a federal investigation revealed his true role in this adventure. He was a broker selling a valuable commodity. In this
instance, it was Teamster patronage. Giacalone could do this
because he had a pipeline into the Teamsters by virtue of his
close friendship with Hoffa. He could lift the telephone at any
time of day or night and reach Jimmy—in Washington, in
Florida, or wherever.

"I want this favor," he would say. And he would get it.

Access to Teamster power brought Tony Jack vast rewards.

By 1976, when a tax evasion trial provided a financial as
well as a personal portrait of him, Giacalone was no longer
"Tony Jack," the king of the streets, counting the daily take
in the numbers and enforcing the collection of usurious loans.
He was Mr. Giacalone, a man of considerable wealth, expensive living tastes—and many business interests. He was also,
as one Detroiter who was intimate with Giacalone's affairs

revealed, "perhaps not the most powerful man in Detroit, but one of the two or three most powerful." He symbolized the new dimension of wealth and power that the Teamsters connection had brought the underworld.

Giacalone's newly acquired importance was evidenced by the major prosecution effort the federal government made against him. The Internal Revenue Service, the FBI, and lawyers from the Detroit Organized Crime Strike Force, headed by Robert C. Ozer, had spent two years tracking down every penny Giacalone had spent from 1968 through 1971, in order to reconstruct his income. The trial itself took over three months, and was Giacalone's third trial on tax evasion charges. A first trial had resulted in acquittal. The second, in 1974, also an acquittal, was a near miss. Giacalone got off when an underworld associate changed his grand jury testimony and assumed responsibility for income that had been ascribed to Giacalone. In its third attempt, in 1976, the government won a conviction, and Giacalone was sentenced to serve ten years for failing to pay $103,000 in taxes. (He appealed, and in mid-1977 was still out on bail.)

In court, Giacalone cut a sharply elegant and regal figure, towering over his average-sized attorneys and associates. Close up, he was a darkly handsome man with a long, hard, unsmiling face set off by fashionably long hair down to his collar, and by dry-blown, fluffed-up muttonchop sideburns. Well tanned and well preserved at sixty-two, Giacalone was obviously concerned with the figure he presented in public. He wore dark tinted glasses in aviator-shaped frames which he changed to match his suits. These, invariably, were of silky material with stitching at the pocket flaps, western style. He favored white-on-white shirts with loudly patterned ties. On the little finger of his left hand was a heavy gold ring mounting a cat's-eye stone, reportedly valued at $20,000. On his feet were oxblood patent leather shoes with bright brass buckles.

From the testimony of some two hundred witnesses—bank-

ers, brokers, accountants, kin, IRS agents, and business associates—a story emerged of a swiftly escalating Giacalone
fortune.

In 1955, two years before Jimmy Hoffa became Teamster
president, Giacalone had told an insurance agent, from whom
he was buying two children's policies, that his yearly income
was $10,000 and his net worth about $30,000. By the early
1960s, Giacalone was reporting yearly income of about
$30,000 and, if his tax returns were to be believed, virtually
all of it came from "speculation," wagering on horses and
football games. By 1971, Giacalone was reporting $280,000
of income in a joint return with his wife. But according to the
IRS, Giacalone was modest. His actual income, as federal
agents were able to piece it together, came to $323,313. Pri-
vately, the revenue sleuths felt even this whopping sum did not
tell the whole story, for they obviously could not uncover
every source of Giacalone's income. They felt they had
tracked down only part of Giacalone's total wealth, which
probably exceeded $1,000,000. Even so, federal agents were
able to show that Giacalone owned $759,840 worth of bonds,
stocks, real estate, and other assets.

Tony Giacalone, onetime king of the streets, had in these
recent years lived like a king, and in the world from which he
had sprung and of which he was still a part, his family was
treated like royalty. When Tony's son, Tony, Jr., was married
in 1970, some 450 guests came to a regal wedding. In a scene
straight out of *The Godfather,* the arriving guests made a
beeline for the gifts table, which was dominated by a large box
made up to look like a wedding present—gift wrapping, big
bow, and all. Into a slot in the side of this box the guests
slipped envelopes containing cash, thus "paying respect" to
Tony the elder. The "respect," as the bride's father testified at
Giacalone's tax trial, came to $104,000.

Until Giacalone moved his legal residence to Florida in

1972, he lived in a three-story, $100,000 mansion in the fashionable Grosse Pointe surburb of Detroit. The grounds sported a pool and combination bathhouse-poolhouse. In the master bedroom of the house was a "panic button" with which Giacalone could touch off a raucous alarm to alert neighbors and presumably his bodyguard if intruders came in the night. All windows were equipped with double locks, and heavy steel gates, padlocked at all times, protected the three entrances.

Even tighter security protected Tony Jack's cash hoard. The subsequent owner testified she had found a closet below a staircase. In it was a concealed panel which opened up on a secret staircase leading down to a windowless room with an outsized safe in it.

Giacalone's home in Florida was a penthouse condominium near Miami Beach. But he kept three Tennessee walking horses in a riding stable in Detroit. His wife, too, had expensive tastes. In preinflation 1968, she spent $7,300 on frocks and additional sums on furs. In one of her dress shops, Mrs. Giacalone prudently paid with bank cashier's checks made out to a "Mrs. Jack Lakeland," presumably to frustrate federal tax snoopers who might be trying to tote up what the Giacalones were spending.

Although based in Florida, Giacalone spent enough time in Detroit to find it worthwhile to belong to two exclusive country clubs there. Here he hobnobbed with the elite of the town and, contrary to locker-room custom, was always addressed as "Mr. Giacalone." In one of these clubs, curiously, Giacalone paid no dues, leading to the suspicion that he was providing the professional service of keeping labor troubles away.

At the same time, Giacalone could afford a third expensive club, the Doral Country Club near Miami Beach, where he was often seen golfing with figures from both the underworld and the straight world.

And finally, Tony Jack Giacalone, living like a king, planned to continue like one in death. For his eternal rest, federal agents found, Tony Jack had purchased a $76,000 "private room" in Detroit's Holy Sepulchre Cemetery. On this he had expended an additional $13,000 for marble imported from Portugal and stained glass windows.

Whence came the wherewithal for the lavish living and the posh preparations for dying?

By 1974, Detroit newspapers were describing Giacalone not only as a Mafia chief, but also as "an investor." Over the years, Giacalone had been in and out of many businesses. He had been involved in a home-delivery juice business and in a pest control firm. (Giacalone used to hand out business cards listing himself as president of an "exterminating company," leading law enforcers to wonder whether this saturnine fellow had a sense of humor after all.) Tony Jack had owned pieces of companies supplying labor to lighterage companies at the Detroit River docks, selling and managing real estate, developing land, finishing and fabricating metals.

For a share in some of these companies, Giacalone may well have paid cash realized from his loansharking and protected-gambling days. But federal investigators suspected that much of his business involvement was similar to his participation in the Integrated Medical Services scheme, that Tony Jack was acquiring pieces of companies by virtue of services he could render through the Teamsters.

Consider a Giacalone adventure we will call "The Case of the 19th Hole" because of the hole a golf course owner dug himself into when he brought Tony Jack in to solve a labor problem.

When the greens of his Royal Scot Golf Course were destroyed in a labor dispute, owner Edward B. Bartoli of Lansing, Michigan, reached for a man who knew his way around in the underworld. This was a friend and onetime neighbor of Giacalone's, Harry Thomas, residing at the Doral Country

Club at Coral Gables, Florida. According to police sources, Detroit's Mafia had suggested to Thomas that it would be prudent for him to leave town after his conviction and imprisonment as a child molester.

Thomas introduced golf course owner Bartoli to Giacalone, who listened to his labor problem. Bartoli had been using nonunion labor to build a bowling alley, nightclub, and restaurant on his golf course grounds. Vandals, presumably building trades members, had forced him to shut down both his golf course and his bowling alley construction. Giacalone's Teamster connection gave him considerable clout in other unions, particularly in the building trades, for word from a Teamster official that his men will deliver building materials through a picket line to prolong or break a strike carries great weight with construction union men. Giacalone was able to deliver that word. The sabotage stopped. The construction of the bowling alley was completed with nonunion labor. The golf course reopened.

But, having poked his nose into owner Bartoli's tent, the rest of Giacalone—plus pals who supplied additional capital and management—soon followed. Giacalone's friends bankrupted the golf course; then Giacalone offered to buy it back at bankruptcy sale price. As an indictment charged later, it was a typical underworld scam. It should be noted that its success depended on Giacalone's access to Teamster power.

How Tony Giacalone spent the day of Hoffa's disappearance was of top priority interest to federal investigators. What they found whetted their appetite to learn even more.

As one government source told me: "If you study Giacalone's daily habits over a long period, you'll never see a day like this [July 30, 1975]. Virtually every minute is accounted for. People are ready to swear and show written records of where Giacalone was and what he was doing."

For example:

Masseur Doug Ryan at the Southfield Athletic Club, where Giacalone hobnobbed with the elite of Detroit, told the grand jury, and later repeated to reporters, that ''Mr. Giacalone had come in during the morning.'' He knew the precise time, 11:10 A.M. When he told Giacalone that he was busy, Giacalone took a nap. ''He slept like a baby,'' the masseur reported. Ryan knew the precise time that Mr. Giacalone awoke (12:40 P.M.) and he went on to tell the grand jury other precise times. At 2:10 P.M., he finished giving Giacalone a rubdown. At 2:25 P.M., Giacalone gave masseur Ryan a tip, and according to the masseur, he left at 2:30 P.M. to get a haircut.

Giacalone is a man who takes obvious interest in his well-groomed, air-blown, abundant hair. But on this day, as a witness told the grand jury, Giacalone dropped in on a barber who had never before done his hair and with whom he had no appointment.

Next, Giacalone visited a lawyer who had offices in the same building that houses the Southfield Athletic Club. The lawyer, too, knew precisely when Giacalone arrived and when he left. Giacalone arrived at 2:30 P.M. and left at 4 P.M.—the crucial period in which Hoffa is believed to have been spirited away. To federal investigators it was more than a coincidence that precisely at that time Giacalone was with a professional man who would have credibility before a jury and could refresh his memory on the witness stand from his daily record of visits from clients. Perhaps even a billing for services rendered on that day.

From Anthony Giacalone himself, federal investigators could learn nothing about his whereabouts on the day of Hoffa's disappearance. Called before a grand jury, he invoked his constitutional right to remain silent.

Chapter Five

"TONY PRO"

ON A JUNE EVENING in 1961, almost fourteen years to the day before Jim Hoffa disappeared, a New Jersey Teamster official left for home from a meeting of his local and was never heard from again. His name was Anthony Castellito, and his job was that of secretary-treasurer of Teamster Local 560 at Union City, New Jersey. Castellito, a popular figure in his local, had announced he would seek to replace Anthony "Tony Pro" Provenzano as president at an upcoming election. He never had the chance. Police theorized at the time that Castellito was murdered and his body buried in one of the many garbage dumps in the area.

Castellito's violent end was not the first in the bloodstained history of Tony Provenzano's Local 560. Nor would it be the last. But it promised to be the most significant. For the Castellito disappearance—long interred in the open files of the FBI and the police of New Jersey and New York—was to come to life a year after Hoffa vanished. On Castellito's ghost, federal sleuths placed virtually their sole hope of breaking the Hoffa murder case.

To UNDERSTAND HOW the ghost of a crime past might trip up
the perpetrators of a crime present, it is necessary to descend
into the murky racket-and-crime-ridden realm ruled by Tony
Pro Provenzano.

When the hapless Anthony Castellito made his bid for the
leadership of Local 560, he was not only threatening Tony
Pro's job, he was threatening a family business as well. Tony
Pro had taken over Local 560 in 1958 via appointment by an
aging predecessor. According to the files of the New Jersey
Commission on Investigation, Tony Pro had gotten his start as
a "capo" (captain) in the crime organization of New Jersey
Mafia boss Jerry Catena. So it is assumed that Tony's "appointment" as head of Local 560 was dictated by the underworld, and that Tony Pro was the caretaker of the mob's labor
rackets in northern New Jersey. Underworld links aren't displayed in Macy's window, but in Tony's case there were occasional slipups. A lawyer once crossed Tony Pro and feared for
his life. When he asked around for the "man to see" to square
matters with Tony, he was told: "See Jerry Catena." The
lawyer did—and lived.

Once inside Local 560, Tony Pro brought in his brothers,
his sisters-in-law, and his nieces: brother Nunzio became
vice-president; brother Salvatore, secretary-treasurer; sister-
in-law Theresa, widow of brother Frank, became office manager; several nieces became clerks. The Provenzanos treated
Local 560—supported by the dues of eight thousand
members—as a wholly-owned family enterprise. Tony upped
his onetime $20,000 president's salary to $95,000. And as an
owner, he didn't even have to work to get paid. While in jail
for extortion—from 1967 to 1970—his wages were put away
for him and turned over to him when he emerged.

But Local 560 was more than a family union business. It
became, under Tony Pro, the hub and enforcer of a crime
empire that spanned northern New Jersey.

Local 560's stewards, making their rounds to check on members' "beefs" at truck terminals and factories in the area became numbers runners, selling bets and making payoffs for a numbers bank housed at the Local 560 union hall. On the premises, too, Local 560 business agents and their pals from outside ran a vast loanshark business that put out money "on the street" and to trucking company operators as well. Also occupying office space in the Local 560 building was one Harold Konigsberg. Known as K.O., because of his huge size and the legend that he had once sparred with Joe Louis, Konigsberg was also known as the "shylock's shylock" because he could squeeze payments from borrowers whom other mobsters had given up on.

Substantial as these union-based rackets were, they were overshadowed in the early 1970s by a bigger source of income—the sale of sweetheart contracts to employers.

More freight is hauled through New Jersey by truck than through any other state, according to Commerce Department estimates. Not only does the state originate some 55 million tons of truck freight yearly, but it is also a corridor for freight to and from New York and New England. And the truck movement of goods to and from New Jersey's ocean piers swells the freight total further.

At first, Tony Pro worked the classical "labor peace" racket. For $200 a month from one employer, as his extortion conviction showed, Tony Pro spared the employer harassment from Tony's own union. It was while waiting for the jury to bring in its verdict in this extortion trial that Tony gave his own insight into himself, saying gloomily to a friend: "Why do I do these things? I guess it's the larceny in my blood."

When Tony emerged from prison in 1970, he found a greater opportunity for larceny. With Jim Hoffa out of power, the Teamster union's enforcement of the terms of the national Master Freight Agreement was left largely to the regional

Teamster barons. Tony had a free hand in making lucrative deals with trucking employers who wanted to cheat on the national freight contract.

Indeed, sweetheart contracts spread like wildfire in New Jersey.

In "Scarface" Al Capone's day, merchants paid tribute to a "protective association" on pain of having their windows smashed or their legs broken. But as Provenzano realized, no force was necessary to ply the lucrative sweetheart-contract racket. The Teamster constitution, molded by Jim Hoffa, protected crooked dealings between union leader and employer.

For example, for more than two decades, Local 701 at New Brunswick, New Jersey, honestly run by a devoted union man, Robert Coar, had a contract with a trucker known as M&G Company. Its sole business was to haul office supplies for a federal agency, the General Services Administration. Then a company called Siegel's Express underbid M&G by a substantial margin and drove it out of business, costing several dozen of Coar's men their jobs. How was Siegel's Express able to do this? A local allied with the Provenzanos permitted Siegel's to pay $1 an hour below the standard contract wage, and another dollar less per hour in fringe benefits.

An honest Teamster local's territory had been raided by a sister local that purveyed sweetheart contracts. Raid victim Robert Coar appealed to the regional Teamster organization, known as the Joint Council, that settles territorial and other disputes between locals. Who headed the Joint Council as president? Salvatore Provenzano, who had stepped up into the job when his brother Tony Pro went to prison.

Of course, complainant Coar got no satisfaction. The Teamster constitution, which gives the regional joint council the final word in territorial disputes between locals, has helped the Provenzanos protect sweetheart deals.

The fear of reprisal is such that few of the honest truckers hurt by competitors' sweetheart deals dare raise their voices. When ten small truckers banded together to raise a $200,000 war chest and sue the Teamsters in an attempt to end the sale of special favors to crooked competitors only three dared put their names on the suit. Yet one trucker not only appeared in the suit, he took on the Provenzanos openly.

The trucker, Robert Kortenhaus, who runs a family trucking business, raised such an uproar at Teamster headquarters in Washington that President Frank Fitzsimmons named a committee to look into the matter. Whom did he name as chairman? Salvatore Provenzano! Kortenhaus then bombarded Salvatore Provenzano with demands that he act.

"Where's the proof?" Salvatore Provenzano wanted to know.

Kortenhaus hired an undercover agent, a truck driver who took jobs with truckers known to be operating under soft deals. Kortenhaus' driver-spy kept records of hours worked and photostatic copies of paychecks—hard evidence of crooked deals.

When Kortenhaus presented chairman Salvatore Provenzano with the proof of sweetheart deals, Provenzano was furious.

"This is Watergate tactics, spying on people," he shouted, and stormed out of the room. The sweetheart deals continued.

TONY PRO HAD BECOME a suspect in the Hoffa murder case almost from the beginning. He had a motive—a profit motive. Hoffa, back in power, would threaten his lucrative sweetheart-contract industry. Too, there was the history of violence in Tony's Local 560.

Tony Pro also had the means to procure a kidnap-murder. Besides the presumed murder of Anthony Castellito, there had been two others in Tony Pro's bailiwick. Armand Faugno, a loanshark associate of the Provenzanos involved in a counterfeit caper with them, vanished without a trace in 1972. Police heard he had been put through a tree shredder. A prosecution witness in Tony Pro's 1963 extortion trial, Walter Glockner, was shot to death outside his home just before he was to have given testimony against Tony Pro.

Also, Tony had threatened Hoffa's life. In Lewisburg Prison, where both had been inmates, the two had quarreled bitterly. "I'll tear your heart out!" Tony shouted at the time. The feud had been resumed outside prison. When the two bumped into each other at an airport, federal investigators learned later, Hoffa and Provenzano went at it with their fists, and Hoffa broke a bottle over Provenzano's head.

Finally, when Hoffa set out for his restaurant rendezvous on his last day, he expected, he told friends, to "sit down" with Tony Pro as well as with Tony Jack Giacalone.

But to convert suspicion into an indictment, evidence is needed. Summoned before a federal grand jury in Detroit, Tony Pro—like Tony Giacalone—invoked his constitutional right under the Fifth Amendment to remain silent on the ground that he might incriminate himself. Federal prosecutors had no evidence on which to proceed further against him.

In a presumed kidnapping and murder, such as Hoffa's, federal investigators proceed on the theory that the crime was the result of a conspiracy, i.e., that more than one person was involved. The strategy, then, is to track down one or more suspects and try to make one of them talk. Unable to learn anything from the two Tonys—Giacalone and Provenzano— federal investigators did what they always do—they waited for a break: a break in the form of an underworld informant who knows something and has something to gain from talking.

Such a break came four months after Hoffa disappeared.

Chapter Six

"WE KNOW WHO DID IT"

HOFFA'S KILLERS, relying on precedent, expected local police to take charge of the case. The federal criminal code does not include the crime of murder—that is left to the states. But the abduction and assassination of a national figure such as Hoffa was an underworld challenge that required a major response. Federal investigators entered the case, using kidnapping—a federal offense—as the jurisdictional entry door.

The federal government spends some $90,000,000 yearly to wage war on organized crime. A headquarters command post at the Justice Department at Washington, D.C., known as the Organized Crime and Racketeering Section of the Criminal Division, deploys seventeen organized crime task forces in the field. These draw on lawyers from the Justice Department, on sleuths from the FBI and the IRS, and on experts from the Labor Department. With backup clerical and research help, this comes to about six hundred full-time antiunderworld operatives.

Some eighteen months after Hoffa's disappearance, organized crime task forces in Newark, New York City, and Detroit had narrowed down their hunt for Hoffa's abductor-killers to a handful of suspects. These became the targets of a pincers movement aimed at squeezing the truth about Hoffa from them—if they knew it.

A HEAVY RAIN had transformed the normally mushy surface of Brother Moscato's garbage dump in Jersey City, New Jersey, into a foul quagmire. But four FBI agents, booted and pressing handkerchiefs to their noses to shut out the acrid methane gas fumes of the fermenting garbage, plodded over the forty-seven-acre wasteland. In a search that had gone on for a week, they had crisscrossed the dump a hundred-odd times. Power-shovel operators from Jersey City's Department of Public Works stood by for word to dig into the mess where, in some places, garbage was packed sixty feet deep.

The FBI agents were armed with a search warrant, which indicated officially that they were looking for the remains of a loanshark, Armand "Cokey" Faugno, who had vanished in 1972. Actually, they were looking for the body of Jim Hoffa.

Suspicion had focused naturally on Brother Moscato's Dump. Its operator, until a few years before, had been Philip "Brother" Moscato, a brawling ex-paratrooper and reputed Mafia associate with personal and business ties to Tony Provenzano. As a friend, Moscato had thrown a big homecoming party for Tony Pro when he returned from prison in 1970. As a business associate, Moscato participated in a loanshark ring operated out of Local 560, now bossed by Tony Pro as secretary-treasurer. And when Tony Pro set up part-time residence in Florida, Brother Moscato moved right along with him. There, as if to flaunt his associations with the Teamsters, Moscato set up a restaurant, Charlie Brown's Steak Joint. He placed it across the street from the offices of the Southern Conference of Teamsters at Hallandale, Florida.

Suspicion had focused on Brother Moscato's dump, too, because New Jersey law enforcers had long suspected that the dump was an auxiliary facility to the Provenzanos' Local 560 union hall. Dissidents or racketeers who ran afoul of the Provenzano union-and-rackets empire were believed to be discarded there—literally thrown into the rubbish heap.

But there was a third and more immediate reason for searching Brother Moscato's dump.

The FBI at Newark had received a message from the New Jersey State Prison at Trenton. An inmate said he had information about the abduction and murder of Jim Hoffa. Felons have often risked their lives as ''stoolies'' to win reductions in heavy time. So the FBI, overlooking no bets, dispatched agents to Trenton. What they heard from the prison inmate sent them hurrying back to their superiors in Newark, who, in turn, relayed their news to Washington.

The informant, it turned out, had an insider's intimate knowledge of affairs at Tony Pro's Local 560. He said he knew the names of three figures in that local who had abducted and killed Hoffa. The body, he said, had been crammed into a fifty-five-gallon oil drum and transported east for disposal in or nearby the Moscato garbage dump. The FBI could not verify this part of the informant's story, because the threat of fire from the methane gases at the dump forced them to abandon their hunt. But they placed such credence in his information that they were soon basing the entire strategy of their investigations on it.

For obvious reasons, federal investigators take great precautions to hide the identity of informants. But the lawyer for the three men whom the informant had fingered discovered the informant's identity and disclosed it.

The lawyer for the three men was William Bufalino. He had long served Hoffa as a lawyer and still retained the two Teamster International jobs he had acquired under Hoffa—those of counsel and general organizer.

How had Bufalino learned the informant's identity? Someone, Bufalino discovered, had been calling the Local 560 union hall asking for Steve Andretta, a business agent. Unable to locate him there, the caller had telephoned a Teamster haunt near Union City, New Jersey. There, he left a message with the bartender:

"Tell Steve that Little Ralph called from the institution."

The "institution" was the New Jersey State Prison at Trenton. Having no trouble identifying "Little Ralph" as Ralph Picardo—also known as Ralph Birche—Bufalino revealed to the press that Picardo was the government's secret witness. Picardo, it turned out, was doing heavy time—seventeen to twenty-three years for procuring a murder. Seeking leniency, he was "singing."

The three men whom Picardo fingered as Hoffa's abductors and killers were Salvatore Briguglio, his brother Gabriel Briguglio, and Thomas Andretta, Steve Andretta's brother.

Salvatore Briguglio was a business agent for Tony Pro's Local 560 and kingpin of the loanshark operations headquartered there. In 1961, Tony Pro had appointed Sal Briguglio, a novice in labor union matters, Local 560's secretary-treasurer. This had reportedly been on orders of New Jersey Mafia boss Jerry Catena. Briguglio had served time for robbery, for extortion, and for counterfeiting food and postage stamps and currency. He had proved his loyalty to the Provenzanos by pleading guilty to the counterfeiting charge to clear the way for the dismissal of a similar indictment against Salvatore Provenzano. New Jersey law enforcers believe he was ordered to "take a fall" for Salvatore, who has no criminal record. Finally, Sal Briguglio was a figure of terror to Local 560 rank and filers because of his reputation for violence. An associate said of him: "Sal could kill a man, then sit down and eat a sandwich."

Sal's brother, Gabriel Briguglio, ran Teamster Local 84 for the Provenzanos. Local 84, state law enforcers believe, was set up by the Provenzanos to deal in sweetheart contracts and to keep these under-the-table dealings away from Local 560. The younger Briguglio had also served time for counterfeiting.

The third man, Thomas Andretta, had no payroll job at Local 560 but was constantly at the union hall. He owned a paper trucking enterprise which owned no trucks and did no carting business; it was believed by law enforcers to be a front for loanshark repayments and employers' bribes. Mostly, Tom Andretta was a driver for Sal Briguglio. He had served three prison terms for theft, counterfeiting, and fencing.

Because Tony Pro was a prime suspect in the Hoffa case, federal investigators believed Picardo's story. True, Picardo had gone to jail in May 1975—two months before Hoffa disappeared. But he said he continued to hear "what was going down at Local 560" because lifelong friends there visited him in prison and told him. Picardo had credibility with federal investigators because he had been an important cog in the rackets operated from the Local 560 union hall. He had posed as the owner of four trucking companies, but only one was legitimate. The other three were fronts for hiding shylock loans and collections. Picardo also arranged loans from the Local 560 pension fund, raking off 20 to 50 percent in commissions and kickbacks.

Finally, federal investigators believed Picardo's information on the Hoffa case because his other information on underworld matters checked out. Picardo gave investigators specific locations where they seized hidden loanshark records.

Other Picardo information put the finger on an interstate stolen-truck operation.

On the strength of Picardo's Hoffa information, the three men he had named—Sal Briguglio, Gabriel Briguglio, and Thomas Andretta—were summoned before the federal grand jury at Detroit. All promptly invoked Fifth Amendment protection against self-incrimination and remained silent.

In recent years, federal law enforcers have relied heavily on a pressure device known as use immunity. A suspect is granted immunity from self-incrimination if he talks. If he refuses, a judge can order him jailed for contempt of court. In the most famous of all use-immunity cases, New Jersey Mafia boss Jerry Catena remained in jail for five years for refusing to answer grand jury questions under an immunity grant. The New Jersey Supreme Court finally freed him.

Now, in Detroit, federal authorities offered use immunity to Steve Andretta, brother of Tommy Andretta.

"Where were you on Wednesday, July 30, 1975, the day Hoffa disappeared?" Steve Andretta was asked.

Rather than answer, Steve Andretta spent sixty-three days in the county jail. When he was ready to talk, he appeared before the federal grand jury at Detroit and provided an alibi for the three chief New Jersey suspects.

"All that day [the day Hoffa disappeared]," said Steve Andretta, "I was playing cards at the union hall with Tony [Pro] and Sal and Gabriel [Briguglio] and my brother Tommy."

Why he didn't say so in the first place and avoid spending two months in jail is a mystery. Whether he perjured himself is another.

With the failure of the use-immunity weapon, the Hoffa investigation was stalled for a year. Then, just as Picardo had brought new life to the investigation earlier, so another felon, doing heavy time in a western prison, revived the Hoffa case with information about another kidnap-murder: that of Tony Pro's onetime secretary-treasurer Anthony Castellito, who had disappeared fifteen years before.

The new informant spoke with authority because, he said, he had participated in the crime. The drama he painted of the Castellito disappearance had the same cast of bad actors as those suspected in the Hoffa case: Tony Pro and Sal Briguglio. With the change of dates, some place names, and supporting characters, the Castellito murder scenario, as spelled out in subsequent murder and kidnapping indictments, was almost identical to that pictured by investigators in the Hoffa case:

In June 1961, Castellito, like Hoffa, was lured to a rendez-vous. According to the indictments, Sal Briguglio was waiting for him at the rendezvous in upstate New York. Briguglio then had no official connection with Tony Pro's Local 560, nor with Harold "K.O." Konigsberg, the "shylock's shylock," who maintained an office in the Local 560 building. To Sal Briguglio, according to the indictment, Tony Pro had prom-ised the job of business agent in Local 560 in return for the murder of Castellito. To K.O. Konigsberg, Tony Pro allegedly had promised $15,000.

While Sal Briguglio and K.O. Konigsberg proceeded to kill Castellito, an associate dug a grave nearby. The killers, seemingly, changed their minds about the interment and, cover-ing up the grave, transported Castellito's body back to New Jersey. In the meantime, Tony Pro had taken off for Florida. Upon his return, as promised, he named Sal Briguglio secretary-treasurer.

Now, in the summer of 1976, the Justice Department had high hopes of breaking the Hoffa case. If convictions could be obtained against Tony Pro and Sal Briguglio in the Castellito case, the government would have them over a barrel—

imprisonment for life. Having nothing to lose, they might shed some light on the Hoffa murder. A long chance, but a chance nevertheless.

Since murder is not a federal crime, the federal government could indict only on the kidnapping charge—a federal offense—leaving the murder indictment to the State of New York. However, another roadblock interfered. When Justice Department Special Attorney William Aronwald of New York City hastened to bring the Castellito kidnapping-conspiracy charge to trial, he ran into a legal problem. The Castellito kidnapping was fifteen years old, and under the government's own statute of limitations, no crime—except one involving the death penalty—can be tried after five years have elapsed.

At the time of the Castellito kidnapping and murder, the federal kidnapping law had called for the death penalty. But Congress revoked the death penalty in 1972. So, in 1976 when the Castellito case came to trial, kidnapping was no longer a capital offense. A U. S. district court judge dismissed the kidnapping indictment and the government's subsequent appeal was denied. The state is now pursuing the muder charge.

Some eighteen months after Hoffa disappeared, then, the government was in a curious position, but one that was not rare in underworld slayings. Investigators believed they had solved the Hoffa murder case, but they did not have the evidence to proceed. An assistant attorney general told a reporter: ''We know who kidnapped and killed Jim Hoffa—and how.''

The Justice Department official named no names, but, as reported in the Philadelphia *Inquirer,* he said that ''evidence and information supplied by underworld informants pointed strongly to New Jersey mobsters—and to persons in the Detroit area who were close to Hoffa.''

The government's theory of the case, as revealed by other sources, was this:

Tony Jack Giacalone set up Hoffa by arranging a fake meeting with Tony Pro Provenzano.

On the day of the murder, three men flew from New Jersey to Cleveland on a private jet, then switched to a small chartered plane and flew to a small landing field in the Detroit area. There, investigators believe, Chuckie O'Brien met the trio and, perhaps unwittingly, drove them to the vicinity of the rendezvous, the Machus Red Fox restaurant.

Hoffa, unsuspecting, got into the car and was driven to a private residence in Detroit. Hoffa was killed, probably by garrotting. His killers left, retracing their return to New Jersey via Cleveland. Several men, other than the killers, disposed of Hoffa's body.

I asked a Justice Department official who was intimate with the daily moves in the Hoffa investigation, "Is the government following any other promising leads—other than those involving Tony Pro, the Briguglio brothers, and Tony Giacalone?"

"No," he replied.

"Then you have all your eggs in one basket?"

"Yes, those are our eggs, and that's our basket," he replied.

PART II

WHO WAS JIMMY HOFFA?

Chapter Seven

WHO WAS JIMMY HOFFA?

INSIDE THE MYSTERY of Hoffa's death, like a riddle within an enigma, is the mystery of Hoffa's life.

Who was Jimmy Hoffa?

The riddle posed itself at my first meeting with Hoffa in the summer of 1955. On asking for an interview, Hoffa had invited me to spend two days with him in Chicago. I could observe Hoffa in action at grievance sessions—usually barred to reporters—involving employers and Teamsters from twenty-three states. I could listen in as he conducted union business via long distance telephone calls, and we could talk. Nothing to hide. All forthright. All open.

Hoffa was only ninth vice-president of the Teamsters then, and since the McClellan Senate Rackets Committee hearings were still three years in the future, Hoffa was virtually unknown except in his hometown of Detroit. Investigation prior to our meeting had revealed Hoffa to be a rapidly rising star in the Teamsters—but also to have been involved in dubious deals with dubious characters.

Except for his gray-green eyes—which simultaneously conveyed intelligence, suspicion, and defiance—Hoffa, face-to-face, seemed an ordinary enough man of the people. His head was somewhat large for his body. His round face, topped by ink-black hair combed straight back and dominated by high cheekbones, might have belonged to an Indian. Short, stubby fingers spoke of forebears who had worked the land. (As I learned later, Hoffa, of Dutch-Irish origin, came from six generations of western Pennsylvania settlers.) Oversized biceps bulged from store-bought clothes. When Hoffa sat down, his pants legs rode up on his shins to reveal the outsized calves of a football tackle. His speech, innocent of the discipline of formal schooling, tumbled out via a high and somewhat nasal voice.

Yet, for all his unimpressive aspects Hoffa emerged under two days' observation as a giant in will, in mind, and in his dominance over those around him. The littlest man in the room, Hoffa seemed to tower over everybody in it. One of his lawyers was to tell me later, "It was beneath Jimmy's dignity to walk into a room without dominating it." Now, as I could see, men who were his seniors in the Teamster hierarchy as well as owners of national trucking concerns listened to Hoffa—then a boyish forty-two—with the deference a junior clerk pays to the senior partner of the firm.

At the grievance-adjustment sessions, Hoffa was only one of three Teamster representatives facing three employer representatives. Yet when a man stated his beef, all heads would turn to "Jimmy," who remained standing at the head of the table throughout the proceedings. Hoffa would bow his head as if sorting out fact from emotion.

"Here's my decision," he would say, and then, to use his phrase, "That would be it, brother!"

In Hoffa's hotel suite, the telephone rang incessantly. Swiftly, he spelled out to Montana the terms that would end a truck strike in the Northwest. By telephone to Seattle, he told

Dave Beck—then Teamster president—of the accomplished fact. In between, he settled union problems in his own bailiwick—Detroit—and gave advice to Teamsters in New York.

Here was a man with larger-than-life abilities doing his thing as an effective labor leader. But on display was another Hoffa, one who seemed to inhabit another world.

In Hoffa's entourage, during the two-day Chicago sessions, was a freckle-faced, redheaded man in his fifties. He walked on his toes like a gymnast and, like Hoffa, was flat-bellied and in fighting trim. He had driven Hoffa from the airport, hung about the hotel corridors while Hoffa was closeted on union business, went out with him to dinner.

Hoffa introduced the redheaded man.

"Meet Paul Dorfman," he said.

Paul Dorfman!

In a magazine article, I had described Paul Dorfman as a onetime Chicago Capone-gang thug who had advanced to more important underworld duties. He had been entrusted with a waste handlers' union when its president was murdered. (He had been booted out of the old American Federation of Labor for running a racket-ridden local that policed a monopoly in the waste-collecting industry.) In my article I had told how Hoffa had channeled Teamster health and welfare fund insurance to a Dorfman family insurance agency that had reaped $1,000,000 of commissions in three years. Since the Dorfmans had withdrawn large sums of cash from their agency, had destroyed records, and would not tell congressional investigators where the cash had gone, it was suspected that the cash had gone to the collector for the Chicago Capone gang. All this I had recorded.[1] But Dorfman put out his hand.

---

1. Lester Velie, "How Welfare Funds Are Looted," *Reader's Digest,* June 1954.

"You shouldn't've written that about me," he said cheerfully.

Questions were racing through my mind as Hoffa watched me quizzically, with the shadow of a smile.

Why did Hoffa flaunt this underworld character to a reporter who, as Hoffa must have known, would be describing the encounter to a national audience?

Did Hoffa see nothing wrong in his relationship with Dorfman?

Or didn't Hoffa give a damn what the world thought?

And there was a bigger question still.

Was Dorfman an underworld watchdog planted at Hoffa's side to keep an eye on him?

When I returned home to New York to write my first magazine article about Hoffa—there were to be seventeen more over the next decade—I tossed sleeplessly, trying to decide who *was* Jimmy Hoffa? Was he a devoted labor leader? Or was he an underworld figure in labor-leader's clothing?

In Chicago, I had asked Hoffa about reports by Detroit union men that he had taken over the Detroit Joint Teamster Council early in his career with the help of hoodlum muscle.

"They did the same thing to me then that you're doing now," Hoffa shot back.

"What am I doing now?"

"You're trying to put me in the mob."

Could I, in good conscience, put this young, boyishly open, and effective labor leader "in the mob"?

Hoffa would often sign his name "James Riddle Hoffa." My troubled sleep was reflected in the title of my article, "The Riddle in the Middle of America's Most Powerful Union."[2]

Senate investigators, criminal prosecutors, and reporters had let in the sun on much of Hoffa's life by the time he

2. *Reader's Digest,* December 1955.

disappeared in July 1975. It was known that Hoffa consorted with gangsters, let them run Teamster locals, lent money to them from Teamster pension funds. Yet, his role vis-à-vis the underworld escaped precise definition. It could not be said with certainty that Hoffa was "in the mob" as were Frank Costello and Lucky Luciano. He was somehow a part of the world of organized crime, but not in it. In death as in life, he remained a riddle.

I had thought that when Hoffa entered prison his saga as a force in American life was ended and that the question about his true role was moot. When he emerged from prison, then disappeared, it became important to continue the search for his true identity as a clue to his death.

Yet, investigating Hoffa dead was considerably more difficult than investigating Hoffa alive. Fear of underworld retribution and Teamster retaliation sealed many lips. So did the federal grand jury investigation into Hoffa's disappearance. And there was the old problem that a Hoffa watcher had to deal with: He was the kind of multifaceted man in whom the eye of the beholder could see what the beholder wanted to see.

To his family, Hoffa was a model husband and father who could do no wrong. To the rank-and-file Teamster member, Hoffa was a folk hero who could do some wrong—he could take from the "big boys." But that was all right, because he took care of the little guy, too. (John English, a former Teamster secretary-treasurer, once said, "If Hoffa and I split the Teamster headquarters in two and each took half, the members wouldn't give a damn as long as we took care of them.") To one of Hoffa's lawyers, Morris Shenker, Hoffa was a "thoroughly dedicated union man . . . one of the straightest, squarest shooters I've ever known." To Edward Bennett Williams, onetime general counsel to the Teamsters, Hoffa was "thoroughly amoral." To Walter Sheridan, who helped Robert F. Kennedy get the goods on Hoffa and then filled a

554-page book with Hoffa's misdeeds,[3] Hoffa was one of the greatest corrupters of his time.

Yet there was a path through this maze of contradictions. It led to nests of underworld characters in Detroit and elsewhere who enjoyed a mysterious power. No union men themselves, they could nevertheless get special favors from union leaders to pass on to businessmen. And they could even make it unnecessary to deal with unions altogether.

If you were a real estate developer whose business life depended on meeting a construction-contract deadline, you found your way to a man in your community who had an office and a secretary and called himself a labor consultant—or had neither office nor job designation, but did have a reputation for delivering the labor favor you wanted. For a fee or a piece of your project, the man would assure you labor peace and the sure completion of your project on time.

How?

The man, it would turn out, was a Mafia-connected character with friends inside the Teamsters: Jimmy Hoffa, or some other Teamster official with the necessary clout. Your benefactor was a power broker from the underworld, selling Teamster power to the upper world. And since the power that the underworld broker sold was really Jimmy Hoffa's power, what did that make Jim Hoffa? It made Jim Hoffa a double agent. Hoffa used his upper-world position to serve the underworld and his underworld connections to serve the upper world.

To understand Hoffa's double-agent role, it is necessary to look briefly at the nature and function of the underworld. By whatever name it is known—whether organized crime, or Mafia, or Cosa Nostra—it exists to serve upper-world needs.

3. Walter Sheridan, *The Fall and Rise of Jimmy Hoffa* (New York, Saturday Review Press, 1972).

The upper world prefers to believe that the underworld is a predatory, criminal octopus that sucks the blood of the communities it infests. With regard to organized crime's extortion or protection rackets, this concept is certainly true. But the larger truth is that the upper world uses the underworld to provide services that the upper world outlaws—but continues to demand.

During Prohibition, when the manufacture and distribution of liquor were outlawed, gangsters organized a vast rum-running and moonshining industry that lubricated millions of consenting adults' throats. Of course, this industry had risks that boosted costs. Federal and local law enforcers had to be paid off; rifle-toting guards had to be hired to protect liquor convoys against hijackers; "hit men" had to be retained to secure and protect sales territory. But the upper world gratefully covered the cost, plus a profit.

When Prohibition ended, the underworld went into the business of providing gambling services: plush casinos and horse books for the well-to-do, betting on the numbers for the poor. The underworld has provided organized prostitution where the straight world has demanded it, and narcotics, too—charging fees commensurate with risks and the size of protection payoffs.

To those underworld services, Hoffa made a major contribution. He turned the sale of union favors into a major underworld industry. Labor racketeering has been with us almost as long as unionism. But access to the power of the country's key union gave a new dimension of power, prestige, and wealth to organized crime figures. The Teamsters can make or break another union's organizing drive or a strike, by honoring a picket line or by crossing it with deliveries. Access to Teamster power gives the underworld leverage in other unions as well.

"Selling labor peace, preventing union organizing, and sweetheart union deals now provide a major source of mob wealth," according to one lifelong student of organized crime, Vincent Piersante, who heads the Michigan attorney general's division on organized crime.

About the underworld brokers of Teamster power in his own Michigan bailiwick, Piersante said: "We are talking about an efficient organization which delivers services. You seek out whomever you know [in the underworld], and he goes to whomever he needs [in the Teamsters] in order to get the job done."

Funneling Teamster economic power to gangsters—who sold it to the upper world—was Hoffa's chief double-agent service to both worlds. But there were others.

For his underworld constituency's monopoly rackets, Hoffa provided Teamster policing power. In Detroit, Cleveland, Chicago, and elsewhere, tavernkeepers had to buy or lease jukeboxes from a distributor, usually Mafia-connected, who had Teamster approval. If a tavernkeeper didn't, Teamster drivers would not deliver beer or food, and Teamster maintenance men would not repair the jukebox.

For his underworld constituents, too, Hoffa provided millions of dollars of loans from Teamster pension funds, which permitted gangsters to broaden their beachhead in legitimate businesses.

To the upper world of trucking employers, Hoffa could provide one of the country's most disciplined work forces. For one thing, Hoffa had a cozy arrangement with truckers, in which they yielded substantial wage increases, knowing that Hoffa would join them in convincing the Interstate Commerce Commission and state tariff bureaus to increase rates and pass along the higher wages to the public. For another thing, Hoffa was closer to his rank and file than virtually any other labor leader and could influence them to keep the trucks rolling.

And where there were rank-and-file rebellions, Hoffa had the hoodlum muscle to douse them.

"Why do you keep hoodlums on the payroll?" a reporter once asked Hoffa, referring to a Teamster local in Tennessee.

"To kick those hillbillies around and keep them in line," Hoffa said.

Chapter Eight

HOW HE
GOT THAT WAY

SELDOM IF EVER, in American public life, had a figure
so highly placed as Hoffa served both the criminal and the
respectable worlds. How did Hoffa come to be cast in his
double role?

The press, the Congress, the courts, the Justice Department,
and even the White House were involved at various times in a
thirty-years' war against Hoffa. What equipment of mind and
energy permitted him to cling to his double role for so long?

Let's start with Hoffa's mind.

Watching Hoffa's mind at work could be a memorable experience. When Hoffa was tried in Chattanooga in 1964, on
charges of conspiring to fix a federal jury, he surrounded
himself with a battalion of fourteen lawyers.

But it was clear that Hoffa was his own chief counsel.
Beside him at the defense table was an outsized briefcase
crammed with documents into which he dipped constantly for
quick reference. Before him was a lined legal pad on which he
furiously scribbled instructions to his lawyers, who would leap

to their feet with motions or objections or demands for a mistrial. No exhibit was introduced into testimony unless Hoffa
perused it first. When one of his lawyers displeased him,
Hoffa would glare until the hapless wretch gave up talking and
sat down. Sometimes Hoffa would growl, ''Pipe down!'' or
''Come on, cut it out! Come back to your seat!''

Six weeks later, when Hoffa was tried again, this time on
charges of defrauding the Teamsters' biggest pension fund,
Hoffa's mind was again in dramatic evidence. The case was of
such head-reeling complexity that Hoffa's own lawyers sometimes had difficulty sorting out the tangled financial facts. But
not Hoffa. Once, when his lawyers were trying to explain a
complex transaction to the judge, Hoffa pushed them aside
impatiently, gave a succinct and lucid account of the deal, and
told the court: ''I tried to tell my lawyers about this, but they
didn't understand.''

Hoffa's prehensile mind was a constant marvel to associates
who never saw him take a note, yet found that he absorbed
facts, compartmentalized them, and spewed them out like a
computer printout when occasion demanded.

To constitutional lawyer Leonard Boudin—who had spent
much of his professional life at labor law—Hoffa was one of
the most knowledgeable men in that field that he had ever met.
Law schools at Harvard, Columbia, and Cornell and technical
universities such as MIT frequently invited Hoffa to lecture.
On one occasion, after listening to Hoffa lecture and answer
students' questions for several hours, an MIT professor
exclaimed, ''Hoffa has an eighth-grade education, and I have
a Ph.D. Maybe I should have an eighth-grade education.''

Transportation executives who negotiated with Hoffa reported that he knew more about transportation industry economics than their own economists—or those of the Teamsters.

To rank-and-file members who, with a little persistence,
could always get to Hoffa on the telephone, ''Jimmy's''

ability to remember their names, the numbers of their locals, and the nature of their problems—was "outa this world."

The mind that was capable of almost total recall was capable of considerable toughness, too. As one of Hoffa's more learned associates put it: "Hoffa had the ability to deflect external stimuli that would have made him uncomfortable." During recesses in trials in which his freedom hung in the balance, for instance, Hoffa would stretch out on the defense table and, seemingly without a care in the world, promptly pop off to sleep.

It was a mind that was forever whirring, forever scheming. At a labor convention in Miami, I heard Hoffa storm at a man who had crossed him: "While you guys are out on the town at night, I'm in my room planning my next move. By the time I go to bed at two A.M., I got you licked."

To be a successful double agent, one must also be a successful artful dodger. During the McClellan Senate Rackets Committee hearings, Hoffa's brilliant, ever-whirring brain served him so well in ducking questions that he could walk away after hours of grilling without having admitted or revealed anything.

Hoffa employed several novel lines of evasive action. Since he couldn't "take the Fifth" against self-incrimination and thus tacitly admit many guilts, he had others do it for him. Pushed into a corner about a shady deal, Hoffa would say he couldn't recall the transaction, but perhaps his partner in it might. The partner, questioned, then would take the Fifth Amendment, saving Hoffa the onus of doing so. Or Hoffa would entangle Bob Kennedy in exhaustive and exhausting quibbles. Here is what Kennedy was up against when he tried to find out whether Hoffa put Minifon "bugs" on Teamsters in order to spy on grand jury proceedings—a crime:

KENNEDY: What did you do with the Minifons [purchased by the Teamsters Union]?

HOFFA: What did I do with them? Well, what did I do with them?

KENNEDY: What did you do with them?

HOFFA: I am trying to recall.

KENNEDY: You could remember that.

HOFFA: When were they delivered? Do you know? That must have been quite a while.

KENNEDY: You know what you did with the Minifons, and don't ask me.

HOFFA: What did I do with them?

KENNEDY: What did you do with them?

HOFFA: Mr. Kennedy, I bought some Minifons, and there is no question about it, but I cannot recall what became of them. I have to stand on the answers I had made in regards to my recollection and I cannot answer unless you give me some recollection other than what I have answered.

If being a double agent required a resourceful mind, it also required a mind with a hole in it—a hole where Hoffa's conscience should have been.

To Hoffa, there was no right or wrong. He liked to say: "You associate with anyone who can make you a winner." In the same way, he believed everything goes—if it works. The schemes that the amoral Hoffa sometimes cooked up were as outrageously funny as they were outrageous.

During his first months in prison in the spring of 1967, Hoffa—frantic to get out—had an inspiration. Why not get prostitutes at Chattanooga to swear that federal agents had hired them to provide professional services to the judge in Hoffa's jury-tampering trial? Such "new evidence" would surely win Hoffa a new trial. To three lawyers who visited Hoffa in prison every Wednesday, Hoffa confided his scheme, taking each lawyer aside to whisper instructions separately. Lawyer A was to coach the prostitutes on the story, paying them to bolster their memories. The ladies would then be brought to Washington where lawyers B and C, who had not been involved in buying the perjury, would take the prostitutes' affidavits.

When lawyer A balked at suborning perjury and besmirching a respected federal judge, Hoffa flew into a rage.

"Goddam you!" Hoffa shouted. "You're afraid of losing your license!"—as if that could be the only reason for the lawyer's reluctance. (Hoffa got other lawyers to go through with the scheme, but it was laughed out of court.)

Hoffa's inability to distinguish right from wrong reached an even more incredible height—or depth—when he named two men with criminal records to serve on the three-man board of trustees that watched over the International Teamsters Union accounts. To attend a trustees' meeting, one of them, Frank Matula, a convicted perjurer, once had to get a three-week furlough from prison.

Hoffa's warped sense of right and wrong was rooted in part in his difficult transition to manhood during a difficult time, the Great Depression of the 1930s.

Although Hoffa's father, a coal mine drill operator, had died when Hoffa was seven, leaving a penniless widow and four children, Hoffa remembered his childhood as a happy one. While food and shelter were modest, there was no desperate hardship. His mother, an indefatigable and courageous woman from whom Hoffa apparently derived his energy, made ends meet by doing laundry and other chores for neighbors and by working in a factory. But when Hoffa left school after the eighth grade, he was plunged into an unjust and cruel world.

As a crate handler in a food-chain warehouse, Hoffa at sixteen often had to wait for hours, unpaid, to see if there was work that night. His hold on the job was precarious, for a tyrannical foreman fired men on a whim. As Hoffa recalled later, firings were so frequent that hungry men formed lines at night waiting their chance to fill a fired man's shoes. Earnings were $15 for a six-day week. The boss was not a benefactor who provided work and the chance to earn one's bread. He was an enemy.

When Hoffa mobilized worker desperation to form a union and then went on to become an organizer for a Teamster local, he found that he had a more potent enemy still—a police force that was subservient to employers.

"My scalp was laid open sufficiently wide to require stitches no less than six times, during my first year as a Teamster business agent," he recalled later. "I was beaten up by cops or strikebreakers at least two dozen times that year."

One of young Hoffa's superiors in the Teamsters corroborated the police brutality in a report to national Teamster headquarters.

"I can remember the time that if [an organizer] went to a coal yard or any other place of business," he reported, "the boss of these companies would call the police . . . and naturally he was picked up and taken to jail. I have seen that fellow come back after his arrest and have his eyes blackened—black and blue marks all over his body by being put through their 'third degree.' "

To the police, a strike picket line was a threat to the peace and security of the state. During one twenty-four-hour period, young Hoffa was hauled from a picket line eighteen times—hustled to the precinct stationhouse, to be released by the desk captain, to return to the picket line and be seized again.

Not only did the cops beat up Hoffa, but they stood by as the boss's thugs did it, too. As Hoffa charged, they also planted weapons in organizers' cars. "Naturally, the police were always right," a colleague of Hoffa's wrote to Teamster national headquarters, "and what chance did we have of proving otherwise?"

So, as a kid, Hoffa was an underdog and a cop hater. As an

adult, he continued to perceive himself as an underdog long after he became a top dog. His hatred of cops was transferred to the whole sprawling apparatus of law enforcement, and indeed, to the entire social order. To Hoffa, the law was a swindle aimed at protecting those who already had theirs—something to be flouted and outwitted by whatever means possible.

Other men suffered early hard times and grew up with respect for the law. Why not Hoffa? The answer lies more in Hoffa's nature than in his nurture. Hoffa was a driven man with a rage for power of Napoleonic dimensions. A friend once pointed out that Hoffa even looked like Napoleon and had a wife named Josephine.

From the time he organized his first union local at age seventeen to the time when he went to prison at age fifty-five, Hoffa was forever rearing an ever-higher edifice of union power.

From his first Teamster local, Hoffa went on at age twenty-one to take over the Detroit Joint Council of Teamsters and, thus, to become boss of the city's Teamsters.

Not one to miss an organizing—or power-accumulation—trick, Hoffa, in Detroit, had watched with fascination as leftist activists in Minneapolis devised and used a "leapfrog" strategy to spread Teamster organization throughout a region. By controlling the truck terminals and warehouses in Minneapolis, they could force truck operators in Des Moines, Iowa, or Kansas City, Missouri—who shipped to Minneapolis—to sign their men into the Teamsters. If they didn't, the Minneapolis Teamsters would not unload their incoming trucks. The newly organized Teamster members could then organize other terminals, and this leapfrogging process could go on and on to the greater power and glory of the Teamsters.

Copying this technique, Hoffa leapfrogged from Detroit Teamster boss to Michigan Teamster boss.

From Michigan it was but a frog's leap into Illinois and beyond. As Hoffa crossed state borders, he invented the area-wide or regional Teamster contract agreement. Before Hoffa, the Teamsters had bargained at most with the employers of one city. Now, with the twenty-seven-year-old Hoffa in the driver's seat as bargaining committee chairman for the Central States Drivers Council, Teamsters negotiated with employers in as many as twenty-three states.

The power building went on even after Hoffa achieved the Teamster presidency. He recast the Teamster constitution to give himself one-man dictatorial powers—to put himself out of reach of conspiring colleagues or rebellious rank and filers. He battled for the right to supplant regional contract negotiations with summit wage-bargaining sessions between himself and truckers from coast to coast. In a dispute he could, theoretically, halt most of the wheels of the country.

"You have as much power as the industrial robber barons of the nineteenth century," reporter Clark Mollenhoff told Hoffa.

"More," Hoffa corrected him.

Hoffa trained for his struggle for power and for his legal wars with the devotion of an athlete training for the Olympics. The exercise that began with push-ups in the morning went on all day. Hoffa would excuse himself from a conference or an interview to get down on the floor and grunt out some push-ups. If you sat at Hoffa's desk, you had to be prepared sometimes to conduct your business with him as Hoffa pounded his desk rhythmically with a right-hand karate chop. With exercise went massages, sometimes two or three times a day.

One advisor, who was at Hoffa's side for years, theorized

that "exercise was Hoffa's transcendental meditation, his way of shutting out his whirling-dervish world."

Luncheons and dinners were training-table affairs: low-calorie crab or cold lobster at noon; well-done steak or beef in the evening, with Hoffa meticulously dissecting away the fat.

Among his hard-drinking and hard-womanizing lieutenants who had fat expense accounts on the road and fat opportunities with which to indulge Rabelaisian tastes, Hoffa was a curiously Puritanical figure. He abjured all alcohol, even beer, and drank no coffee. He took no joy in night life. Once, while abroad, his companions prepared for an evening out. "I'm going to bed," Hoffa announced. "There's nothing much in this town, anyway." The town was Paris.

Hoffa didn't smoke, and in smoke-filled conference rooms he would rise from time to time to empty ashtrays and open windows. Sex away from home was out-of-bounds, too, not only because Hoffa was a highly moral family man, but because energy had to be husbanded for physical demands that would have wilted a John Bunyan—or a Rasputin.

Once when Hoffa showed special sass and vinegar while testifying before the Senate Rackets Committee, I remarked to one of his aides: "Hoffa must have rested up for today's session."

"Are you kidding?" the Hoffa man said, stifling a yawn. "When we got through here yesterday afternoon, we flew to West Virginia for a night meeting of a local there. Then we got on a plane for Detroit, and arrived about midnight for a rally of Hoffa's local. We didn't get back here until four this morning. That guy, Jimmy, he just ain't human."

With physical fitness and endurance went physical courage. When a would-be assassin—who said he had a message from God—shot at Hoffa during his trial for jury tampering, lawyers and U.S. marshals dove for safety under chairs and benches. But Hoffa dove, instead, at his assailant, knocking him down. The assassination weapon turned out to be an air gun, but Hoffa, not knowing this, had not hesitated to look into the face of death.

Had Hoffa possessed the patience—or conscience—to play the game straight, he would have achieved a historic place in labor and public life. Like George Meany, he could have held that place into venerable old age.

As Hoffa saw it in his autobiography, he failed because "I made two disastrous mistakes in my life." The first, according to Hoffa, was coming to grips with Robert F. Kennedy to the point where we became involved in what can only be called a blood feud." The other was to name Frank E. Fitzsimmons as his successor.

But Hoffa had made a bigger mistake still. He had taken a shortcut by accepting help from the underworld.

Chapter Nine

LIFE
WITH THE MOB

LONG BEFORE HOFFA'S desperate bargain with the underworld cost him his life, it exacted a heavy price. Like Faust, Hoffa had saddled himself with a treacherous and corrupting partner. Hoffa's Mafia pals exploited the weakness of his wife, Josephine. They plotted to rob Hoffa. They used a close friend of the family to spy on him. And they turned Hoffa into a man at war with himself—a battleground of clashing demands and loyalties.

From 1961 through 1964, the FBI had an electronic bug in the ceiling of a business office occupied by Detroit Mafia enforcer Tony Jack Giacalone. This recorded conversations between Giacalone, his brother Vito, and others. The FBI also planted an eavesdropping device in the apartment of Giacalone's mistress, Sylvia Paris, the mother of Chuckie O'Brien. The Detroit News published transcripts of taped conversations from both bugs in mid-1976.

These showed that Tony Giacalone was in virtually daily contact with Hoffa—either by telephone himself, or through Sylvia Paris. She and her son, Chuckie O'Brien, had lived in the Hoffa home and were regarded by the Hoffas as "family." Sylvia Paris handled the Hoffas' personal finances, paid their bills, ordered furniture for them. So she was in a position to spy on Hoffa and to report his every move to her lover, Giacalone.

Sylvia Paris' and Anthony Giacalone's contacts with Hoffa proved very useful to the mob. Hoffa approved a pension loan and arranged introductions as part of the Detroit mob's plan to move into Las Vegas.[1] He paid a lower court judge $15,000 to dismiss a charge that Giacalone had tried to bribe two policemen.[2]

Sylvia Paris, long a friend of Josephine Hoffa's, found ways of drawing Josephine even closer. She arranged consolation for Josephine Hoffa during Hoffa's long absences from home. According to an FBI memorandum based on the tapes, "Giacalone, who visited Sylvia almost daily, began bringing a friend, Tony Cimini, known as 'Nino' or 'Tony Long' to provide companionship to Josephine Hoffa."

And Hoffa's Mafia pals did something else for Mrs. Hoffa. They exploited her drinking problem.

As the FBI tapes revealed, Sylvia Paris, Tony Giacalone, and Tony's brother, Vito, made plans to get Josephine drunk and rob a safe in Hoffa's Washington apartment while he was out of the city. Seemingly, the Detroit mob had reasons to suspect that it contained a considerable hoard of cash.

In November 1963, according to the tapes, Vito Giacalone proposed to his brother, Tony:

"While you're in there [the Hoffa apartment], I'll go cabareting with her [Josephine] for a couple of hours."

---

1. Alerted by the bugged conversations, federal authorities blocked one deal and sent Vito Giacalone to prison for an attempt to buy a hidden interest in a gambling casino.

2. The judge, now dead, delayed the case in an effort to kill it. Giacalone was ultimately tried and freed.

"You don't have to go cabareting. Drink right there," Tony replies. "Yeah, knock her out . . . knock her out. Leave the bottle in bed with her. That's better yet."

"Sylvia says it's got to be [in] that closet," Tony Giacalone reports, in one conversation. Sylvia Paris had apparently cased the Hoffa apartment.

And in February 1964, Tony Giacalone is speaking to Vito:

"Now, the way it looks, what we got to do . . . Josephine goes back to Washington, I'll send Sylvia there . . . we got to make a trip to wine and dine her.

"Now you [Vito] can go down there [Washington], and she [Josephine Hoffa] wants to zoop it up. Fine, you make her zoop it up . . . now when she is zooped up . . . I'll be down there . . ."

A later transcript revealed that Tony Giacalone stole some money from the Hoffa bedroom, but the plot to break into the Hoffa safe apparently fell through.

Hoffa suffered this treachery at a time when he was honoring his part of the bargain with the underworld. He was making Giacalone and others in the Detroit Mafia rich by permitting them to sell Teamster favors.

In fact, it was due to Hoffa that there even was a marketplace for the sale of such favors. For years, Detroit has had an exclusive luncheon club where, curiously, everything is on the house. It is located in a brick office building on one of whose walls is emblazoned the name of Market Vending, Detroit's biggest distributor of cigarettes, candy, and other vending-machine items. Two Detroiters, described in Senate testimony as Mafia business administrators—Rafael "Jimmy Q" Quasarano and Pete Vitale—run Market Vending, although the company was sold to a Cleveland outfit in 1970. Some twenty-odd guests sit down in the Market Vending dining room. Because Mafia associates of Jimmy Q and Pete Vitale—among them, Tony Giacalone—have taken lunch there, the place has come to be called a mob hangout. It is also a Teamster hangout.

Rubbing shoulders with the Giacalones, the Quasaranos, Vitales, and others are presidents of Teamster locals and business agents. While vice-president of Detroit Local 299, Frank E. Fitzsimmons came to the club regularly. Even after he went to Washington as an International vice-president, he showed up occasionally at the mob hangout, usually in tow of his great friend the late Maxie Stern, labor racketeer.

Businessmen have been glad to accept invitations for lunch at Market Vending. It has brought them close to labor and gangster power that could make or break their businesses. And it has brought them into contact with go-betweens who could make deals for that power.

One person seen there was Leonard "Lenny" Schultz. Lenny once served a prison stretch for fencing stolen goods. On emerging, he went to his friend Maxie Stern, who was a strong-arm man for Jim Hoffa as well as for Mafia Don Pete Licavoli. Maxie gave Lenny $500 and some advice. "Go into labor."

Since Lenny Schultz's prison stretch barred him from union activity, he went into labor relations instead. He read up on unions, opened an office in a downtown office building, and became a "labor consultant" associate of Tony Jack Giacalone.

When the chairman of the board of a furniture chain was found in the trunk of his car with his head almost severed from his body, investigation showed that he was on his way to a meeting with his labor consultant—Lenny Schultz. Investigators reported that Lenny was a close friend of Tony Giacalone's, and that Tony seemingly held an interest in the furniture company. For, as investigators reported, Tony Giacalone and Lenny Schultz hosted parties at their homes for officials of the furniture company. The murder of the board chairman remains a mystery. The mystery deepened when the company was sold to lawyers who had participated with Tony Giacalone in obtaining Teamster business for the Integrated Medical Services scheme, already described.

One "labor consultant" who didn't have far to go for lunch in the Market Vending mob hangout was the veteran "Babe" Bushkin, who, according to McClellan Committee testimony, once carried the bag in a $17,500 payoff to the Teamsters by a laundry owners' association. Jim Hoffa, Bob Kennedy charged, got $5,000 of this. But witnesses who had told investigators of the bribe in private would not repeat it in public before a committee hearing. Babe Bushkin was still at his old game of labor consultant. From an office in the Market Vending building he served a supermarket association in its dealings with the Teamsters. It was a service that derived its value from Bushkin's old friendship with Hoffa.

Along with the Teamster favors that Hoffa turned over to fixers or middlemen like the Giacalones, the Lenny Schultzes, and the Babe Bushkins, who sold them to employers, there was the direct assist to gangsters in legitimate business. Through Hoffa, gangsters could enjoy an "edge" over competitors.

"The edge." I first came across this phrase while investigating the gangster invasion of New York City's garment district. By terrorizing and sometimes murdering union organizers, gangsters in the dress business kept out the International Ladies Garment Workers Union and gave themselves the edge over unionized competitors who paid union scale wages. In Detroit, thanks to Hoffa, the Mafia didn't have to use terror to enjoy the edge.

When Joseph Barbara, Jr., son of the Barbara who hosted the Mafia's Appalachin, New York, summit meeting of 1957 and son-in-law of mobster Pete Vitale, formed a rubbish collecting company with Vitale in Detroit in 1962, he had no trouble dislodging competitors of long standing.

How did young Barbara and Pete Vitale do it? True, their company, Tri-County Sanitation, well financed, entered the field with the latest labor-saving equipment. But more important, Hoffa gave Barbara, Jr. and Vitale a crucial edge. In the heart of his Teamster empire, where everything that rolls is organized, Hoffa let Tri-County operate nonunion. As Senate testimony showed, Barbara and Vitale were using nonunion drivers fully eighteen months after Tri-County was founded—some of their drivers getting $40 less weekly than the Teamster-organized drivers of competitors. Ultimately, when Tri-County dominated the Detroit area's commercial rubbish-removing field and no longer needed the edge provided by nonunion labor, Hoffa organized the company's drivers.

If Hoffa gave to the underworld, he also received something in return. The underworld's part of the bargain became evident with Hoffa's very first step up the Teamster ladder—his move from leadership of a single Teamster local to the control of all of Detroit's Teamsters. At nineteen, Hoffa had run for the presidency of the Detroit Joint Teamster Council, which then headed up three locals (today there are fourteen). He had received only four of the twenty Joint Council delegates' votes, but he made himself president anyway.

"I just walked in and took over," Hoffa later said. Inside the Teamsters there was a more plausible explanation. The fist-swinging kid had muscle behind him that even the hard-bitten Teamsters in the Joint Council had to respect.

This muscle was at Hoffa's service as he moved up from city to state to regional Teamster power.

Convicts leaving prison could find employment with Hoffa as "organizers" or as strong-arm men to repel the goon squads of antiunion employers. One "organizer," an armed robber by the name of Frank Kierdorf, pressed into service by Hoffa on leaving prison, died promptly in the line of union-organizing duty. He burned himself fatally while setting fire to a nonunion cleaning and dyeing establishment.

The Mafia had also supplied Hoffa with hoodlums to subdue rank-and-file rebellions that threatened his power.

When rebelling members at Pontiac, Michigan, held a protest meeting aimed at wresting the local from officers indicted on charges of taking bribes from employers, Hoffa stormed up from Detroit with a caravan of twenty cars loaded with toughs wielding lead pipes and wrenches, intent on smashing the threat to Hoffa's satellites. Deputy sheriffs armed with machine guns repelled Hoffa but, undeterred, he persisted in the use of terror and union trusteeship (union martial law) to keep control of the local.

And when Hoffa felt the time was ripe—in the mid-1950s—to extend his Midwest influence beyond Chicago, the Italian mobs in Chicago and Detroit provided him with the O.K. and the gunmen to take Teamster control in St. Louis from the Irish Buster Workman gang there.

The Workman gang dominated the St. Louis Joint Council of Teamsters and were threatening to seize a local from the man who had built it—Harold Gibbons—who was to become a Teamster power later.

As Harold Gibbons recalls it, "Jimmy came into town with his boys. He had the O.K. of Chicago [the Chicago Capone gang] and of Detroit [the Mafia, there headed by Joe Zerilli] to oust the Workmans. He said to them: 'Get out and stay out. Whatever you choose to do to us, we'll do double to you.'"

Then Hoffa said to Gibbons:

"Arm your men. Shoot the first son of a bitch who comes here [Gibbons' union hall] to take over." Gibbons armed his men. And for six weeks thereafter, Hoffa also kept a gunman at Gibbons' side to protect him. The Workman gang retreated.

So began a curious friendship and working partnership. Gibbons was an intellectual who had studied at the University of Chicago. He had been the protégé of Roosevelt liberals and had gone into unionism as a cause. Now, he harnessed his brain and union savvy to help push Hoffa up the Teamster ladder. Egghead Gibbons and Dead End Kid Hoffa made an odd couple. Side by side (they shared a Washington office and a Washington apartment), they ran the Teamsters for ten years—until Hoffa went to prison in 1967.

Just as Jimmy "had the O.K. of Chicago and Detroit" when he came to St. Louis, so he "had the O.K." when he came to New York City, Cleveland, Philadelphia, and other cities to build a political machine to win the Teamster presidency.

Hoffa needed support from New York for his presidential ambitions. Gangsters John "Johnny Dio" Dioguardi and Tony "Ducks" Corallo formed six shadow unions—i.e., paper unions without members. Hoffa then wangled six Teamster charters for them from the then president, Dave Beck. With these paper locals in their pockets, Johnny Dio and Tony Ducks named fellow gangsters as delegates to New York City's Teamster Joint Council and so seized control of it. When Jimmy made his move for Teamster president, he could count on a big pro-Hoffa delegation from New York.

Teamster presidents are elected by delegates to a convention held every five years. These delegates consist primarily of officers of Teamster locals—the president, secretary-treasurer, the trustees and business agents. As in New York City, Chicago, and Detroit, big city crime organizations that controlled Teamster locals elsewhere provided Hoffa with a core of delegate strength to the convention of 1957. Hoffa did the rest.

First, he used his delegates to take over the convention credentials committee, which controlled the seating of delegates. When Hoffa was elected president on the first ballot, congressional investigators—alerted by rebel rank and filers—descended on Miami's luxurious Eden Roc Hotel in search of the credential committee's minutes.

"They have been accidentally burned," the investigators were told. "A maid threw them into the incinerator."

But what had been taken for the incinerator turned out to be a laundry chute. In the bowels of the hotel, intact, were the incriminating minutes. They revealed that at least 561 delegates had been seated fraudulently. More than half the delegates, it turned out, had no business being there. Indignant rank and filers sued to throw out the election. But Hoffa, once in, remained in.

Hoffa made no bones about his friendship with and admiration for the gangsters who had helped bring him to power. He would rarely arrive at an airport in the East without being greeted by a waiting Johnny Dio, the much-jailed New York City gangster. Hoffa's and Dio's wives were friends, too. And when Hoffa testified before the McClellan Senate Rackets Committee, he would take lunch with Johnny Dio—ostentatiously, almost, inasmuch as Robert F. Kennedy and his committee staff frequented the same restaurant.

Hoffa was also a devoted and protective friend of Tony Pro Provenzano. As a fellow inmate of Provenzano's at the Lewisburg Penitentiary, Hoffa saved his friend's life when Provenzano became seriously ill with a stomach ailment. Hoffa threatened the warden with a lawsuit and unwelcome public attention to prison conditions unless Tony Pro was removed to an outside hospital for surgery. Hoffa prevailed.

Hoffa's children, Jim and Barbara, grew up with those of Tony Jack Giacalone. To Hoffa, Giacalone and others like him were upstanding, honorable, decent people. Indeed, Hoffa trusted the Giacalones, the Provenzanos, the Johnny Dios, and the "Paul the Waiter" Riccas as he did few men in the upper world. When he did trust someone in the straight world, it was because they, in turn, had won that trust by services to the underworld.

Morris Shenker, who knew Hoffa intimately, told this writer: "I was one of the few straight people he trusted. Why? Because I had defended and won the trust of the men Hoffa trusted, the Frank Costellos and others."

With trust went admiration. Like Hoffa, his underworld friends were cop haters. They successfully defied and frustrated the law-enforcement machinery that Hoffa held in contempt. They made the upper world stand and deliver to them limousines, tailored clothes, country homes, and Florida retreats.

And with admiration went respect. His underworld friends had the power that helped make Hoffa "a winner."

Chapter Ten

THE HOFFA
MONEY MYSTERY

IN A RUSSIAN morality tale, a peasant, told he can have all the land he can cover on foot from sunrise to sunset, keeps running until he falls dead from exhaustion as the sun sinks below the horizon.

In a curious way, Hoffa's death, like that of the Russian peasant, also stemmed from greed. Because of two avaricious schemes—a secret trucking business and a secret Florida land promotion—Hoffa went to jail. For want of freedom, his Teamster presidency was lost. For want of the presidency—and its power—underworld loyalty was lost. And for want of underworld loyalty, Hoffa's life was lost.

Others' greed, nurtured by Hoffa, played a part in his downfall, too. Just as Hoffa had made a deal with the underworld to achieve power, so he permitted local and regional Teamster barons to feed at numerous Teamster troughs to win and hold their support. When Hoffa emerged from prison and sought to regain the Teamster presidency, his onetime followers proved more loyal to their riches—their plural payrolls, *la dolce vita* expense accounts, and kingly pensions—than to the father of it all, James R. Hoffa. They chose, prudently, to side with the man in power, Hoffa's successor, Frank E. Fitzsimmons.

Since Hoffa's lusting after riches played so important a role both in his life and death—and in setting the moral tone of our biggest union as well—the size and origin of Hoffa's fortune are worth exploring.

Although intimates of Hoffa's believe he accumulated millions, the full extent of his fortune may remain as much of a mystery as his disappearance. For one thing, Hoffa was as secretive about his financial dealings as the most secretive of his Mafia friends. He paid for everything in cash, abjuring the use of checks that might leave tracks for congressional and Internal Revenue Service snoopers to follow. For another thing, Hoffa rarely revealed his presence in a business, but preferred the role of silent partner.

For instance, it was not known, except by his family and a few intimates, that Louis Linteau, the man who was the last to hear from Hoffa the day he disappeared, was Hoffa's partner in an airline limousine service. Linteau was a onetime Teamster official who had served a prison sentence for accepting employer bribes. Hoffa had secretly invested in Linteau's taxi service at Pontiac, Michigan; he kept desk space and spent much time there after leaving prison. Just as secret was Hoffa's suspected part-ownership of two Las Vegas gambling hotels, of other real estate, and of caches in Swiss banks. And until Hoffa's protégé, Chuckie O'Brien, boasted about it, none knew that Hoffa owned a shirt factory in Jamaica—which he turned over to Chuckie.

Finally, Hoffa's own family was as reticent about his wealth as Hoffa himself was. Hoffa's son, Jim, told me that his father's estate was limited to his pension settlement, the family home at Lake Orion, and a condominium in Florida.

Yet the elder Hoffa's hints to interviewers as well as educated guesses by informants who knew some of Hoffa's financial secrets indicate that he had amassed substantially more.

"Are you a millionaire?" one interviewer asked.

"I would say," Hoffa replied.

QUESTION: We have heard that you and Jimmy, Jr., got into a discussion on money and you commented, "How many men can come up with two million in cash immediately?"

ANSWER: I would say, exactly right.[1]

Hoffa was not exaggerating. When he disappeared, federal agents checked his bank accounts on the tip that he had withdrawn all of his cash and fled the country. The tip proved false. Hoffa's cash had not been disturbed. In one safe deposit box, agents found $600,000 in currency. Secret Swiss bank accounts probably contained much more, according to Walter Sheridan, onetime head of the Justice Department's Hoffa unit, which dug up the evidence for two criminal convictions against Hoffa.

A man who can lay his hands on $2,000,000 cash immediately, as Hoffa intimated he could, obviously owns much more than that.

A Hoffa lawyer and confidant for more than thirty years waved his hand to encompass the substantial hotel sitting room in which we were talking some thirteen months after Hoffa's disappearance.

"If you could fill this room with hundred-dollar bills from wall to wall and from floor to ceiling," he said, "you might have an idea of how much Jimmy accumulated."

"Well, how much?" I pressed.

"About twelve million, as a guess," he said. "I know about some of the pension-fund deals he was involved in."

Ironically, because of Hoffa's secret money habits, his family may never fully inherit his wealth. For instance, when

1. Interview with James R. Hoffa by Jerry Stanecki, *Playboy*, December 1975.

Hoffa bought an interest in a Pennsylvania hard-coal mine in 1976, he is reputed to have made two payments totaling a reported $600,000—in cash. Presumably, Hoffa obtained some document of ownership in return. But the family, a year after Hoffa's disappearance, couldn't find that piece of paper. Nor were there, of course, any canceled checks to prove Hoffa's transaction. Meanwhile, the chief owner of the mine contended that Hoffa never did buy an interest.

Similarly, Hoffa's son-in-law, Robert Crancer, told me the family does not know what other secret pieces of ownership Hoffa may have acquired. Making an estimate of Hoffa's estate for the purpose of paying death taxes or probating a will posed problems for the family and for the Internal Revenue Service.

How much did Hoffa really leave to his heirs? The picture emerged that the wily Hoffa, dealing only in cash, had squirreled away pieces of ownership in secret hands. Unless these came forward voluntarily, what they held would be lost to the Hoffa family. Hoffa may have outsmarted himself and robbed his family of a considerable portion of their inheritance.

Hoffa's accumulations coincided with two periods of growth. One was Hoffa's own growth in the Teamsters, which opened up increasing opportunities for multiple Teamster payroll checks and regal pensions as well as for the sale of favors to other union men and to employers. And as the reserves of the Central States, Southeast and Southwest Areas Pension Fund—the Teamsters' biggest—grew, so did Hoffa's opportunities. As dictator of investment loans he realized kickbacks both in cash and in pieces of the borrowers' businesses.

Self-enrichment through the sale of Teamster favors began when Hoffa was still only a state Teamster power. When (as part of a larger inquiry into the jukebox monopoly racket), a county grand jury looked into the affairs of a Detroit union representing jukebox maintenance men, it found on the union's payroll the wives of Jim Hoffa and his pal, Owen Bert Brennan.

The jukebox local was not in the Teamsters. It was an independent affiliated directly with the parent American Federation of Labor. Hoffa's and Brennan's wives did no work for the local and never went near the union hall. But weekly, each received a $100 check. The jukebox union's president testified that he had borrowed from the Messrs. Hoffa and Brennan, and this was how he was repaying it. The trouble was that the alleged loan came to $2,000, but payments at the time of the grand jury inquiry already totaled $6,000.

"I figure, the money was well spent," the jukebox union president explained to the grand jury (which published the testimony).

"Why?"

"Because they [Hoffa and Brennan] are big men. They can help me a lot."

It was clear that the "help" that the jukebox local was buying from Hoffa and his pal was the economic power of the Teamsters—the dread secondary boycott with which the Teamsters can cut off businessmen's supplies by refusing to take them through union picket lines.

Employers could be grateful to Hoffa, too. Again, the gratitude would be channeled secretly through his wife. As congressional testimony showed, one of Michigan's biggest truckers and employer of drivers formed a company to rent out hauling equipment, saying, "I'm going to put some friends in business." The friends were the "Misses Josephine Poszywak and Alice Johnson," actually the wives of Jim Hoffa and Owen Bert Brennan. The wives, again, did not go to an office; they solicited no business and kept no accounts. All this was done by the trucker's accountant. The Teamster bosses' wives had only one chore: to ask by telephone for dividends. At the time I learned about this matter, in 1955, the dividends had come to $62,000 in four years.

As Hoffa climbed the Teamster ladder, opportunities arose for self-enrichment via Teamster payrolls, and Hoffa cashed in handsomely by granting himself the highest salaries in labor history. At the time Hoffa went to prison in 1967, he was receiving $87,500 in pay as Teamster president; with travel allowance, this exceeded $100,000, and was more than the salary then paid to the President of the United States and also 30 percent more than the $70,000 paid to the president of the 13,700,000-member AFL-CIO, George Meany.

Hoffa also took prudent retirement measures. A pension program known as the Family Protection Plan covers all those on the Teamster International payroll, from president down to secretaries and janitors at Teamster headquarters. In 1966, Hoffa amended this plan so that a handful of officials, including himself, could qualify for retirement at full pay or with a fortune in severance pay. Hoffa, choosing the severance settlement, came away in 1971 with the equivalent of twenty-two years' pay at the time of retirement—or $1,700,000. From the Detroit local of which he had been president, Hoffa also drew a $41,000 yearly pension. And there was still more to sweeten the Hoffa family's take. For two of the three years in which Hoffa lived to enjoy his pensions, his wife Josephine was on the International Teamster payroll for $48,000.

Mrs. Hoffa's job for the International, as well as the timing of her appointment, raised some interesting questions. The job, created in 1972, was that of director of the women's division of DRIVE, the Teamsters' political arm. Mrs. Hoffa's chief chore was to make occasional speeches to Teamsters' wives urging them to become politically aware. Terrified of the speaker's platform, Mrs. Hoffa would race through an occasional thirty-second speech and sit down.

Why did Teamster president Fitzsimmons entrust Mrs.

Hoffa with a task for which she was only modestly qualified? And why did he create the job at the time that Hoffa was leaving prison?

When Hoffa went to prison in 1967, he held on to his presidency but gave up his pay. Instead, there was an agreement to pay Mrs. Hoffa a living allowance of $40,000 yearly. Mrs. Hoffa never received this sum during Hoffa's imprisonment. Mysteriously, however, a $40,000 yearly payment to Mrs. Hoffa appeared in the Teamsters' annual report during the first year of Hoffa's freedom, 1972.

Could Hoffa have bargained out the $40,000 payroll spot for his wife in return for his agreement to step down as president and clear the way for Fitzsimmons? Fitzsimmons would not comment, and a former secretary-treasurer of the Teamsters—who was in a position to sign payroll checks—would only say, "I can't read a man's [Fitzsimmons'] mind," In any case, Fitzsimmons abolished Mrs. Hoffa's job in 1974, indicating it wasn't much needed in the first place.

IN THE EARLY 1960s, at about the beginning of his second term as Teamster president, Hoffa woke up to the discovery—perhaps not altogether unexpected—that he was the master of an El Dorado, an abundant gold mine. Magically, this hoard of gold would not diminish with the mining, but would grow bigger year by year. This was the Central States, Southeast and Southwest Areas Pension Fund, covering 400,000 Teamsters in twenty-three states.

I first reported on Hoffa's operation of the Central States fund in 1962, in an article called "The Strange Saga of James Hoffa, Banker."[2]

I found that the fund, negotiated by Hoffa and fed by employers' contributions, already had a reservoir of

2. *Reader's Digest*, August 1962.

$125,000,000 of investment cash in it, and this was rising at the rate of almost $100,000,000 yearly (by the time Hoffa went to prison, the pension fund would have $325,000,000 in reserves, and by 1977 the staggering sum of $1,400,000,000).

Instead of turning the pension fund's investment management over to a bank or an insurance company as most unions do, Hoffa dictated that investments be made directly by a board of trustees equally divided between his union subordinates and employers. (Two of the union trustees had criminal records. Two of the employers, I found, were borrowing from the fund, thus making them subject to Hoffa's will.) Instead of investing the pension fund's reserves in securities, Hoffa went into the lending business to finance land development schemes, business loans, hotels, and other construction.

Hoffa became a banker with lending power equal, in time, to that of a major bank. And as banker, Hoffa could do favors and win powerful friends—in the Mafia and out—to extend his own power. He could enrich himself and members of his family as well.

Hoffa was fascinated by his role as banker and took an increasing amount of time and energy from his union duties to tend to it. Once, when some thirty officials of Hoffa's Teamsters and Harry Bridges' Longshoremen's Union were meeting to solidify their newly formed joint Western Warehousemen's Council, Hoffa was called to a telephone for a party-line conference on a pension-fund loan. In full hearing of the assembled union men, Hoffa embarked on a long and acrimonious debate over the sale of a bankrupt hotel and the granting of a further loan. An eyewitness observed: "The result was both tragic and hilarious. Bridges delivered a class-solidarity speech while Hoffa played the big investment banker in the background."[3]

3. Ralph C. and Estelle James, *Hoffa and the Teamsters* (New York: Van Nostrand, 1965).

Hoffa "the big investment banker" was also Hoffa the big tollgate keeper, levying tolls on some who sought pension-fund loans.

Kickbacks are made in cash and are not proclaimed in the financial pages of your newspaper. So the extent of the payoffs to Hoffa, like so much of his financial dealings, may never be known. Yet, like the tip of an iceberg, some of what Hoffa was collecting surfaced in criminal trials that brought convictions for pension fraud.

One of the schemes that started Hoffa on the road to disaster was a Florida land promotion. The plan was to sell lots to re-tiring Teamsters and make a fortune for Hoffa and other insiders. As usual, Hoffa's participation was a secret. It consisted of a 22.5 percent interest and was held in trust for Hoffa by a nominee. When the venture foundered, Hoffa came to the rescue with $500,000 from his Detroit Local 299 treasury. And when the project continued to sink, Hoffa knew what to do to bail himself and his friends out. He imposed 10 percent kickbacks on a number of pension-fund loans, and used the proceeds to pay off the land scheme's debts and retrieve his Detroit local's money.

In Hoffa's subsequent trial for pension-fund fraud in 1964, one businessman who borrowed $3,300,000 to finance a Miami hotel testified that he was asked for a 10 percent cash kickback. When he said he couldn't afford it, he was told to increase his loan application so that $300,000 could go to Hoffa, via two go-betweens.

"They told me they had to have it immediately, because Hoffa was raising hell and was expecting it," the borrower testified. The go-betweens also told him they hoped no harm would come to him (the borrower) because "these boys play rough."

The prosecution convinced a federal jury that borrowers of

some $20,000,000 of Teamster pension-fund loans either kicked back cash to Hoffa and company or diverted part of their loan proceeds to his land development venture. Hoffa and six codefendants were found guilty.

A series of six trials that began four years later, in 1968, cast further light on Hoffa the investment banker and tollgate keeper. An undercover agent for the FBI and CIA, assigned to spy on the underworld, found that some of New York City's most lurid characters—including Tony Ducks Corallo and James "Three Finger Brown" Plumeri—were wallowing in a new source of cash: kickbacks for arranging loans from the Teamster pension fund. At a subsequent trial, the undercover agent, a lawyer named Herbert Itkin, testified that the Mafia characters didn't keep all of the kickback cash. They divvied it up with Hoffa. The bagman, he testified, was the pension fund's then accountant, David Wenger.

Just as the role of banker fascinated Hoffa, so did Las Vegas as a stage on which to play that role. Under Hoffa, the Teamster pension fund poured $170,000,000 into Nevada. gambling enterprises.

What profit, if any, Hoffa personally realized from his early loans to Las Vegas figures is not known. But federal investigators had reason to believe, and an informant close to Hoffa has confirmed to me, that in later deals Hoffa got a piece of the action, i.e., hidden ownership in at least two hotels.[4]

Always the strong family man, Hoffa did not neglect to throw some juicy deals, financed with Teamster pension-fund loans, to members of his family.

Few horseplayers ever made a bigger killing on a long shot than Hoffa's son-in-law, Robert Crancer, and daughter, Bar-

4. For a more detailed description of Hoffa's involvement in Las Vegas, see Chapter 23, The Golden Godfather of Las Vegas.

bara, did when they put $50,000 into a racetrack, financed with Teamster pension-fund loans, and came up with a $1,202,632 profit.

In the spring of 1965, son-in-law Crancer's lawyer, Gene Zafft of St. Louis, wrote a confidential memorandum to Hoffa (then out on bail pending appeal of two convictions, one for pension-fund fraud). The letter outlined Zafft's understanding of a deal to purchase the Charles Town racetrack in West Virginia and the role of a $4,000,000 Teamster fund loan in it. The letter, with marginal comments in Hoffa's handwriting, was found in his old Detroit Local 299 office after Hoffa's disappearance. It proved that son-in-law Crancer knew that a Teamster loan was in the works when he bought into the deal for a nominal $50,000—getting a 20 percent interest in a racetrack that was purchased for $5,300,000.

Principals in the racetrack deal, too, were pals of Hoffa's who had been deeply involved in prior Teamster pension-fund deals. One was Irvin Kovens, brother of Calvin Kovens, who was convicted of pension fraud along with Hoffa in 1964. Irvin Kovens had refused to testify at that trial on the ground that his testimony might incriminate him.

When the Charles Town racetrack was sold in 1971 and the Crancers' participation in the giant profits became known, both Irvin Kovens and the Crancers insisted there had been no connection between their interest in the racetrack and the granting of the Teamster fund loan. Kovens pointed out that Crancer's purchase of his share in the track preceded the granting of the Teamster loan by more than two years. But the Teamster pension-fund file, as well as the telltale letter to Crancer's father-in-law, Hoffa, indicated a loan was in the works at the very inception of the racetrack deal.[5]

5. The SEC, checking the deal for fraud, could find none. The loan to the Kovens-Crancer group is being repaid by the corporation to whom they sold the racetrack.

Hoffa's passion for riches had, over the years, thrown him into business partnerships and deals with assorted dubious characters, among them Allen Dorfman. Dorfman was the stepson of Paul "Red" Dorfman, who introduced Hoffa to the Chicago Capone mob, and he was also the man to whom Hoffa entrusted the Teamster pension fund when he went to prison. "When this man speaks, he speaks for me," Hoffa had told subordinates. So Dorfman had spoken for Hoffa until he, too, went to prison in 1973 for extorting money from a pension-fund borrower. But what was good enough for the father, Hoffa—in the way of a business partner—was good enough for the son, James P. Hoffa. When Dorfman went into the high-risk-loan business in New York, one of his associates, it turned out, was James P. Hoffa. (The business was soon dissolved.)

Hoffa did, however, at one time mistake a coal mine for a gold mine and sank a reported $600,000 into it. "I'll make a billion!" Hoffa told a Washington lobbyist-friend. "The Japanese are hunting for coal mines, and we've got them."

The "we" with whom Hoffa associated himself was a typical bunch of financial adventurers in a typically complicated Hoffa financial involvement. As *Overdrive,* a truckers' magazine based in Los Angeles, pieced together the story, Hoffa's associates were "persons connected [in prior years] with high risk, gray area companies, with Teamster pension fund loans, with criminal investigations and . . . with alliances with organized crime figures."[6] The coal mining company, said *Overdrive,* "was apparently funded by a company operating out of the Bahamas, frequently a stopping-off point for cash entering or leaving the United States."

One of Hoffa's partners in the coal deal was a Jim Durkin, whom Hoffa met in jail.

6. *Overdrive,* August 1975.

Like the peasant in the Russian fable, Hoffa kept pursuing riches until the day he died. Shortly before his disappearance, for instance, Hoffa sought to make a quick killing as promoter of a rock and roll festival. The idea was to lease the Detroit Lions stadium at Pontiac, which seats eighty thousand, hire some rock performers, and watch the money roll in. But Hoffa disappeared while negotiations were still going on. Hoffa's lifelong drive for riches, paralleling his drive for power, involved him with unsavory characters and deals that were bound to attract the attention of the press. Exposure in the press was bound to attract the attention of congressional investigators. This ultimately resulted in one of the most dramatic confrontations in the annals of Senate investigations and federal crime prosecution: the struggle between James R. Hoffa and Robert F. Kennedy.

Chapter Eleven

THE MONKEY ON HOFFA'S BACK

I N THE SPRING of 1964, Jim Hoffa received a message from the man he regarded as his mortal enemy, Robert F. Kennedy.

Kennedy had warred on Hoffa for seven years: first as Senate investigator, then as U. S. Attorney General and architect of the criminal prosecutions against Hoffa. Kennedy had just won his first great battle in that war: Hoffa's conviction for jury tampering and an eight-year sentence. Now, within two weeks, Hoffa would go on trial again, this time on charges of defrauding the Teamsters' Central States pension fund. Conviction could mean another five years.

Kennedy's message—delivered by the late Johnny O'Rourke, a Teamster vice-president and friend of the Kennedy family—was as electrifying as it was unexpected. For in it, Bob Kennedy offered Hoffa amnesty.

If Hoffa would step down from the Teamster presidency and out of union work altogether, he would serve virtually no time in prison. As courier O'Rourke spelled it out, a swift parole would reduce Hoffa's jury-tampering sentence to a few months at most. As for the pension fraud charges, they would be dropped, and the coming trial would be called off.

Hoffa's response, according to two lawyers who were with Hoffa at the time, was a raging tantrum.

"You double-crossing mother f———!" Hoffa roared at the aging O'Rourke, some twenty years Hoffa's senior. "That son of a bitch [Kennedy] is trying to take my union away from me, and you're making yourself a party to it!"

Hoffa had thrown another such memorable tantrum some seven years before. It was during the early days of the McClellan Committee hearings when pressure was building against Hoffa to cleanse his union of gangsters. Hoffa's then public relations advisor, Eddie Cheyfitz, had been holding forth to Teamster officials in Hoffa's Woodner Hotel suite in Washington about the need at least for a token cleanup.

"If only one ex-criminal were to be dropped from the Teamsters in each of a dozen key cities, it would do wonders for Hoffa's name," Cheyfitz was saying.

At this point Hoffa entered the room, listened until he got the drift of Cheyfitz' discourse, then flew into a rage.

"Who do you think you are, firing guys out of the Teamsters!?" he stormed.

Several years later, Edward Bennett Williams, then Teamsters general counsel, also tried his hand at separating Hoffa from his hoodlum pals. Finding himself alone with Hoffa at Teamster headquarters at the end of a working day, Williams suggested to Hoffa that chance had placed a great opportunity in Hoffa's hands to rid himself of at least a selected group of embarrassing associates.

"A federal court has ordered you to clean up the union, and you are under the jurisdiction of a board of monitors that checks your every action," Williams reminded Hoffa. "So you have a great umbrella. All you have to do is to say the court forced your hand."

But Williams, a master in the courtroom, could not convince Hoffa. A shouting match ensued.

"I may have my faults," Hoffa yelled, "but being wrong ain't one of them!"

When Williams returned home, quivering, his six-year-old son greeted him with: "Hey, Dad! Where did you get the shiner?"

"What shiner?"

"The one under your right eye."

On examination, it turned out that Williams had literally burst a blood vessel trying to get Hoffa to drop some mobsters.

Neither Edward Bennett Williams nor Cheyfitz nor Bob Kennedy was aware of Hoffa's terrible secret—his trial by the Detroit Mafia and his desperate bargain. In exchange for underworld support he would provide Teamster favors. Dropping the Teamster presidency or shedding underworld supporters would break Hoffa's desperate bargain. Hoffa had put a monkey on his back, and he would carry it as long as he lived.

To retain his underworld ties, Hoffa—by early 1957—had already used the considerable political and financial resources of the Teamsters to prevent or abort three congressional investigations.

Four years before, a Kansas congressman, Wint Smith, was beginning to unravel Hoffa's underworld entanglements when he suddenly called off his investigation. To reporters Smith would only say, raising his eyes ceilingward, "The pressure comes from way up there, and I just can't talk about it."

Hoffa had put pressure on truckers who contributed heavily to Republican campaigns and these, in turn, had put pressure on the Republican National Committee.

But in 1957 Hoffa faced a new threat. The press had begun to illuminate some of the murkier corners of the empire Hoffa was building. The *Reader's Digest* had introduced Hoffa— then a little known Teamster ninth vice-president—to its national audience in 1955. Clark Mollenhoff of the Cowles newspapers, who subsequently won a Pulitzer Prize for his Teamster reporting, had waged a campaign to convince the then thirty-year-old Robert F. Kennedy that an investigation into labor racketeering could turn into the biggest investigation in Senate history.

By 1957, Bob Kennedy's legal and investigating experience had been minimal. He had served as an assistant U. S. attorney in Washington, then as assistant counsel on Senator Joseph McCarthy's controversial Permanent Subcommittee on Investigations. Now, as chief counsel of the Senate Labor Rackets Committee,[1] Kennedy knew little of organized labor. His knowledge of the Teamsters was limited to a tour of Teamster headquarters, opposite the Capitol, which had been arranged by Teamster public relations man Eddie Cheyfitz. But Bob Kennedy was hungry to make his name in public life. To this, when Kennedy learned more about Hoffa, was added a zeal to "get Hoffa" that bordered on religious fervor.

To Kennedy, Hoffa became the embodiment of evil, the "enemy within the gates," who harbored within the Teamsters, as within a Trojan horse, pillagers from an alien world— the underworld. Kennedy felt that these, if unchecked, would soon be at the controls of the country's economy. Hoffa became an obsession with Kennedy. As one writer put it, Bob Kennedy was Captain Ahab, Hoffa was Moby Dick.[2] With a staff of forty investigators and forty-two accountants, Bob Kennedy gave chase while the nation looked on.

To Hoffa, Bob Kennedy was a "spoiled brat," a boy sent to do a man's job. Hoffa delighted in his early encounters with Kennedy in showing, by feats of strength, who was the man and who the boy. Hoffa's first face-to-face encounter with Bob

1. Formally known as the Senate Select Committee on Improper Practices in the Labor and Management Field.
2. Victor S. Navasky, *Kennedy Justice* (New York: Atheneum, 1971).

Kennedy was at a dinner in the home of Hoffa's public relations advisor, Eddie Cheyfitz. As Hoffa reported gleefully to an intimate later, it wound up in an Indian (arm) wrestling match in which—Hoffa reported—he easily "put down Bobby." When FBI agents arrested Hoffa the day after the dinner on charges of buying secret McClellan Committee documents, Hoffa, in court, bumped into Bob Kennedy, who had come to witness the arraignment.

What did the two men talk about?

As Hoffa recalled it, they compared the number of push-ups each could do. And in his autobiography, published in 1975, Hoffa told happily how he had roughed up Bob Kennedy in a restaurant when Kennedy allegedly had accosted him rudely.

Yet, boy or no boy, Bob Kennedy posed a perilous problem to Hoffa. With his investigators poking into every nook and cranny of Hoffa's private and public life, Kennedy was bound to uncover underworld ties and ask questions about them. If Hoffa answered truthfully, he faced underworld retribution. If he lied, he risked a perjury indictment.

So, on the eve of Hoffa's first appearance before the McClellan Committee, he debated strategy with five lawyers, assembled around the giant desk in Hoffa's oak-paneled office.

The easiest way out, Hoffa was advised, was simply to take the Fifth Amendment. This might cause Hoffa some momentary embarrassment, but it would soon blow over.

Hoffa rejected the suggestion. To refuse to answer on the ground that his answers might incriminate him would surely result in having Hoffa and the Teamsters booted out of the parent AFL-CIO, something Hoffa wanted desperately to avoid. Also, Hoffa had been destroying the records of his Local 299 at the end of each yearly audit. Suppose he was asked why—and had to say that the answer might incriminate him? Also, once he invoked the Fifth Amendment, he couldn't pick and choose the questions he would answer. Having answered one, he must answer all.

"To hell with it," Hoffa decided. He would invoke no constitutional amendments.

"Any time I can't stand up to that spoiled brat I'll quit," he said. "Besides, he isn't the brightest fella in the world, and he's got to investigate for weeks and weeks to find out what we already know."

Hoffa, with his computer mind, seldom took notes on anything and prided himself on a total recall memory. Yet, as a witness, Hoffa remembered so little about his own affairs or those of his union that a senator remarked, "Mr. Hoffa, you have one of the best forgetteries in the business."

Hoffa was at his forgettable best—or worst—when pressed about underworld infiltration into the Teamsters.

Asked why he conspired to get Teamster charters for Johnny Dio, the New York City Mafia figure and extortionist, Hoffa fumbled and brought out: "To the best of my recollection, I must recall with my memory, I can't remember."

Later, Hoffa said, "Maybe I did look silly. But there was a reason for it." He couldn't peach on his underworld friends.

The McClellan Committee hearings were an important but not decisive battlefield in the Hoffa-Kennedy war. The Senate could not remove Hoffa from office nor send him to jail. That could be done only by the courts.

In a court struggle that began while the McClellan Committee hearings were still on, Hoffa's refusal to shed his underworld burden almost cost him the Teamster presidency.

The key to Hoffa's election to his first term of office in 1957, as we have seen, was the Hoffa-controlled credentials committee, which permitted the seating of fake delegates who swung the election to Hoffa.

A subsequent rank-and-file suit to set aside Hoffa's election resulted in a compromise settlement. Hoffa would be permitted to hold office as "conditional president" if he submitted to the surveillance and orders of three monitors. When Hoffa resisted monitor demands that he kick out his underworld followers, a federal court ordered Hoffa to stand trial which could remove him from office.

Hoffa turned to the circuit court of appeals to block the trial and possible removal from office. On the day the appeals court was to hand down its decision, Hoffa, waiting in court, had tears in his eyes. His face twisting to restrain a sob, Hoffa asked the lawyer at his side, Jacob Kossman, "Am I going to lose the union?"

The lawyer, towering above Hoffa, reached down to put his arms around Hoffa's shoulders and said: "There, there. It'll turn out all right."

It had not occurred to Hoffa, even at this dire moment, that all he had to do to retain his presidency was to jettison some of his underworld followers.

But as lawyer Kossman had said, things turned out all right. The circuit court of appeals, seemingly tired of the endless litigation that Hoffa's battle with the monitors had generated, ordered the monitors to wind up their affairs. Hoffa had escaped, but he still had his enemy to deal with—and his underworld burden to hamper him.

In 1960 Kennedy was no longer counsel to a Senate committee that was powerless to do anything to Hoffa except embarrass him with its revelations. Now, Bob Kennedy was the United States Attorney General, in charge of the federal government's prosecuting machinery. And in the White House, backing up "Bobby," was his big brother, John F. Kennedy, the President.

For both, putting Hoffa behind bars was unfinished business.

In one of his first moves as attorney general, Bob Kennedy set up a special unit in the Justice Department. It came to be known as the "Get Hoffa unit"—to sift evidence and obtain criminal indictments against him. Taking charge was ex-FBI man Walter Sheridan, who had acquired an encyclopedic knowledge of Hoffa's doings while serving as top McClellan Committee investigator. He was soon keeping tabs on Hoffa's movements twenty-four hours a day. Hoffa's life became a nightmare of suspicion and irrational fears. As Hoffa told the Teamsters convention of 1961, he believed that FBI agents followed him everywhere, tapped his telephone, opened his mail. He warned each delegate to study the man or woman beside him; the person might be an FBI spy. Hoffa warned, too, that female FBI agents prowled the hotel corridors and bars intent on seducing delegates and obtaining information from them.

Hoffa also told an MIT professor that the FBI beamed listening devices on him from a half mile away, aided by an invisible powder they had rubbed on his clothes.

The Hoffa unit pored over many of Hoffa's deals, many of his pension-fund loans. At the same time, fifteen federal grand juries around the country began to sift McClellan Committee testimony and the Hoffa unit's findings with the aim of bringing criminal indictments against Hoffa's subordinates.

Soon, Teamster officials began to fall like tenpins, among them vice-presidents Tony Provenzano of New Jersey and Bill Presser of Ohio, as well as the treasurer of Hoffa's Local 299—plus several dozen others who were convicted of crimes ranging from the destruction of subpoenaed records to extortion.

As for the chief target, Jim Hoffa, it took Hoffa to get Hoffa. And the underworld did its part. The Kennedy Justice Department's first case against Hoffa provided a prime example. The Justice Department's Hoffa unit had labored and brought forth a mouse—an indictment charging Hoffa had permitted an employer to put his wife into the trucking busi-

ness. This constituted a misdemeanor under the Taft-Hartley
Act. If proved, it would be punishable by a fine and, at most,
by a few months in jail. A slap on the wrist.

Yet Hoffa showed up for the misdemeanor trial in
Nashville, Tennessee, as if he were defending himself against
a charge of murder. In his entourage were nine lawyers,
among them two masters of criminal law, Jacob Kossman
from Philadelphia, and Morris Shenker from St. Louis. In his
entourage, too, were Chuckie O'Brien, then serving Hoffa as
messenger and bodyguard, plus Allen Dorfman, Hoffa's
bridge to the Chicago Capone gang, and "Babe" Triscaro and
John "Skip" Felice, representing the Ohio Mafia.

On its side, the Justice Department had rarely deployed so
much legal and backup firepower for a misdemeanor case.
Three Justice Department lawyers came down from
Washington to assist the U. S. attorney at Nashville. Walter
Sheridan of the Hoffa unit took up an observation post in the
Federal Building. He reported back at least once daily to Bob
Kennedy, who, although preoccupied at the time with the
Cuban missile crisis, was always available to Sheridan on the
telephone. From the FBI in Washington, too, came several
dozen agents to beef up the local FBI. In Hoffa's previous
trials—none of which had resulted in a conviction—there had
always been questions about extracurricular influence on the
juries. This time, the feds would not be caught napping.

They weren't.

Hoffa's trial on the misdemeanor charge ended in a hung
jury, seven-to-five for acquittal, but Hoffa's pals and Hoffa
himself had been busy improving his chances and the feds had
a spy planted in Hoffa's inner circle of lawyers and well-
wishers who was ready to testify that Hoffa and company had
tried to fix the jury. A grand jury indicted Hoffa and four
others on the charge. By arranging their own justice, Hoffa
and his underworld pals, including his mob-connected friend

Allen Dorfman, had escalated a misdemeanor charge into a felony indictment.

To Chattanooga for the jury-fixing trial, Hoffa brought fourteen lawyers—and two tin boxes. One box was kept at the Patton Hotel, Hoffa's headquarters, and the other at the Andrews Hotel, where some of his entourage stayed. Into these boxes, emissaries from the mobs lodged in Las Vegas gambling casinos poured cash estimated by one of Hoffa's lawyers at "hundreds of thousands of dollars."

The Teamsters' aging secretary-treasurer, John English, had grown increasingly reluctant to pay out union money to finance Hoffa's personal problems. So the Mafia came through for Jimmy—to pay lawyers' fees, secretarial help, printing costs as well as a substantial fee and expenses to an expert in detecting electronic surveillance, Bernard Spindel. Spindel brought a ton of equipment to Chattanooga to listen in on the radio communications between FBI agents who were maintaining tight surveillance of Hoffa and company.

This surveillance was so galling to Hoffa that, in the midst of a grim trial, Hoffa decided to turn himself into Puck and play a prank on the FBI.

One evening, Hoffa's codefendant, Allen Dorfman, emerged from the Patton Hotel, knowing that the FBI was staked out across the way and taking pictures of the comings and goings of Hoffa's friends. Dorfman looked warily—and guiltily—around him. He entered his car and drove to a dark side street where he parked and waited.

Moments later, Hoffa and Chuckie O'Brien left the hotel, each carrying a large traveling bag. With them was a Hoffa lawyer, William Bufalino, with a tightly rolled package under his arm. This trio, too, looked self-consciously about them for the benefit of the FBI cameras, entered a car, and drove to a rendezvous with the waiting Dorfman. On their heels, as their electronics expert later told them, FBI agents were filling the air with excited instructions to each other.

At the rendezvous, Dorfman leaped from his car, slammed the traveling bags brought by Hoffa and his friends into the luggage carrier, and sped off from a screeching start. Hoffa, O'Brien, and Bufalino, in turn, sped off in the direction of the Chattanooga airport.

At the airport, Bufalino deposited coins in two lockers and left his tightly wrapped package—containing old newspapers—in one of them. Hoffa and his two playmates then boarded the Teamsters' twin-jet-engined six-seater Lockheed plane and flew off to Memphis, where they alighted and remained long enough for waiting FBI agents to spot them. They then returned to Chattanooga. In their absence someone had struggled with the tangled knots on the package and, finding the hoax, had seemingly thrown the package back into the locker without troubling to hide the effort to untie it.

Hoffa roared.

The laughter continued back at Hoffa's hotel, where Dorfman was waiting for them with three traveling bags—all empty.

But the jury-tampering trial itself gave Hoffa little to laugh about. Although Hoffa was surrounded by some of the country's most able criminal lawyers, it soon became evident that Hoffa was his own chief counsel—and enemy. As his own lawyer, Hoffa did what no seasoned defense lawyer would do. He attempted to try the judge, U. S. District Judge Frank Wiley Wilson. Wilson, a tall, gentle-voiced man, patrician in bearing, was widely known and respected in Tennessee. Hoffa directed a remorseless stream of abuse at the judge. It began during the preliminary rite of selecting a jury and continued for seven long weeks. At Hoffa's instigation, his lawyers berated the judge for operating a "drumhead court-martial," suggesting that the court's actions smacked of "Stalinism, Hitlerism, Mussolinism." As the lawyers poured vituperation on the judge, Hoffa would lean back, a broad happy grin on his face.

On the twelfth day of the trial, the prosecution called a surprise witness. Up the courtroom aisle strode a tall, athletic figure whose red face and red neck contrasted with the somber black of his Sunday suit. Hoffa took one look at the man and went gray. He turned to a lawyer beside him and gasped: "My God, it's Ed Partin!"

Hoffa knew Edward Grady Partin as a rough, tough secretary-treasurer of a Teamster local at Baton Rouge, Louisiana. He also knew that Partin had been in Nashville during Hoffa's trial there a year before. At that time Hoffa had let Partin in on some secrets.

"We're going to get to one juror," Hoffa had confided, according to testimony, "or try to get to some scattered jurors." What Hoffa didn't know was that Partin had become an undercover agent for the Department of Justice.

And Partin had a grievance against Hoffa. The Teamsters' bonding and insurance agent had revoked a bond for Partin just as he was being bailed out on a kidnapping charge arising from Partin's removal of two children from their home in behalf of a friend involved in a divorce. Partin had had to remain in jail. Freed shortly before Hoffa's Nashville trial, Partin came up to be with Hoffa—and to spy on him.

Now, at Chattanooga, Partin was "singing" against Hoffa.

"One day," testified Partin, "Hoffa told me, 'I may want you to pass something around for me.'"

"Then," Partin continued, "he put his hand behind his back and hit his pocket."

Another time, Partin testified, Hoffa said, "I'd pay $15,000 or $20,000—whatever it costs to get to the jury."

For five days, Hoffa's lawyers hammered at Partin. But the

longer they cross-examined him, the more details he dredged up about his spying adventures in the Hoffa camp.

In the end, the jury believed Partin. The sentence was eight years in federal prison and a $10,000 fine.

Six weeks later, Hoffa went on trial on charges that he and seven accomplices had diverted Teamster pension fund money to Hoffa's own use. Again, as in Nashville and Chattanooga, Hoffa's underworld ties showed.

The case was tried in Chicago, home of the Capone mob. Some of its plug-uglies comprised a curious cheering section at the trial. Led by the veteran Capone gangster and labor racketeer Joey Glimco, who had a record of thirty-six arrests—twice in connection with murders—they staked out seats on the two front benches and glared at the jury. Or they roamed the corridors, spitting near government attorneys and investigators. Once, Glimco approached a government man and offered to throw him over a guard rail to the ground floor, five stories below.

Despite the terror in the courtroom, or perhaps because of it, the verdict, once again, was guilty. The sentence was five years. The man who had seemed invincible only six months before now stood on the brink of the abyss. With the sentence in the jury-tampering case, Hoffa faced thirteen years in prison.

For three years, Hoffa, his Teamster bar association of several dozen union lawyers, his Teamster lobbying organization, plus newspaper owners who had borrowed money from the Teamster pension fund, battled in the higher courts, and on Capitol Hill to ward off prison. In vain. On March 7, 1967, Hoffa began to pay the first installment on his bargain with the underworld. The second installment, his life, would be paid later.

Chapter Twelve

THE
END BEGINS

WHEN JAMES R. HOFFA arrived as usual at the Teamsters' marble and glass Washington headquarters at 8 A.M. on March 6, 1967, the telephones were already jangling. Although it was only 5 A.M. on the West Coast and 7 A.M. in the Middle West, over-the-road drivers who had been tooling their giant rigs through the night were calling Jimmy collect from all points of the compass.

When a rank and filer called, Hoffa would try to squeeze out the time to take the call.

"Those people are important," he would say to exasperated conferees whose business with Hoffa had been interrupted.

Usually, drivers called to seek Jimmy's intercession to settle a beef against a business agent or employer. Jimmy would take the man's name, the number of his local, then call the Teamster vice-president in the area and order him to "get on the ball."

Now the calls had another purpose. Tomorrow was the day Hoffa would go to prison. And the words in each call were virtually the same.

"I've parked my rig beside the road," a voice would say from a pay station at Shawnee, Oklahoma, or at Boulder, Colorado, or at Waukesha, Wisconsin. "They're railroading you, Jimmy. Say the word, and I won't move out of here until they give you a break."

For months, the union's monthly magazine, *The International Teamster,* had hammered away at the theme that Jimmy Hoffa was being framed by a hostile government and power-greedy politicians intent on turning Hoffa into a political prisoner. Hoffa, an effective orator, had used the same theme to arouse union audiences around the country. Now, as prison gates yawned for their leader, truck drivers from coast to coast were talking up a general work stoppage over their citizen's band radios. Such a stoppage could halt the delivery of food and raw materials and, if prolonged, could affect millions.

Hoffa had reason to believe that this was more than a shadowy threat. It was a virtual certainty.

On the prior Saturday, members from Detroit's fourteen Teamster locals—15,000 men and women strong—had jammed the city's convention center, Cobo Hall, intent on voting a general strike as a demonstration "in behalf of Jimmy." Detroit's Teamsters deliver milk for babies and chauffeur hearses to cemeteries. They drive the city's buses, haul away completed cars from the auto factories, and bring parts and raw materials to them. Teamsters store goods in warehouses, sell goods in retail stores, pump gas, take dictation in the city's public offices. Such a strike would have shut down Detroit.

Several advisors had urged Hoffa to sanction the strike secretly, then go on television and call it off—to demonstrate his power and his responsible leadership. But Hoffa had hastened from Washington and had pleaded at the mass meeting: "You people stay on the job. That's the best way you can help me."

Hoffa, who was five feet five and one-half inches tall and conscious of his stature before an audience, would sometimes raise himself up on his toes when emphasizing a point. Now, raising himself on his toes and flailing his arms, Hoffa had vowed, "I'll be back! The union will go on!" Some beside Hoffa on the platform thought they saw his eyes glisten and feared he would choke up. But he finished to the shouted encouragement from his followers: to whistles, cheers, and— among some of the women Teamsters—tears. Detroit's wheels had continued to roll. The city had not gone dead.

Now, at the Teamster headquarters in Washington, it wasn't a city that was being threatened. It was an entire country.

On the oversized desk of his home local, No. 299 in Detroit, which Hoffa had continued to run after he was elected Teamster president, Hoffa kept an eighteen-inch plaster-of-paris arm and hand with the middle digit raised ceilingward in an obscene gesture. On his desk, too, was a wooden plaque with raised letters that proclaimed, *Illegitimi non carborundum!* Hoffa never tired of translating it for visitors: "Don't let the bastards grind you down!"

What a laugh! What a grand gesture it would be to "give the bastards the finger" with a calamitous national strike. But Hoffa, a political animal, sensed he could not blackmail an entire nation.

Into the telephone Hoffa barked: "No strike! No strike! Keep moving! Don't f—— up my chances of getting out soon!"

As usual, Hoffa had rolled out of bed at 6:30 A.M. and begun his thirty-odd push-ups before he was fully awake. But an oppressive leaden weight inside his flat belly told him that this would not be a usual day. It would be one of the most trying in his turbulent life.

Hoffa had showered and toweled himself vigorously until his body, still hard at fifty-five, glowed. He had dressed perfunctorily, as always. First, he had pulled on the white cotton socks that were his hallmark. He wore them because they cost only 79 cents a pair. The gray wool-and-dacron suit had been bought off the rack with an eye toward economy, too. He rarely paid more than $85 for his suits. They fitted him indifferently, and provided a sharp contrast to the flashy $300 tailor-made jobs his colleagues at Teamster headquarters affected.

Hoffa's daughter, Barbara, an attractive woman of twenty-five, had flown in from St. Louis to be with her father and busied herself with breakfast. Hoffa was proud of Barbara and liked to refer at union rallies to her degree in sociology and her Phi Beta Kappa key. To show his gratitude, Hoffa had made an exception to his penurious habits and put on a $20,000 wedding when Barbara had married Robert Crancer, the son of a St. Louis steel producer, three years before. Some of Michigan's most respected people, including judges and corporate chiefs, had attended. Some of the guests were not so respectable. Tony Pro Provenzano had come up from New Jersey and Tony Jack Giacalone was there as well. The Johnny Dios of New York could not attend: Johnny Dio was in prison serving an extortion sentence. The night before the wedding, Jim and Josephine Hoffa had hosted a dinner at Detroit's then fashionable Living Room restaurant for a few selected guests, among them the Provenzanos and the Giacalones.

That had been three years and three criminal trials ago. Now, at breakfast Hoffa made small talk with his daughter and with his son, Jim, a onetime all-state football tackle at high school. Young Hoffa had just graduated from the University of Michigan Law School and, while waiting for his bar exam results, was serving as a legislative intern with the Michigan State Legislature under a Ford Foundation fellowship grant.

Father, son, and daughter finished breakfast which, for Hoffa, seldom varied from grapefruit, toast, two soft-boiled eggs, and a cup of tea—no coffee. Too early for such stimulation. Seven-thirty A.M. rolled around. Hoffa tiptoed into his wife's bedroom to say good-bye. Under the stress of the coming separation, Josephine had suffered a mild heart attack several days before and, asleep, looked exhausted, pale, and fragile. Hoffa touched his lips to her forehead and tiptoed out.

On taking over the Teamster presidency ten years before, Hoffa's aides had urged him to travel in a chauffeur-driven Cadillac as his predecessor, Dave Beck, had done; but Hoffa felt this did not quite fit the image that his rank-and-file members had of "Jimmy Hoffa"—one of their own hard-bitten breed. So now, Hoffa and his son and daughter wedged themselves into Hoffa's Pontiac convertible. With Hoffa at the wheel, they began in silence the twenty-minute drive from the Ambassador's Row section on Massachusetts Avenue in which the Hoffa apartment was located to the Teamster headquarters across from the Capitol. Occasionally, as if to interrupt her father's gloomy thoughts, Barbara, sitting beside Hoffa, squeezed his right arm in a gesture of family support.

By midmorning Hoffa's deeply carpeted, oak-paneled office—with thirty-three volumes of Senate Rackets Committee hearings prominently displayed in recessed bookshelves—had filled up with regional Teamster leaders who stood about as at a wake or kept vigil with the condemned man as he waited for word from Teamster lawyers who were seeking a last-minute stay of sentence, which never came. Most of the union's executive board, consisting of the secretary-treasurer and fourteen vice-presidents, was there. The ancient John English, an incorruptible man who had kept a firm hand on the union's treasury under three Teamster presidents, glowered in a corner, his long, leathery face longer than ever.

"Oh, that I should see this day!" he had lamented in his vain plea to the AFL-CIO convention a decade ago that had expelled the Teamsters. "Oh, that I should see this day!" his troubled old eyes seemed to say now.

Vice-president Harold Gibbons, tall, handsome, and famous as the Teamsters' egghead, hovered respectfully about his old companion-in-arms, Jimmy. Gibbons had worked at Hoffa's side as executive vice-president for years, had shared an apartment with him, and was the logical choice for caretaker president when Hoffa went to jail. But Hoffa, envying Gibbons his good looks, his stature, his skill with words, and his forceful way with a union audience, had feared to leave the union with Gibbons. Hoffa had never trusted intellectuals, anyway. So he tapped one of his own kind for caretaker president, the artless, untutored Frank E. Fitzsimmons, whom Hoffa had raised up from the obscurity of a local vice-presidency in Detroit and brought to Washington a few years before.

Standing about were men, too, who had made momentary headlines during the Senate Rackets Committee hearings eight years before. Big Bill Presser, the Ohio Teamster tsar, who had gone to jail for eight months rather than show the Senate Rackets Committee his union records, had brought his son, Jackie, whose bulging waist indicated he would soon outdo Big Bill in size. Presser was grooming Jackie to take over the family union business in Cleveland if the ruling Frank Scalisi crime family gave the O.K.

One man had come whom Hoffa would rather have had stay at home. This was Salvatore, brother of Tony "Pro" Provenzano. Salvatore Provenzano, himself under indictment on charges of counterfeiting food stamps (later dropped), was an unhappy reminder of what soon lay in store for Hoffa. He had become vice-president when his brother, Tony Pro, had vacated the job to go to prison for extortion. Tony was at Lewisburg, where Hoffa would go the following day.

And flanked by two bodyguards was a fierce-faced gent by the name of Frank Chavez. He had come up from his Teamster fiefdom in Puerto Rico with the publicly avowed purpose of assassinating Senator Robert F. Kennedy, the source, he said, of all Jimmy's woes.[1] The FBI, learning of Chavez' intentions, had put him under twenty-four-hour surveillance when he arrived in Washington and checked into the Continental Hotel—equally near to both the Teamsters headquarters and Senator Kennedy's office. The FBI need not have bothered. Hoffa had summoned Chavez several days before and had pleaded with him to drop his wild plot. It would only worsen matters for everybody. "Give me that goddam gun," Hoffa had ordered. And the fiery Latin had handed it over. Hoffa should have asked for the guns of Chavez' bodyguards as well, for two months later Chavez would himself be murdered by one of them.

As the day wore on, some of Hoffa's well-wishers urged him to "take the wraps" off the drivers.

William E. Bufalino, a Detroit Teamster lawyer who rarely left Hoffa's side, had coined a jingle:

"They gave you the blame" (they railroaded you) "but you won't play the game" (fight back by letting the drivers strike).

But against this and other urgings to halt the country's wheels, Hoffa set his face. It wasn't only that he recoiled instinctively from blackmail that he knew would be futile. He had never, either as a Teamster vice-president or president, called a regional, let alone a national, strike. Hoffa hoarded power, using it sparingly, just as he used his money.

Hoffa had been clearing out his desk, and in his top right-hand drawer he came upon a silver money clip with the initials J.R.H. Some well-wisher, who didn't know Hoffa's money habits, had given it to him. True, Hoffa used no wallet, nor ever wrote a personal check; he carried cash. But it was always

1. For a more complete account of the Chavez plot against Robert F. Kennedy, see Walter Sheridan, *The Fall and Rise of Jimmy Hoffa* (New York, Saturday Review Press, 1972).

in a crumpled wad—sometimes as much as several thousand dollars, stuffed into his right-hand pants pocket.

Hoffa tossed the money clip to Bill Bufalino. "I won't be needing this where I'm going," he said.

Some of the secretaries were sobbing openly as the day ended. Hoffa put his arm around the shoulder of a stenographer, Alice Busby.

"You'll get on," he said gently. "Suppose I had died?"

Throughout this day Hoffa had maintained his public image of the unperturbed, purposeful strong man. But his face had been a mask, hiding a distraught man at the darkest moment of his life. Inside strong man Hoffa was another Hoffa, boiling with the suppressed emotions of fear, frustration, and rage.

During the preceding month, when Hoffa had not been on public display, he had been a raging, irrational wild man.

The night before, while working on last-minute motions for new trials and for stays of execution, Hoffa had terrorized a six-man team of lawyers with a virtual nonstop tantrum. The men against whom Hoffa ranted were respected by legal colleagues in their communities, and some were of national stature. Morris Shenker of St. Louis, big, gruff, and solid, had achieved fame as a criminal lawyer as far back as the Kefauver crime investigation days of the 1950s. Jacques Schiffer and Dan Maher had made reputations in New York and Detroit. But Hoffa's temper made no distinctions.

Since Hoffa had been through nine criminal trials, he had acquired considerable legal knowledge and now was reading and revising every brief his lawyers wrote. When Hoffa discovered at 2 A.M. that his secretaries had gone and there was no one to type up his corrections, enraged, he picked up a heavy oak conference-room chair and hurled it across the room. Luckily, no head full of legal brains was in the way.

Once, the distraught Hoffa had interrupted the legal skull session to ask his lawyers, in turn, how much time he would have to serve before he was eligible for parole. He had been sentenced to two consecutive terms of eight and five years each for jury tampering and for union pension fraud. Morris Shenker, making a rapid calculation, said: "Twenty-two months, Jimmy."

Jacques Schiffer said it would probably be twenty-four months.

Hoffa turned to William Bufalino, who had done his homework by consulting the federal statutes and doing the necessary arithmetic.

"It will be thirty-four months at least, Jimmy," Bufalino said.

"You f——— bastard!" Hoffa stormed at him. "You son of a bitch. You've given me ten extra months!"

"Don't eat yourself up, Jimmy," Bufalino had remonstrated mildly.

But "eating himself up" was something Hoffa couldn't help.

Hoffa was already a union leader, banker, politician, wielding combined power rarely held by any American other than a President of the United States. But he had further, soaring plans, and these had been—so Hoffa felt—unjustly interrupted.

For example: Hoffa had added some 500,000 members to the million-man union he had inherited. It was not only the biggest, richest, and most effective union in the world, but it had taken on a kind of critical mass and was growing explosively in areas far removed from the original teamsters, drivers of horse-drawn wagons.

The unorganized security police at airports Hoffa arrived at would clamor for Teamster membership. "When are you going to get us a raise, Jimmy?" These and air stewardesses, professional football players, public employees, and farm workers were ripe for the plucking. Hoffa liked to talk of a Teamster union that would soon pass the two-million mark.

As a banker, Hoffa had at his disposal some $300,000,000 of reserves from the Teamsters' biggest regional pension fund, that of the Central States, Southeast and Southwest Areas. Not only were these lendable reserves piling up at the rate of about $100,000,000 yearly, but Hoffa dreamed of taking over all the Teamster pension funds from coast to coast to swell his lending power further. He planned to invest these pension funds in banks, to control at least one bank in every major city.

As a politician, Hoffa had deployed Teamster funds and members' votes to help elect judges in Detroit and a U. S. senator from Ohio. He had organized a Teamster political arm called DRIVE (Democrat, Republican, Independent Voter Education), whose lobbying muscle was respected on Capitol Hill.

Then there was Hoffa's personal wealth, whose further accumulation would be interrupted.

Now, interrupted in mid-career, he was literally devouring himself. Several weeks before, Hoffa, who had rarely experienced a day of illness in his life, had been ordered to George Washington University Hospital. The diagnosis was bleeding ulcers.

Being Hoffa, he had tried to keep this illness secret, just as he had kept his marginal diabetes secret. He wanted the world to believe he was above such human frailties. And, of course, on being discharged from the hospital, Hoffa had disregarded doctors' orders to slow down his whirling-dervish activity.

The blizzard of legal papers that Hoffa and his lawyers had generated in the final two weeks had failed to win a new trial or stay the execution of the sentences. So had the pressure from Capitol Hill, which Hoffa and his lobbyists had orchestrated. As evening fell on his last day at headquarters, his

lawyers brought word that a federal district court judge had
denied Hoffa's plea for several weeks' time in which to finish
an important piece of unfinished business—his negotiations
for a new national truck drivers' contract.

That night, back in his apartment, Hoffa talked on and on
about his unfinished work as Barbara and Jim interposed occasional reassuring words that he would soon return to pick up
where he had left off. The arrival of a doctor to tend to the
ailing Josephine Hoffa interrupted Jimmy's dialogue.

The following day, as Hoffa gave himself up to the U.S.
marshal at Washington, he paused on the federal courthouse
steps to shout to reporters: "I'll be back!"

Indeed, he was so confident that he would be back, and
soon, that he took the presidency of the Teamsters Union to
prison with him. The union's executive board had studied the
union's constitution. A prison term was interpreted as "travel
for a rest period to conserve one's health." During the "rest
period" Hoffa fully intended to run the Teamsters from
prison.

As the gates of Lewisburg Prison swung shut behind him,
rank and filers in scores of Teamster locals around the country
were listening to a recording Hoffa had distributed several
days before.

"I'll be back" was the defiant message.

But for Hoffa, the end had begun.

Chapter Thirteen

NO. 33–298 NE

LEWISBURG FEDERAL PRISON, on the banks of the Susquehanna in mid-Pennsylvania, lies behind grimy gray walls that hide from the world gang rapes, maimings, torture killings, and other forms of cruel and inhuman punishment barred by the Constitution of the United States.

Hoffa came to this "hell on earth, only worse," as he later described it, in March 1967 to serve the first of two prison terms totaling thirteen years, less time off for good behavior.

As Hoffa passed through the gates, he seemed "deeply sedated," one of the two lawyers with him recalled. Hoffa, seemingly in a daze, did not raise his eyes to a face that looked down on him from a second-story window as the Hoffa party marched toward the reception center in the prison's administration building.

But one of Hoffa's lawyers did see the face at the window and shouted up:

"Hi, Cousin Tony!" (The word "cousin" is common to salutations in the Mafia and does not necessarily denote blood kinship.)

Anthony Provenzano had preceded Hoffa into Lewisburg by about a year. His iron rule over the Teamsters and much of the loansharking and numbers rackets in northern New Jersey had been interrupted by a conviction for extortion. Tony Pro knew the ropes and was master of a number of prison privileges. For one thing, he had finagled his way to a coveted assignment in the prison's "honor unit." These were rooms formerly occupied by bachelor members of the prison staff. As a result of this privilege, Tony slept on a bed instead of a cell cot, and behind unlocked doors instead of bars; instead of the exposed toilet bowl in a cell, he enjoyed privacy in a bathroom down the hall. And instead of the ordinary prison fare, which inmates charged was often cold and foul-smelling, Provenzano ate what the staff ate, thanks to a chit from the prison doctor. Tony had his coterie and, since prisoners ate four to a table at Lewisburg, Tony and his group could eat together—and alone.

Tony took Hoffa under his protective wing. He seated Hoffa at his table, wangled special food for him, showed him how to get into the "honor unit" later. More important, Tony Pro and his group protected Hoffa against the sexual abuse and violence that was a commonplace in the prison.

With him, Hoffa had brought into the prison his temper and the easily triggered stream of abuse that went with it. He was seething with frustration at the loss of his freedom. Both "mouthy and edgy," as fellow inmates described him, Hoffa would court disaster by shouting "nigger son of a bitch" at a black inmate or "spick bastard" at a Puerto Rican one. A prison cafeteria spoon or a slab of metal stolen from a prison shop and honed to razor sharpness could provide a lethal "shank." Four inmates were "shanked"—knifed fatally— during Hoffa's stay. Without the protection of Tony Pro and his coterie, Hoffa could have been the fifth.

Similarly, but for Hoffa, Tony Pro would not have survived Lewisburg. When the barrel-chested Provenzano fell ill with a stomach ailment and faded to a ninety-pound bag of bones, Hoffa threatened prison officials with public exposure and a lawsuit unless Tony Pro was removed to an outside hospital. With surgery there, Provenzano recovered.

Two disasters befell Hoffa while in prison. One was the theft of his union. The other was a violent quarrel with Provenzano. Its origin is one of the mysteries Hoffa left behind him.

In Hoffa's autobiography, *Hoffa, the Real Story,* published after his disappearance, Hoffa related that the quarrel stemmed from Provenzano's claim to a generous Teamster pension. However, Hoffa's intimates, as well as his family, doubt that he actually authored this account. There are grave errors in the autobiography—errors that Hoffa's total recall would not have permitted him to make. Hoffa's son believes the quarrel stemmed from Hoffa's failure to deliver a Teamster pension-fund loan to Tony Pro. Although Hoffa sent word out approving a loan for a Provenzano restaurant project, the deal was not consummated.

Federal investigators believe there was a more profound reason: that Hoffa, looking ahead to his own release and return to his union, had asked Tony Pro to get out of the Teamsters for "everybody's good."

"Your name is heavier than mine," Hoffa told Tony Pro, according to a Hoffa lawyer. "Why don't you stand aside?"

Which of these versions is true—if any—is not known. What is known is that when Hoffa and Provenzano were both out of prison, there was another encounter in which Provenzano flew into a murderous rage, shouting: "I'll tear your heart out!" And, according to one informant, Provenzano threatened Hoffa's grandchildren, as well.

HOFFA WAS CONVINCED, as the prison gates slammed shut behind him, that it would be only a matter of weeks, certainly no longer than a few months, before they would swing open for him.

"Almost immediately on arrival, Hoffa came to me and began to talk about parole, about getting out," his social caseworker, Olymp Dainoff, recalled. "He was obsessed with the idea that he had been framed, that he was a political prisoner and had no business being in prison."

Hoffa was confident that Teamster legal and political muscle and Mafia financial muscle would spring him. It was this confidence that permitted him to bear up under the humiliating transformation from the man whom other men had approached with trepidation for three decades and whose word could bring fortune or disaster to the man whose prison number was 33–298 NE.

At the U.S. marshal's office in Washington where he had given himself up, Hoffa had submitted stoically as irreverent hands had strapped ten pounds of leg irons around his ankles. Around his flat middle, they had snapped on an iron bellyband and had run chains from it to his shackled legs and manacled hands.

As Hoffa later put it he had been shackled "like a wild animal." On his ride to Lewisburg and during the customary initial period of isolation—twenty terrifying hours alone behind an iron door—Hoffa perceived that prisons are meant to break a man and render him unfit to return to the outside world.

Outside, Hoffa had lived spaciously. In the executive suite at Teamster headquarters, he had trod on carpeting an inch thick, looked out from his desk at an office several times the size of the usual living room, and reached it or left it via a private elevator. A French chef had prepared Hoffa's lunch. Hoffa convened Teamster executive board meetings at the most elegant hotels in Miami. It was his favorite city and he had spent a week there every month.

At Lewisburg, this wide and handsome world narrowed to a cell seven and a half feet wide and ten feet long. A bunk bed, a locker, and a chair occupied most of this space, leaving some three feet by three feet to contain the restive body and spirit of Jim Hoffa.

Certain that his prison stay would be brief, Hoffa took his Teamster presidency into prison with him, fully intending to run the giant union from behind bars. One of Hoffa's heroes, Joe Fay, had run the Operating Engineers Union while doing a stretch for extortion; why couldn't he do the same?

As part of his plan to run the Teamsters from prison, Hoffa had named two men who, he was sure, would carry out the orders he would send out to them. To his side, on his last day of freedom, Hoffa had called four men, three of them Teamster officers and intimates of long standing. Until Hoffa brought him to Washington as a national vice-president, Frank E. Fitzsimmons, a jowly, heavy-bellied, avuncular figure, had been an obscure vice-president of Hoffa's home Local 299 in Detroit. Around Teamster headquarters, Fitzsimmons was known as Hoffa's "gopher," one who would "go fer this and go fer that." Hoffa showed his contempt for Fitzsimmons with frequent tongue-lashings, and one Teamster wag quipped: "Hoffa uses Fitz to strike matches on."

Yet Hoffa trusted "Fitz," who was from Hoffa's own violent world. Unlike the whirlwind Hoffa, he would rather play golf than work at his union job. Thus he seemed to have little ambition and was not likely to defy Hoffa's long-distance dictation. This was the man Hoffa named to be caretaker or, more precisely, the conduit for his orders.

The other three men were involved in activities that affected underworld interests. Frank Murtha, aged and ailing, was secretary-treasurer of the Central States, Southeast and Southwest Areas Pension Fund, which had lent millions to some of the uncleanest hands in America. National vice-president Bill Presser, Ohio Teamster tsar, was Hoffa's link to the powerful John Scalisi crime family in that state.

Allen Dorfman was the fourth man at Hoffa's side. Dorfman, a muscular six-footer of forty-four, glib, hard-eyed, and flashily tailored, wasn't a Teamster officeholder or even a member. But it was about this man's shoulder that Hoffa put an arm and said: "When this man speaks, he speaks for me."

What he would speak about—for Hoffa—was loans from the Central States pension fund.

Hoffa, going off to prison, had made sure that a major underworld interest in the Teamsters would be protected. For the man who would speak for Hoffa on the granting of pension-fund loans was the stepson of the late labor racketeer Paul Dorfman, Hoffa's conduit to the Chicago Capone gang. Dorfman would also be the man Mafia figures would see for other favors that had to be cleared by Hoffa. Through Dorfman, Hoffa would keep his bargain with the underworld.

In addition, Hoffa needed and had a trusted courier who would faithfully carry his bidding to his two caretakers. Since only kin and lawyers could visit Hoffa, the courier had to be a lawyer. Hoffa had the ideal man in William E. Bufalino. A fanatic Hoffa servitor, Bufalino had seen as little of his own family over the years as Hoffa had because of his selfless and unbroken attendance on the orbiting Hoffa.

Although he took his presidency to prison with him, Hoffa had his pay suspended, a rare bow to rank-and-file opinion. He knew his wife Josephine would not want for anything. Friends in the underworld would see to that.

While Hoffa had contempt for lawyers individually, he respected them collectively. Until his final two trials, lawyers had held off the full might of the federal government through thirty years, seven other criminal trials, and a half-dozen congressional investigations. Occasionally, lawyers had magically extricated Hoffa from certain disaster. One time, Hoffa was caught in the act of passing money and receiving McClellan Committee documents from a double agent—employed by both Hoffa and the committee. But Edward Bennett Williams, a master courtroom strategist, had gotten Hoffa off. Now, in prison, Hoffa was sure his lawyers would find the legal key with which to unlock the gates.

So, each week Hoffa devoted two full visiting days—from 8 A.M. to 3:30 P.M.—in strategy sessions with five lawyers, while ten others outside were busy implementing the strategy devised inside. Each Friday, Hoffa would emerge into the prison visiting room in his prison garb of denim shirt open at the collar, khaki pants, and black, plain-toed shoes. Waiting for him would be Morris Shenker, his chief counsel. Hoffa's son, a fledgling lawyer fresh from his Michigan bar examination, was usually with Shenker. Hoffa and Jim and Shenker would retire to a corner table especially reserved for them to assure privacy.

Around the same table on Tuesdays, three other lawyers would put their heads together with Hoffa. One was Frank Ragano, a mob mouthpiece who himself would go to prison later for evading taxes on commissions from Teamster pension-fund loans. Another was Jacques Schiffer, a New York City lawyer who had served sixty days in prison on a contempt-of-court charge arising—as a federal judge said—from Schiffer's effort to disrupt and cause a mistrial of Hoffa's trial for jury tampering. The third lawyer was Bill Bufalino who also doubled as courier to Fitzsimmons.

Hoffa, usually self-controlled in public, could not hide his frustration at the meetings with his lawyers. He tapped his fingers nervously on the table or squeezed a Coca-Cola can until it was a piece of crushed and twisted metal.

Through his lawyers, Hoffa generated a tidal wave of "Spring Hoffa" activity before the federal courts, on Capitol

Hill in Washington, and elsewhere. At the courts, Hoffa blew
up a storm of motions for new trials. To one such motion,
Hoffa appended affidavits from twenty Chattanooga prostitutes. *Life* magazine asserted that its reporters "have found
conclusive evidence that Hoffa's pals, some in the union,
some in the mob," had raised a $2,000,000 "Spring Hoffa"
fund. This, according to the magazine, had been put at the
disposal of Louisiana Mafia chief Carlos Marcello to pay anyone who could wreck the government's jury-tampering conviction against Hoffa.

Chief target of the case-wrecking effort was Louisiana
Teamster Edward Grady Partin, whose testimony had convicted Hoffa. Partin, who had reported Hoffa's jury-bribe at-
tempts to Walter Sheridan of the Justice Department, continued to report to Sheridan on Hoffa's efforts to get him to
change his testimony. If Partin would swear that the government had bugged Hoffa's defense lawyers, a Marcello associate told Partin—and Partin told Sheridan—"the sky would
be the limit. It's worth at least a million bucks. You'll be put
in charge of all loans [from the Teamsters Central States pension fund] in the south."

Money and favors to "spring Jimmy" seemed inexhaust-
ible. Some $100,000 in legal referral fees were turned over to
Senator Edward Long of Missouri, who investigated alleged
wiretapping activities by Robert F. Kennedy.

At a party attended by some Teamster officials and their
friends, the Washington *Post*'s society reporter, Maxine Che-
shire, accosted Allen Dorfman. "I've heard you are here to try
to get Jimmy Hoffa out of jail," the society reporter said.

"That's right, baby," said Dorfman. "I'm here to buy anyone who can be bought. Are you for sale?"

As weeks passed without results, Hoffa, almost beside himself, would badger his lawyers relentlessly. Once, he lashed
out at Bufalino: "Goddamit, you got me in here, Bill

Bufalino, you and Morris Shenker. Now you get me out of here!''

Instead of getting him "out of here," some of Hoffa's lawyers took to substituting promises for performance.

"We'll get you out in ninety days," Hoffa was told repeatedly.

The promises were due in part to the belief that a magic affidavit or motion for a new trial would turn the trick. But some of the promises were self-serving. Three of the lawyers who saw Hoffa in prison had either profited handsomely by arranging pension-fund loans for others or were themselves borrowers. Now, by playing on Hoffa's desperate hopes, some of the lawyers wangled further fat loan commitments and further fat finders' fees.

"It got to be so bad," one non-loan-seeking lawyer said, "that some of the lawyers came into the prison with loan applications in their back pockets."

In the four and one-half years that Hoffa held on to his Teamster presidency in prison, pension-fund loans for real estate development and land purchases expanded by $228,000,000. Much of this vast new lending had Hoffa's personal approval.

Trying to impose his will on union affairs from behind prison walls was just as maddening to Hoffa as his unsuccessful "free Hoffa" efforts. On going to prison, Hoffa had been yanked traumatically from negotiations with employers for a national contract that would set wages and benefits for truck drivers from coast to coast. These negotiations were important to Hoffa, not only for the bread-and-butter issues that would be bargained out, but for the further development and refinement of the national bargaining mechanism known as the Master Freight Agreement. Hoffa regarded the national contract as the keystone to the edifice of union power he was building. With it, he could bring truckers all over the country to their knees. Looking into the future, Hoffa could see himself bar-

gaining out a national pension fund—covering all the country's drivers—and, thus, piling up lendable reserves that
would stretch his stature as a banker to J. P. Morgan size.

To have to abandon the completion of his masterpiece to
other hands was gall and wormwood to Hoffa. So, from prison
Hoffa sent out instructions to David Previant, the Teamsters'
general counsel and chief negotiator in Hoffa's absence. When
Bufalino returned with reports of the negotiation's progress,
Hoffa would rage at him that his orders were being disobeyed.

Hoffa found further cause for frustration when he tried to
place discharged convicts on Teamster payrolls. Hoffa, on the
outside, had always lent an ear to an ex-con who could beef up
a Teamster local's goon squad. Now, on the inside and moved
by compassion at the suffering around him, Hoffa tried to help
inmates who needed a job as a condition of winning parole. He
would shout at courier Bufalino to get on the phone to regional vice-presidents all over the country to find the needed
employment. If a departing inmate needed a stake, Hoffa
would seek one for him, too.

"Call Bufalino," he would say, giving the man Bufalino's
unlisted Detroit telephone number. Bufalino would find himself groping for the telephone at all hours of the night to hear
some unfamiliar voice say: "Jimmy says it's all right for you
to give me a thousand dollars."

After some six months of this, Hoffa lost his courier.
Bufalino, fed up, told Hoffa off in a letter:

"If you continue to act the way you do in prison, either you,
Jimmy Hoffa, or I, Bill Bufalino, will go crazy."

Chapter Fourteen

EXPLORING
THE WRECKAGE

SOME SIX MONTHS after Hoffa entered prison, he emerged briefly into a late September Pennsylvania countryside that reminded him painfully of his own northern Michigan at leaf-turning time. But the stab of pain was only momentary. Despite the fact that he was manacled again to two federal marshals, Hoffa was euphoric. His tireless lawyers had convinced the United States Supreme Court to send his pension-fund conviction back to the trial court for a review of Hoffa's charge that the FBI had obtained evidence against him by illegal wiretaps.

Testimony on this charge had been taken several weeks before, and now Hoffa was on his way to Chicago to hear the judge's decision.

Should the judge rule in Hoffa's favor, there would be a new trial of the pension-fraud case. This could open the way, too, for the retrial of the jury-tampering case in which Hoffa also had alleged illegal FBI electronic surveillance. So it was an ebullient Hoffa who arrived at the federal courthouse in Chicago.

"I'll be out in ninety days!" he told a Washington lobbyist friend.

The friend had brought Josephine Hoffa to the court session, and there was a brief emotional embrace. Chuckie O'Brien was on hand, too, with a freshly pressed suit of clothes for Hoffa. Allen Dorfman was there, as well as a crowd of well-wishers who had come "to shake Jimmy's hand" and to assure him they would be expecting him back at Teamster headquarters soon.

In a room behind the judge's chambers, Hoffa was permitted to shed his shackles and hold court again, moving among his friends like a successful candidate at a victory celebration.

But the euphoria and the celebration were premature. The judge's decision was as shattering as it was terse:

"The convictions of none of the defendants [including Hoffa] were tainted by the use of evidence improperly obtained."

The motion for a new trial was denied. The prior sentences were reimposed.

Utterly crushed and near tears, Hoffa submitted to the humiliating ritual of manacling for the return trip to purgatory.

Hoffa's journey to the Chicago court had ignited rumors, both in Washington and Detroit, that Jimmy "would soon walk." When these proved unfounded, Fitzsimmons and others at Washington Teamster headquarters became convinced that Hoffa was in for a long stretch and began to pay less attention to his long-distance dictation.

As for Hoffa, back inside Lewisburg he began to come to terms with his role as a numbered inmate and to fashion some means of getting through the prison day and the prison years.

OUTSIDE, HOFFA HAD USED exercise as one way of shutting out his troubles with investigators, prosecutors, and courts. But he also did it with union work, with loan making and politicking that took up twelve hours of his day six and a half days a week.

Now, except for the two visiting days, prison time was as endless as prison space was limited. Hoffa's prison job was to clean, press, and sort guards' uniforms. He had been assigned to this because, as the warden said, "No one would dare steal from Hoffa." The job took seven hours a day, leaving a void of eight others before lights out at 10 P.M.

To fill these, Hoffa plunged into a world he had scorned outside, the world of books and ideas. On the outside, Hoffa had surrounded himself socially with mugs from the under-world. But in the upper world of union administration, he was flanked by intellectuals. His executive vice-president was Harold Gibbons, a onetime Socialist theoretician who had been educated at the University of Chicago. "Egghead" Gib-bons had, in turn—with Hoffa's approval—brought in other intellectuals to help administer the union.

Hoffa used these men but mistrusted them, just as he mis-trusted other men of book learning—his lawyers. Although Hoffa had been a careful reader of the New York City and Washington newspapers and absorbed, in addition, a daily digest of magazine and newspaper news prepared by his staff, he had as an adult read but one book, Robert F. Kennedy's *The Enemy Within*—painful reading, since Hoffa was the chief enemy in it.

Now, with the help of his Phi Beta Kappa daughter, who selected books for him—two copies of each title, one for Hoffa, another for the prison library—Hoffa read voraciously.

"Whether he was in his cell or in the recreation yard, you could always see Hoffa with his nose in a book," his warden, Noah Alldredge, recalls.

Being Hoffa, he tolerated no fiction and read only such books as would help him understand and confront the world more effectively when he got out.

Hoffa became a scholar of economics, gulping down economist Peter Drucker's *The End of Economic Man: The Concept of the Corporation.* Interested in the future, he read *Future Shock* and *The Greening of America,* which discussed the impact of the "youth culture" on American life. Hoffa was not as enthusiastic about this impact as the author was. Upset by what he read about the rebellion of the young in the late 1960s, Hoffa told his warden: "Dammit, what's happened to the good old values of honesty and hard work?"

In the role of underdog in which he had always cast himself, Hoffa suffered with the Indian martyrs in *Bury Me at Wounded Knee.* He read and identified with the lives of John L. Lewis and Eugene V. Debs, the Socialist leader who was imprisoned as a conscientious objector during World War I.

The plight of those around him—when Hoffa lifted his eyes from his legal troubles—provided him with additional uses for his time. Lewisburg had been built in 1932 to hold 1,050 prisoners, but was now jammed with twice as many. Lifers, homosexuals, gunmen, forgers, burglars, jostled each other in the crowded exercise yard. Prison jobs were available to only one-half of the inmates. Heroin, hashish, marijuana were freely available for those who could pay with money or cigarettes. Sexual abuse was rampant, and men pleaded for transfers to other prisons to escape rape and worse. Many inmates were armed. "If you have a metal bunk, you have a knife," Hoffa said later.

Hoffa worked hard to defuse a continuously explosive situation. He formed a committee that brought beefs directly to the warden. For a time he helped alleviate at least one evil: the serving of cold, rotting food, which Hoffa described as crawling with maggots.

Every convict is forever working on a legal brief that will spring him. Hoffa organized white-collar inmates into a writing team that prepared briefs for the less-schooled felons.

Hoffa edited the briefs.

On visiting days, Hoffa continued to work with his lawyer, Morris Shenker, on efforts to win a parole or a pardon—anything that promised to turn him loose. But, more and more with the passing of time, he devoted his visiting days to exploring with his son, Jim, the wreckage of his life.

Jim, who resembled his father in muscular bulk, was an obedient and devoted son. As an all-state football tackle at high school, he was wooed by Michigan State's coach, Duffy Dyer. But the elder Hoffa, forever surrounded by violence himself, was terrified that his son might get hurt.

"You're going to college to get an education, not to play games," Hoffa told his son. Young Hoffa played no games.

Now, to the visits with his son, Hoffa would bring the torment that kept him awake after lights out at 10 P.M. What had gone wrong? Hoffa would ask himself. In the darkness, Hoffa would replay the events of his rise and fall and grope toward an answer: Perhaps his early bargain with the underworld had been a mistake.

On the outside, Hoffa had liked to say, "I may have my faults, but being wrong ain't one of them." Now, in lengthy monologues, Hoffa admitted to his son what he could admit to no one else.

"My association with the mobs has hurt me, no doubt about it," Hoffa said. "It gave Bobby Kennedy the handle to immobilize me, put me in jail—uproot me from my union work. But I'm coming back," Hoffa said.

He vowed he would shed his mob ties, break with the gangs, run the kind of union that could be readmitted to the company of respectable labor people—the AFL-CIO. "And make my mark in labor history," Hoffa said.

But to other visitors, such as FBI agents, Hoffa would say nothing about breaking with the mobs. The FBI suspected what Hoffa's closest associates knew—that stored in Hoffa's computerlike brain was an exhaustive Who's Who of the underworld: who bossed what and where; who was involved in what rackets; who committed what crimes. Of Hoffa, a knowledgeable Las Vegas insider said, "If Jimmy talked, a dozen leading citizens in this town would be destroyed overnight." But to the FBI, Hoffa had nothing to say.

Perhaps he would break with the mobs—when he got out. But in prison he would not blow the whistle on anyone. That was against his code and against his tradition.

Meanwhile, the long prison days turned into weeks, then into months and years. From the outside, assurances kept arriving in the form of scores of letters weekly that rank-and-file members and loyalist Teamster officials "are behind you, Jimmy." Occasionally, there were other reminders. On his fifty-seventh birthday, an airplane flew low over Lewisburg, trailing a banner: "Happy Birthday, Jimmy!"

But, along with the remembrances, Hoffa began receiving disquieting signals that not only was his freedom slipping away but his union as well.

Chapter Fifteen

ET TU, FITZ!

T HE FIRST SIGNAL that the International Brotherhood of Teamsters was slipping from Hoffa's grasp came midway through his prison stay in 1969. The Teamsters' aged secretary-treasurer, John English, was retiring. Hoffa, still president of the Teamsters, sent word from behind bars to caretaker Frank E. Fitzsimmons:

"Name Harold Gibbons."

Fitzsimmons sent word back, "I can't."

Why not?

The Chicago Capone gang, it turned out, had another candidate. Its conduit to the Teamsters, Paul Dorfman, an old friend and business associate of Hoffa's, had called Fitzsimmons.

"You know the deal!" Paul Dorfman barked.

His memory refreshed, Fitzsimmons named the Capone gang's designee, a regional Teamster official from Chicago, Tom Flynn.

This was a triple blow to Hoffa. Fitzsimmons, his caretaker, had defied him. So had Paul Dorfman, the labor racketeer who had introduced Hoffa to the Chicago Capone gang. Worst, this was the first overt move by Fitzsimmons to keep Hoffa loyalists out of key positions of Teamster power.

Fitz, so Hoffa began to suspect, had been bitten by the presidential bug. He wanted for himself the Teamster presidency that Hoffa had left in his care.

Later, Hoffa wrote that naming Fitzsimmons as caretaker of the Teamsters was one of his biggest mistakes; he should have named Harold Gibbons instead. What he left unsaid was that the Mafia would never have approved Gibbons.

True, Gibbons had done much for Hoffa. Back in 1956, Gibbons had masterminded the convention strategy that had elected Hoffa to his first term as president of the Teamsters. As executive assistant to Hoffa, Gibbons, "the brain," gave class to Teamster headquarters and ran the union when Hoffa was in the field. A talented orator himself, Gibbons helped polish Hoffa's speechmaking style. He had also helped improve Hoffa's public image by involving him in good works. When Hoffa was at his lowest public rating during the McClellan hearings, Gibbons induced him to raise money for an Israeli orphanage. Hoffa went to Israel, was greeted by the then premier, Golda Meir, and saw his name inscribed on the James R. Hoffa Children's Home.

But as candidate for caretaker, Gibbons had a fatal flaw. He was squeamish about the company that Hoffa kept. When Hoffa broke bread with the likes of Abe Gordon or Johnny Dio, Gibbons would excuse himself and leave the table. Similarly, when Hoffa had business to transact with gangsters at Teamster headquarters, Gibbons would step away from the common office he shared with Hoffa.

A caretaker of Hoffa's Teamsters who was squeamish about underworld characters obviously couldn't fill the job. Fitzsimmons, on the other hand, was quite comfortable in unclean company. When Fitz was a vice-president of Detroit Local 299, he would be seen often with Detroit gangsters at their hangout in the Market Vending Building. Fitz was on intimate terms with Jimmy Q Quasarano, Pete Vitale, and other Detroit mobsters. So Hoffa didn't let Fitz's modest qualifications for heading the country's biggest union stand in the way of the caretaker appointment.

Like Hoffa, Fitzsimmons had little formal schooling. But, unlike Hoffa, he lacked the assets of mind and energy that Hoffa brought to the Teamster presidency. Fitzsimmons' limitations showed up most dramatically on the rare occasions when he met the press. His disordered syntax had reporters gasping, "What's that again?"

In answer to a reporter's questions about deregulating highway transport, Fitzsimmons once replied: "There are so many numerous things in it. With deregulation, there would be no responsibility to service rural areas. If a man lived in Podunk and bought a piano, so far as his daughter was concerned from Arkansas, he would have to get his own truck or mule to get the piano to Podunk."

Fitzsimmons was also extremely gullible and relayed to reporters whatever his flacks told him to say. During the Teamsters' effort to break the United Farm Workers union, Fitzsimmons had this to say about the farm workers' leader, Cesar Chavez, who was then paid $100 a month by the union and subsisted largely on the produce of his own garden: "Why don't you guys [the reporters] ask Chavez about how he gets out of his Lincoln limousine a mile away and how he changes from his tuxedo into work pants when he goes visiting the farm workers?"

How had this limited man gotten so far in the Teamsters?

Hoffa provided one answer in his autobiography. "He was a guy I took off a highway truck and hand-carried all the way from shop steward to general vice-president."

Part of the hand-carrying consisted in keeping Fitzsimmons out of jail. Back in 1958, according to Senate Rackets Com-

mittee testimony, when Fitzsimmons was indicted on a charge
of accepting an employer payoff, Hoffa contributed heavily to
the reelection campaign of the Detroit judge who would try
Fitzsimmons. Some of the campaign contribution, earmarked
for television advertising, went directly to the judge, according to committee testimony. The indictment against Fitzsimmons was dismissed.

Fitzsimmons owed Hoffa a double debt of loyalty, and it
was on this loyalty that Hoffa had relied in naming Fitzsimmons caretaker. Yet the job's powers and perquisites—to
which Fitzsimmons was becoming happily accustomed—put
great strains on old loyalties.

For the perquisites were of eastern potentate proportions.
First, there was the regal salary of $125,000 yearly.[1] To this,
as the Teamster constitution dictated, were added unlimited
expenses, permitting the Teamster president to travel anywhere on the planet in pursuit of rest and recreation and to take
his wife, his secretaries, and anyone else he thought necessary
with him. A $3,500,000 jet plane was at Fitz's disposal, as
were three homes—in Washington, D.C., Florida, and
California.

With this royal living went the equally royal elbow rubbing
with the mighty of the earth—the President of the United
States, for instance. And perhaps best of all, the Teamster
presidency, as the torpid Fitzsimmons perceived it, didn't require much work. More energetic men could run it, permitting
Fitzsimmons to devote himself to serious business—golf. (So
serious that Fitzsimmons, arriving once at La Costa, California, and finding he had left his golf clubs behind in
Washington, sent his jet plane across the continent to bring
them.)

---

1. This was increased to $155,000 at the Teamsters 1976 convention.

Added to the unfolding betrayal by Fitzsimmons, as Hoffa perceived from prison, was that of another friend who owed much to Hoffa. This was William "Big Bill" Presser, the Ohio labor racketeer who had served a prison term for destroying union records sought by Senate investigators and who later was to be convicted of accepting employer bribes.

From Hoffa, Presser had received in 1951 a Teamster charter that permitted him to control a jukebox racket monopoly. Backed by Hoffa, Presser had advanced to vice-president and had become boss of all Ohio's Teamsters. In Hoffa's absence, Presser had risen still higher. When Hoffa's pension-fund caretaker, Allen Dorfman, went to jail for extortion, Presser became the man to see about loans from the Teamsters' Central States pension fund.

Although Fitzsimmons was supposed to take his orders from the imprisoned Hoffa, Presser had become Fitz's closest advisor. Before and after Teamster executive board meetings, the two men could be seen in close and confidential confabs.

It was Presser, so Hoffa learned, who had put the presidential bug in Fitz's ear. Now the wily Presser was not only helping the sluggish Fitzsimmons to run the union but was giving Fitzsimmons pointers on how to capture the Teamster presidency for himself.

Hoffa should not have been surprised that, in his absence, there would be plotting against him. After all, in 1957 he had done a bit of quiet betraying himself. David Beck, Teamster president at the time, had been tottering under the blows being dealt him in the initial McClellan Committee hearings. Hoffa helped to shove Beck into oblivion by arranging to have Beck's own lawyers feed discrediting information to Committee counsel Robert Kennedy. Beck, disgraced, abandoned the Teamster presidency, so clearing the way for Hoffa's election.

Now, barely a decade later, Fitzsimmons used his friend

President Richard Nixon to topple Hoffa from the Teamster presidency, just as Hoffa had used Bob Kennedy to topple Beck.

If Fitzsimmons was to achieve the Teamster presidency, it was vital that Hoffa remain in prison until after the July 1971 Teamster convention. For, with Hoffa in prison, chances were excellent that Fitzsimmons could seek and win the presidency himself. This meant that a parole or a presidential pardon before July 1971 had to be blocked at all costs. Then, if Hoffa was sprung later, Fitzsimmons could remain president only if restraints were attached to Hoffa's release—restraints that barred him from reentering union politics and regaining his office.

This is precisely how things turned out. Why they turned out that way requires a visit to some of the murkier corners of Richard Nixon's Watergate White House.

Chapter Sixteen

THE WATERGATE WHITE HOUSE HELPS STEAL A UNION

W HEN COURT EFFORTS failed to spring Hoffa during his first year in prison, his underworld pals moved the "Free Jimmy" battle to another arena: the White House.

With Richard Nixon heading for the presidency, Las Vegas gambling interests thought it a good bet to put a bundle into his 1968 campaign. Contributions, made secretly and in cash, came to more than $1,000,000, according to Las Vegas sources. In return, the boys from Las Vegas received assurances from Republican campaign figures—who said they had cleared it with "Dick"—that a pardon would be forthcoming as soon as feasible after Nixon took office on January 20, 1969.

Sure enough, some seven months after the Nixon inaugural, the lobbyist and public relations grapevine in Washington was vibrating with reports that "the fix was in" and that Hoffa would soon be free.

This time the reports had substance. For, as one eyewitness reported, the wheels began to grind both in the Justice Department and at the White House to produce an early pardon for Hoffa.

The eyewitness was Clark R. Mollenhoff, a distinguished journalist who had joined the first Nixon Administration as a special counsel to the President with a special mission: As ombudsman—a protector of the public interest—he would ferret out corruption and bring it to Nixon's attention.

Ombudsman Mollenhoff had been on the job only a few weeks (he was to quit in frustration after a year) when he received a phone call from his friend Walter Sheridan, who had left the Justice Department but still maintained his own Washington intelligence network. Sheridan said that he had heard from Teamster and Justice Department sources that Hoffa would be freed within several weeks as "part of a deal made during the 1968 presidential campaign."

"I'm told John Mitchell and John Ehrlichman have something to do with it, and I'm told it has been cleared with Nixon," Sheridan said.[1]

Mollenhoff found it hard to believe Sheridan's news. In a conversation with Nixon during the 1968 campaign, Mollenhoff had asked "direct questions about any deals with Hoffa" and had been assured by candidate Nixon that there were none. Nixon, as Mollenhoff recalled, had agreed that Hoffa was "a menace to the labor movement."

Seeking to verify Sheridan's report, Mollenhoff sent an inquiring note to an administration colleague, presidential assistant John Ehrlichman. A reply came back via a young Ehrlichman assistant: "Mr. Ehrlichman says you should not concern yourself with the Hoffa matter. He is handling it himself with John Mitchell" (then attorney general).

So Walter Sheridan's information was accurate, after all!

---

1. As related in Clark R. Mollenhoff, *Game Plan for Disaster* (New York: Norton, 1976).

Mollenhoff telephoned Ehrlichman and was told brusquely: "The President does not want you in this. It is highly sensitive. Mitchell and I have it under control."

Mollenhoff then whipped off a memorandum seeking to persuade Ehrlichman that a pardon for Hoffa would have disastrous political consequences. The press, he pointed out, was looking for just such a cause. When no reply came, Mollenhoff—despairing of blocking the pardon—turned to other matters. To his amazement, the pardon move was dropped.

Why did the Nixon White House drop the early pardon for Hoffa? Who blocked it?

It was somebody who could do what Nixon's own anticorruption ombudsman, Clark Mollenhoff, could not do: penetrate the Berlin Wall erected by Ehrlichman and H. R. Haldeman, get to the President, and change his mind.

The man who blocked Hoffa's release was Nixon's special counsel for labor affairs, Charles "Chuck" Colson. And behind Colson was Hoffa's caretaker, Fitzsimmons—taking care that Hoffa remained in prison.

For what follows, I am indebted to a Washington underground figure—a combination lobbyist, go-between, and arranger—whose pipelines into power sources in Washington win him big-money clients. He would talk only on the condition that he remain anonymous. We'll call him Mr. Middleman.

As cultivator of power sources, Middleman had wooed and won Hoffa's friendship and that of Hoffa's family as well. The friendship had paid off. Hoffa had favored Middleman with substantial loans from the Teamsters' Central States pension fund and with introductions to other Teamster powers and to Mafia powers as well. When Nixon took office in 1969, Middleman—an assiduous "spring Jimmy Hoffa" promoter—sought out another arranger like himself, but with a pipeline to the biggest power source of all, the President of the United

States. This was Murray Chotiner, Nixon's early political mentor and architect of what came to be known as Richard Nixon's dirty tricks. Chotiner's relationship with Nixon was for hire. He once intervened to block the deportation of a white slaver and racketeer, Marco Reginelli of New Jersey.

Chotiner was setting up a law practice at the time. He promised Middleman to intervene for Hoffa in return for some lucrative legal business that Middleman promised to throw his way. And, of course, should Hoffa be sprung, there would be further handsome rewards from Hoffa himself.

But when Chotiner began his labors in behalf of Hoffa, he made a disturbing discovery. Despite the fact that John Mitchell at the Justice Department and John Ehrlichman in the White House were clearing the way for a pardon, another member of the Nixon team, Nixon's labor advisor, Charles Colson, was working quietly behind the scenes to block it.

A shadowy tug-of-war now ensued with Colson at one end, Chotiner at the other, and Hoffa in the middle. Shortly before the 1969 Thanksgiving, Murray Chotiner was so sure he had won that he reported jubilantly to Middleman: "Mr. Hoffa will be eating turkey at home this Thanksgiving!"

The word had come right from the Oval Office, Chotiner said.

For Middleman, this news was too important to be conveyed to the Hoffa family by telephone. So he flew to Detroit and raced from there to the Hoffa home on Lake Orion, where he delivered the electrifying news to a weeping Josephine Hoffa. Together, Middleman and Josephine Hoffa then called Lewisburg Prison and asked officials there to tell Hoffa he would be home for Thanksgiving.

But Hoffa did not eat Thanksgiving turkey at home. Nor Christmas pudding, either.

Colson, so Chotiner told Middleman, had thrown a last-minute monkey wrench into the pardon-Hoffa plan. As the

President's advisor on political relations with organized labor, Colson seemingly had persuaded the President that a bird in the hand—Fitzsimmons at Teamster headquarters—was worth more than a bird in the bush—Hoffa in prison. Fitzsimmons, the only major labor leader supporting Nixon, had to be listened to. He was.

Fitzsimmons' desire to keep Hoffa in prison had been confirmed by Colson himself.

In November 1971, Colson told Clark Mollenhoff that "Fitzsimmons had made no pitch [to get Hoffa out of prison] . . ." and that Colson *"had concluded that Fitzsimmons would be content to run the Teamsters Union with Hoffa safely in prison"* [italics added].

The Nixon Administration put the 1968 campaign commitment to spring Hoffa on the back burner. There it remained until the beginning of Hoffa's fourth year in prison, in March 1971. On March 31, Hoffa would take his second plea to the U.S. Parole Board (the first, during the prior October, had been summarily denied).

This hearing was crucial to Hoffa and Fitzsimmons alike. For the Teamster presidential convention of 1971 was only three months away. If the parole board freed Hoffa, there was little question that he would be reelected to the office, which he had never relinquished. With the exception of Fitzsimmons and Big Bill Presser, Hoffa had the loyalty and support of the thirteen-man Teamster executive board whose endorsement virtually assures reelection by convention delegates. Hoffa also had wide rank-and-file support. Washington *Post* reporter Ken W. Clawson wrote at the time: "Jimmy holds all the cards."

For Fitzsimmons, who had already once headed off Hoffa at the pass—the White House—it was vitally important that Hoffa remain in prison at least through the convention. Since it was quite possible that Hoffa could be reelected even if he remained in prison, it would be better if Hoffa gave up his presidency altogether, prior to the convention.

The U.S. Parole Board is an independent body, presumably insulated against White House and Justice Department pressure. Whether the White House, under Nixon, and the Justice Department, under John Mitchell, influenced the parole board's Hoffa decision in early 1971 is not known. What is known is that the parole board began—in advance of the hearing—to show an interest in Hoffa's future plans, if paroled.

A parole board examiner traveled to Lewisburg a week before the hearing and asked Hoffa what work he intended to pursue if freed. Without hesitation, Hoffa replied he planned to resume his Teamster presidency.

At the subsequent parole board hearing, board members gave no ultimatum to Hoffa to quit his Teamster presidency as a condition of parole, but their questions to Hoffa's lawyer, Morris Shenker, and to Hoffa's son and daughter, who had come to plead that their mother was seriously ill and that their parents should be reunited, hinted strongly that there would be no parole until Hoffa dropped his union offices. Parole was denied.

At the Justice Department, too, as Hoffa's son and fixer Murray Chotiner made the rounds, seeking to rekindle a pardon drive, the story was the same as before the parole board. Come back after Hoffa relinquishes his union jobs.

With this pressure from Fitzsimmons' friends in the Nixon Administration came treachery.

During the 1971 Easter season, Hoffa received a furlough to visit his wife at the University of California Medical Center at San Francisco, where she was being treated for a heart ailment. Word that Hoffa "would be on the outside" for four days preceded him. Arriving in San Francisco, Hoffa played host to everybody who was anybody in the Teamsters—among them Frank Fitzsimmons, then caretaker of the Teamsters for Hoffa.

Fitzsimmons, it turned out, had a proposition for Hoffa. If Hoffa resigned from the Teamster presidency, he would get a pardon. The White House had assured Fitzsimmons of this. Fitzsimmons would then stand for president and be elected. Then as Hoffa left jail, Fitzsimmons would call a special election, nominate Hoffa, and restore him to office.

Fitzsimmons made his proposition to Hoffa in the sitting room of Hoffa's hotel suite. Hoffa excused himself, went to the suite's bedroom, and called his lifelong friend Nick Morrissey, a Boston Teamster.

Hoffa explained the deal to Morrissey and added: "Fitz tells me he can get me a pardon. He's been working for more than a year on it. But I will have to resign everything."

"You are a damned fool," Morrissey told Hoffa. "Don't do it. You're nobody once you step down and give away your power."

"Jo is sick," Hoffa said. "My kids are after me. They want me out of the box."

Hoffa was now confronted with an agonizing choice: further months or perhaps years in prison purgatory—or freedom at the price of giving up the Teamster presidency. He decided for freedom and Fitz's proposition. Back in prison, Hoffa scribbled a note—so short that it seemed the act of writing must have caused him excruciating pain. It read:

"I agree not to be in organized labor as a [sic] officer."

Hoffa signed the note, and his lawyer, Morris Shenker, bore it to Fitzsimmons, who, along with his executive board, was waiting at Miami Beach. Within minutes of receiving the Hoffa resignation, Fitzsimmons convened the Teamsters executive board and was elected interim president to serve until the convention, now only two and one-half weeks away.

Someone else seemed to have been waiting for word from

Hoffa. Although it was late June, Richard Nixon was conveniently nearby at the winter White House at Key Biscayne. Within minutes after Fitzsimmons had been elected interim Teamster president, Nixon entered the executive board's meeting room and sat down beside him. Rubbing elbows with Nixon was Big Bill Presser, who only several months before had pleaded guilty to accepting bribes from employers. Also rubbing elbows with the President of the United States were other Teamster vice-presidents with criminal records and mob connections.

"My door is always open to President Fitzsimmons," President Nixon said.[2]

Meanwhile, although Hoffa had relinquished his union offices, his prison ordeal continued. The parole board convened a special hearing a month after the Teamsters convention elected Fitzsimmons to a full five-year term as president. Hoffa's son, Jim, fully expecting he had a deal that would promptly free his father was greeted by a hostile board instead. Now parole board members asked questions about the elder Hoffa's ties to the underworld. Young Hoffa emerged white and shaken—and empty-handed. His father, he was convinced, had been entrapped into relinquishing the Teamster presidency. Architect of that trap, young Hoffa suspected, was Fitzsimmons, who was influencing Nixon Administration decisions through his man in the White House, Chuck Colson.

Fixer Murray Chotiner redoubled his efforts to win a Hoffa pardon from his political protege, Nixon. He argued that Hoffa had wide rank-and-file support that could mean votes for

2. The White House door, seemingly, was just as open to Fitzsimmons and company under Nixon's successor, Gerald Ford. On the day after President Ford delivered a lecture on the need for morality in high government places, his secretary of labor, William Usery, appeared before the June 1976 Teamsters convention at a Las Vegas gambling hotel to praise the Teamsters' leaders. Some of these, including Fitzsimmons, were at that moment under subpoena in the Labor Department–Justice Department investigation into Teamster pension-fund fraud.

Nixon in the approaching 1972 presidential election year. As evidence of this vote potential, Nixon received a "free Hoffa" petition signed by 250,000 Teamster members and brought to the White House by Senator Norris Cotton (R.-N.H.).

As Hoffa's commutation became a certainty, Fitzsimmons slept more and more fitfully of nights. True, he—Fitz—was now the elected head of all the Teamsters. But Hoffa, being Hoffa, could be expected, when freed from his prison Elba, to march at once on Teamsters headquarters.

Indeed, as Fitzsimmons heard, Hoffa was already making plans in prison. Hoffa had sent word out to David Johnson, president of Detroit Local 299 and an old Hoffa strong man and friend, that he, Hoffa, wanted to be named assistant to Johnson on emerging from prison. Johnson had sent word back, "No sweat."

Hoffa, who could never be assistant to anybody, wanted, of course, to take over Local 299—his old home base—and use it as a power base from which to mount a drive to regain the Teamster presidency. Fitzsimmons knew of Hoffa's plan through one of his sons, Richard, who was a vice president of Local 299.

But Fitzsimmons and Colson found a way to frustrate Hoffa's comeback plans when he was freed by presidential commutation two days before Christmas in 1971. How Fitzsimmons and Colson did it was revealed by an aide of Fitzsimmons' who had a front seat at the performance.

The aide was William Carlos Moore, who headed the Teamsters' political arm, DRIVE. As the union's lobbyist before Congress and elsewhere in Washington, he had the job of winning support for freeing Hoffa.

As Moore told me, and as he also attested in an affidavit used by Hoffa in a lawsuit: "Teamster officers, rank and filers as well as the friends and family of Jim Hoffa, put a great deal of pressure on Fitz in late 1971 to secure Hoffa's release from prison. He was always being asked what he was doing about it. So, Fitz lectured me a good deal about how to lobby for Hoffa.

" 'We would like to have Hoffa released from prison,' he kept telling me, *but we want to make sure that he won't return to the Teamsters or the labor movement* [italics added].' "

Once, while in Fitzsimmons' office, Moore went on to relate, "Fitz put in a call to Chuck Colson in the White House."

Moore recalls these words by Fitzsimmons:

"Chuck, Hoffa should be released from prison, but I think it awfully important a condition be placed on him that he won't be free to seek office and participate in the labor movement."

Both Fitzsimmons and Colson have denied such a conversation.

Yet when Hoffa emerged from prison, precisely such a restraint was placed on him. On pain of being returned to prison, Hoffa was to stay out of union affairs until 1980—nine years away, when Hoffa would be sixty-eight.

As a postscript to the White House capers that helped Fitzsimmons win and hold the Teamster presidency, it is interesting to see how Fitz rewarded his friends, Chuck and Dick, for their efforts in his behalf.

One of the more famous Nixon Watergate tapes has President Nixon complaining to presidential counsel John Dean about lawyer Edward Bennett Williams. He was, at the time, counsel for the Washington *Post,* which was beginning to unravel the Watergate scandal. The tape reveals Nixon as saying: "I don't want to be in Edward Bennett Williams' shoes after the election [in 1972]. We are going to fix that son of a bitch, believe me, we are going to. We've got to, because he is a bad man."

Lawyer Williams' standing with Nixon did not improve when the Democratic National Committee retained him to sue the Committee to Re-Elect the President (CREEP) for

$2,000,000 damages for instigating the Watergate break-in. (CREEP settled for $500,000.)

At this point, in late 1972, Fitzsimmons—seeking to aid his friend Nixon—started sending word to Williams, who had been general counsel for the Teamsters for sixteen years.

"Maybe the Teamsters account doesn't mean anything to you," Fitzsimmons would tell Williams. "But if you persist [in the Watergate suit], the Teamsters will have to reconsider their relationship with you."

The "relationship" brought a $100,000 yearly retainer to the Williams law firm. When Williams continued to disregard the warnings from Fitzsimmons, his law partner, Raymond Bergen, who handled much of the Teamster account, received a call from Colson at the White House.

"I am going to get the Teamster account in several months," Colson confided to lawyer Bergen. "I'd like you to come with me." There would be plenty in it for everybody, Colson intimated.

Colson then continued: "You may think that it won't look good if you abandon Williams and come with me, but we can solve that. We can make you assistant secretary of labor for six months. This will create a suitable hiatus—then you can resign and come with me."

Both Bergen and Williams resisted the Colson-Fitzsimmons carrot and stick. On January 1, 1973, Edward Bennett Williams was fired as general counsel to the Teamsters—a job he had held since he saved Hoffa from jail in the McClellan Committee spy case of 1956. Charles Colson took Williams' place.

As Hoffa charged in a lawsuit later, this $100,000-a-year job was the payoff to Colson for aiding and abetting the Fitzsimmons conspiracy to rob Hoffa of the Teamster presidency. Two years after Hoffa's disappearance, the FBI was investigating reports also, of payoffs to Nixon administration officials.

PART III

THE LAST DAYS OF JIMMY HOFFA

Chapter Seventeen

RACE
WITH DEATH

OR JIM HOFFA, the Christmas of 1971 was the best of times and the worst of times.

He was home for the holidays. Nothing could be better. But he was to discover that he was still a shackled man. Nothing could be worse.

During four prior Christmases, Hoffa's wife, son, daughter, and son-in-law had spent a few frustrating hours with him in a prison waiting room jammed with inmates' teary wives, restive children, chin-up-if-it-kills-you parents. When his family left for the wide, free world outside, Hoffa had summoned up all of his will to restrain himself from battering his head against the prison's concrete walls.

But now, on December 23, 1971, that was all behind him. Hoffa's son-in-law, Robert Crancer, had been waiting in a nearby Lewisburg motel for the expected word of a White House pardon. When it came from the prison at 4 P.M., Crancer had hurried over to the prison warden's office, where Hoffa awaited him.

Even at this moment of deliverance, Hoffa's thoughts were

on one track: getting back to his life's work, the Teamsters. Was there anything in the presidential pardon that would block him from this?

By the time Crancer arrived, Hoffa had already perused the document that freed him. It was a standard parole form (as Hoffa produced it in a lawsuit later) and stipulated the standard parole conditions: Hoffa must report monthly to a parole officer, obtain permission before leaving the Detroit area, refrain from consorting with ex-convicts. Not a word against resuming union activity.

Hoffa then asked the warden, Noah Alldredge, to telephone the pardons attorney at the Justice Department in Washington, to inquire whether he knew of any restrictions. Word came back: The pardons attorney knew of none. (Both the warden and the pardons attorney denied such a conversation later, but the President's then counsel, John Dean, supported the Hoffa version.)

With steps as light as his heart, Hoffa almost ran from the prison. He paused only long enough at a pay telephone outside to call an old Teamster friend in Boston, Nick Morrissey, to spread the joyous news that he was "on the outside." With his son-in-law, Hoffa then drove to nearby Williamsport, Pennsylvania. There, a Teamster jet was waiting, sent at the urging of Hoffa's loyal friend Teamster vice-president Harold Gibbons. Waiting beside it was Frank E. Fitzsimmons.

Had Hoffa been able to see behind Fitzsimmons' spectacled pumpkin face and look into his mind, he would have learned a shattering secret. Fully six weeks before Hoffa's release, special White House counsel Charles Colson had called in Clark Mollenhoff, who by then had resigned from his ombudsman's job in the Nixon Administration. Colson pledged Mollenhoff to secrecy until the news was released officially. He then told Mollenhoff that Hoffa would receive a presidential pardon by Christmas but *would be barred from further union activity for some time*. And what Colson knew about the Nixon Administration's intentions toward Hoffa, Fitzsimmons knew, too.

Unaware of Fitzsimmons' secret, Hoffa and his son-in-law took off in the Teamster jet. It touched down at Detroit to pick up Hoffa's son, Jim, then headed for St. Louis, where his wife, daughter, and granddaughter, Barbara Jo Crancer, would be waiting. On the flight to St. Louis, Hoffa's thoughts raced along faster than his agile tongue. He was a bit soft in the body. Prison had put some twenty pounds on him. But prison had not broken Hoffa's spirit nor punctured his soaring vision of his place in the scheme of things. He must hurry back to Detroit after the holidays. By arrangement from prison, a union job was already waiting for him—that of assistant to the president of Detroit Local 299. It would be the platform from which to launch his comeback.

Upon arrival at the modest six-room Crancer home at Glendale, Missouri, outside St. Louis, Hoffa was swept up in a turbulent crowd of reporters and television cameramen. But instead of the expected questions about prison life and his plans for regaining office, the reporters were shouting questions about the conditions of Hoffa's pardon.

"What conditions?"

A reporter read Hoffa a news bulletin: "The President has commuted Hoffa's combined consecutive sentences to a term of six-and-one-half years, upon the condition that [Hoffa] *not engage in direct or indirect management of any labor organization prior to March 6, 1980 on pain of recommitment to prison*."

Hoffa was stunned, then outraged.

Had there been no presidential pardon, Hoffa, counting time off for good behavior, would have been eligible for mandatory release in 1974—two years away—with no strings attached. But the conditional pardon barred him from union activity until his two combined sentences, totaling thirteen years, would have run their course in 1980. By then he would be sixty-eight.

In prison, Hoffa had convinced himself he was a political prisoner, the victim of the Kennedy brothers' political ambitions. Now, with Nixon in office, Hoffa felt he was still a political prisoner, the victim of Nixon's political alliance with Fitzsimmons. To Hoffa, the two were in league to immobilize him as long as possible.

As Hoffa tossed sleeplessly in the unaccustomed softness of the pull-out sofa bed in the Crancer rumpus room, he brooded that, to obtain justice, he would have to go back to those very institutions he had been battling for three decades—the Congress, the Justice Department, the courts. Was he doomed to be forever entangled with lawyers and the law?

The answer, unknown to Hoffa, was yes—until the very last day of his life. On that day, a circuit court of appeals would still be deliberating Hoffa's plea that the restraints against his union activity were unconstitutional. After Hoffa's disappearance, constitutional lawyer Leonard Boudin, who had been handling Hoffa's case, said: "Had the case been decided a year earlier, Hoffa would have been a union official [in Teamster Local 299]. With Hoffa speaking and campaigning, the underworld might have seen Hoffa as a winner, and he might still be alive today."

The drama of Hoffa's destruction would unfold inexorably: while Hoffa was immobilized, Fitzsimmons would use the Teamsters' presidential powers (the power to reward as well as punish) to separate Hoffa from his following. Hoffa, being Hoffa, would not know when his cause was lost. He would rock the boat and even threaten to upset it—by breaking the underworld code of silence. The underworld, in the boat with Fitzsimmons, didn't want it rocked. Hoffa's fight to shed the pardon's restraints so that he could hold on to his following would turn out to be a race against death.

In prison, Hoffa, chafing and bitter, had done what convicts describe as "hard time." Although he lost himself in reading and in helping departing convicts with jobs outside, there were long stretches when time stood still; when Hoffa turned inward and when, as a prison official put it, "incarceration ate at him like an acid."

To be free yet not free was, for Hoffa, to continue to serve hard time.

Hoffa's lack of freedom was borne in on him almost daily. Once when *New York Times* labor writer A. H. Raskin suggested to Hoffa that they make the rounds of Miami warehouse loading docks to give the reporter a chance to observe Hoffa chatting with Teamster rank and filers, Hoffa said: "Got to find out from the parole man first."

But the parole man could not tell Hoffa whether such hob-nobbing constituted "indirect union management." For Hoffa to guess wrong might mean a return to the slammer. So the talks with the rank and filers were off.

Hoffa couldn't even park his car without running the risk of violating the conditions of his pardon. Parking lot attendants, recognizing Hoffa, would ask his help to form a Teamster local. Hoffa would gun his car and flee.

An intelligence network made up of old Hoffa loyalists kept Hoffa abreast of political currents inside the Teamsters. But communications posed problems. To the telephone calls that poured into his home at Lake Orion or at his Florida condominium (an interview with Hoffa by my research associate, Jennifer Bolch, was interrupted by six telephone calls), Hoffa would say cryptically: "Don't talk from that phone. I'll call you back."

Hoffa carried pocketsful of coins and did a good deal of telephoning from pay stations.

And if Hoffa had an intelligence network, so did Frank Fitzsimmons. Since Hoffa had to obtain his parole officer's permission to leave Detroit, then call in to a parole officer at his destination, Fitzsimmons' informers were forever checking up at parole offices all over the country to see if they could catch Hoffa in a parole infraction. It was as if an army of gumshoes had Hoffa under round-the-clock surveillance.

Those galling and crippling restraints had to go. But how?

A lawsuit could eat up years as it dragged its way through a district court, then a circuit court of appeals, then the U.S. Supreme Court. A shortcut lay through the Justice Department. But as sometimes happens with shortcuts, Hoffa could get lost. For one thing, the Nixon Administration was happily in bed with Fitzsimmons, its only major labor supporter. For another thing, the man who had put in the fix with Nixon that freed Hoffa—Murray Chotiner—had died the day after Hoffa's release. For those who see omens in such things, the place of Chotiner's death had its own mystic meaning; Chotiner, the man who freed Hoffa, died by crashing his car into a tree in front of the home of Robert Kennedy's brother, Senator Edward Kennedy.

However, Hoffa had to try the Justice Department route first, before appealing to the courts. And when he did, he was—as expected—told to get lost. To Hoffa's plea to the department's pardons attorney to unshackle him on the ground that no other labor leader had ever been subjected to such a conditional pardon, the pardons attorney gave a curt "No."

And from the then attorney general, Richard G. Kleindienst, who played golf with Frank Fitzsimmons, came a public rebuff. Kleindienst did not even wait for Hoffa to appeal directly to him. On reading a newspaper report that Hoffa meant to make such an appeal, Kleindienst let it be known: "I have informed Mr. Hoffa that the conditions set forth in his commutation are not negotiable. Therefore, there is no need for a meeting . . . the Government will move quickly to enforce all aspects of the conditional commutation [if] Mr. Hoffa does not abide by the conditions imposed on him.''

Hoffa, the man who had trampled on other men's rights, now searched for a lawyer who specialized in defending such rights. He found his man in federal court in Los Angeles, defending Dr. Daniel Ellsberg in the Pentagon Papers case (subsequently dismissed). This was the scholarly constitutional lawyer with a national reputation, Leonard Boudin.

For Boudin, Hoffa provided a new kind of lawyer-client experience. ''I had never had a client offer—let alone argue—legal strategy with me before,'' Boudin recalled. But Hoffa, already knowledgeable in criminal law, had spent his days since leaving prison in hitting the law books in search of constitutional issues that applied to his conditional pardon. To Boudin's amazement, Hoffa discussed, ''with considerable background knowledge,'' some of the legal routes that his case might take.

As Boudin recalls, Hoffa came to the heart of the problem: ''Can the President of the United States impose restraints on the way a man makes a living when he pardons him?''

When Hoffa and Boudin filed suit against then U.S. Attorney General William B. Saxbe to find out, they simultaneously lifted the curtain on some doings that were bizarre even for Nixon's Watergate White House.

For openers: The attorney general usually advises a President on whom to pardon, and how. However, in Hoffa's case, the attorney general wasn't even consulted. In an affidavit, former Attorney General John Mitchell stated: ''Neither I as Attorney General, nor to my knowledge, any other official of the Justice Department, initiated or suggested the inclusion of any restriction in the Presidential commutation of James R. Hoffa.''

Furthermore, swore John Mitchell: ''President Nixon did

not initiate with me or suggest to me that restrictions on Mr. Hoffa's activity in the labor movement be a part of the commutation.''

Who, then, had done it?

John Dean, the President's counsel.

And the affair took on an air of Byzantine intrigue when Dean—as he later admitted under oath—agreed with the Justice Department's pardons attorney that Hoffa should not be told of the pardon conditions before he left prison.

As Hoffa charged later, Charles Colson, who was to be rewarded with $100,000 of yearly Teamster legal business, had cooked up the strategy of inserting the restraints at the last minute and keeping them secret from Hoffa.

"Colson and Fitzsimmons figured I would refuse to leave prison if I knew I was being barred from union activity," Hoffa said.

Hoffa lost the first round in his court battle. U.S. District Judge John Pratt did not accept the allegation of White House intrigue nor Hoffa's argument that no President could abridge his right to ply his union trade. Starting the second round, Hoffa's lawyer, Boudin, pleaded with the circuit court of appeals to give Hoffa's case its earliest attention. Instead, the court put the case on its regular calendar, and Hoffa waited.

Some two and one-half years had passed since Hoffa had left prison. While chafing under the law's delays, he found his chief surcease through working with his hands and back at his five-acre summer place at Lake Orion. As a labor leader, Hoffa had not known physical labor for thirty-five years. Now he gathered calluses on his hands chopping down trees, draining the lake's overflow from his land. He hammered, sawed, and nailed together an addition to his summer house.

When his three grandchildren visited, Hoffa would spend a happy hour at his workbench repairing their toys. He rode the children around on his power lawnmower or watched anxiously as granddaughter Barbara Jo took her first canter on the horse he had bought her for Christmas.

Every month or so, Hoffa would take three- or four-day swings around the country's college campuses and lecture halls or appear on television talk shows to give his own vivid plea for prison reform.

The National Association of Justice, organized by a former convict, C. Edward Lawrenson, had recruited Hoffa as chief lecturer and fund raiser. To Hoffa, this was an opportunity to remain in the public eye. But he also enjoyed the contact with the audiences, particularly with college students, with whom he uniformly made a hit. In a rambling, off-the-cuff forty-minute speech, chiefly about his own experiences, Hoffa would tell them: "Put a twenty-one-year-old first offender in with homosexuals and murderers; if he's between twenty-one and thirty, he's a subject for rape and he sure as hell will be if he don't have a knife to protect himself. They come out of an ordinary prison, raped. It's why John Dean didn't want to go in. . . . I gave all this before the congressional committee. And murder! A guy working out on a punching bag. This was when I was there. Some man comes up. Gimme the bag. No. The guy gets a knife, comes back, kills him. The man already had two life sentences. What do you do, give him three?"

Hoffa's lecture tours gave him an opportunity for unobtrusive talks with loyalists who would come to the lectures, then remain to report how support for him was holding up in their areas.

But in his lecture swings, toward the end of 1974, Hoffa sensed that something ominous was happening. Fewer and fewer Teamster leaders who had clung stubbornly to Hoffa's cause were showing up.

For Hoffa, time was running out.

Chapter Eighteen

BROTHERHOOD OF GREED

FOUR MONTHS BEFORE he vanished, Hoffa received ominous news. Charles "Chuckie" O'Brien, whom Hoffa regarded as "more of a son than a protégé" and who—in turn—called Hoffa "Dad," had donned an I'M FOR FITZ button and had gone over to the side of "Dad's" mortal enemy.

For three years, Hoffa had held together a hard core of loyalists. Like reserve troops, these could be thrown into the battle for the Teamster presidency, once Hoffa was free to resume union activity. Now, Chuckie's defection indicated that Hoffa's support was crumbling. Crumbling not among the rank and file, but where it counted: among officeholders like Chuckie, who was both a business agent of a local and a "general organizer" for the International.

Hoffa could come into any town in the country and fill its biggest hall with rank and filers screaming their heads off for "Jimmy." But, as far as his comeback to power was concerned, it did him no good. For, irony of ironies, Hoffa had shut out the rank and filers—who could have been his chief strength—from having a voice in electing a Teamster president.

Between Hoffa's comeback effort and the rank and filers stood a monster Hoffa himself had created. This was the Teamster constitution, the body of laws by which the union is governed. Hoffa had remolded it in 1961 with the aim of keeping himself in office for the rest of his life.

Soon after achieving the Teamster presidency, Hoffa asked and answered a few basic questions:

QUESTION: How do you control a union of two million-odd men and women?

ANSWER: You control the union convention, held every five years, which elects you and fellow national officers, which passes laws or amends old ones, and which is the supreme court for settling intraunion disputes.

QUESTION: How do you control the convention?

ANSWER: You control the delegates.

QUESTION: How do you control the delegates?

Hoffa did it with two far-reaching amendments to the Teamster constitution. The first was to limit convention attendance virtually to Teamster officialdom only. The second was to permit officers—both local and international—to hold more than one union job. This made many of them rich, but not independent. Hoffa controlled the source of their affluence. Along with the considerable powers the Teamster president already enjoyed—the power of the purse, for example, and the power to settle disputes that could make or break a man or an entire local—the new constitution made Hoffa an absolute ruler.

But the constitutional monster that served Hoffa could serve his successors, too. Now, as master of the monster Hoffa had created, Fitzsimmons was using it to destroy Hoffa. In the battle for delegates to the Teamster convention of 1976, Fitzsimmons was separating from Hoffa even those he considered part of his family. Like Chuckie O'Brien.

Everything that Chuckie owned—both his Teamster jobs, which brought him more than $40,000 yearly in salaries and expenses; the gift of a shirt factory in Jamaica; Chuckie's schooling in union work; his very freedom from jail—Chuckie owed to Hoffa.

How did Fitzsimmons turn him against his "Dad"? By using a stick and carrot made available to him by the constitution Hoffa built.

In the service of Hoffa, Chuckie as business agent for Local 299 had been campaigning there to help keep the pro-Hoffa faction under control. Wearing his other hat as general organizer for the International, Chuckie had also traveled around the country doing what Hoffa, under restraints, could not do: seek delegate support for Hoffa.

None of this had been lost on Fitzsimmons' espionage network. Chuckie, Fitz was told, "was causing trouble." So the troublemaker was called into the presence of Fitzsimmons, who had the power of life or death over Chuckie's career with the International. Fitzsimmons could name any number of "general organizers" and so create activists who would spend most of their time on Fitz's business—the business of getting reelected. Conversely, Fitzsimmons had the power to fire a general organizer at whim, without having to account to anybody. A six-word telegram would do it: "Your services are no longer needed."

Fitzsimmons had not fired Chuckie. But he had put him on ice by banishing him to the Teamsters' Siberia—Alaska.

There, out in the cold and cut off from friends and family, Chuckie had languished for three months until Jimmy again came to his rescue. Unable to appeal directly to Fitzsimmons, Hoffa had gone instead to one of the two men who ran the union for Fitzsimmons. This was Ray Schoessling, a respected Teamster vice-president from Chicago and later secretary-treasurer. Schoessling had interceded with Fitzsimmons to end Chuckie's banishment. But as a precaution against pro-Hoffa activity, Fitzsimmons had limited Chuckie's movements to a district in Michigan. To travel elsewhere required Fitzsimmons' permission.

The banishment was the stick. Now came the carrot.

The next thing that Hoffa knew Chuckie was packing to go as far from Alaska as the length of the continent permitted, i.e., to Florida. There, he would base himself at the new home of the Teamsters Southern Conference at Hallandale, where Tony Pro Provenzano, Tony Jack Giacalone, New York racketeer Harry Davidoff, and others of similar stripe already resided in elegant condominiums. With Chuckie's happy move to the Florida fleshpots went a handsome promotion. He was to supervise twenty-six Teamster construction locals in the South. Also, Chuckie's credit cards, lifted by Fitzsimmons, were restored.

And that's how Chuckie had come to desert his dear old dad.

General organizers who would not desert Hoffa were dismissed summarily. When Boston Teamster Nick Morrissey, a lifelong Hoffa friend, wanted to know from Fitz, "Why are you destroying me?" Fitzsimmons replied:

"If you're loyal to Hoffa, you're disloyal to me. Hoffa wants my job. I want you to know that Hoffa is not coming back, and that I'm the boss."

As his following faded, Hoffa could brood that in his 1961 effort to make himself Teamster president for life, the biggest boomerang of all was the constitutional amendment that transformed the International Brotherhood of Teamsters into a brotherhood of greed. This was the Hoffa brainchild that gave express permission to Teamster officials to hold more than one union job—so opening up new vistas of multiple salaries and multiple expense accounts and pensions. At the same time, Hoffa set an example of inflated union-leader salaries that would have made Samuel Gompers, father of the labor movement, spin in his grave.

Hoffa gave himself a 50 percent raise, boosting his $50,000 salary to $75,000. (Fitzsimmons, by 1976, was paying himself $155,000.) The combination of high salaries and multiple jobs created a newly affluent class of union officialdom, many of whom received more pay than the President of the United States. They sported Florida condominiums for the winter, palatial diggings for the year-round, limousines, "periodic rests" at the country's fanciest spas. One Teamster vice-president, Big Bill Presser of Ohio, could do what most millionaires don't do: On her birthday in 1975, he gave his wife a $40,000 Rolls-Royce.

All of this affluence had depended on Hoffa's benign sufferance. With rank and filers' dues payments, Hoffa had tied Teamster officeholders to himself with bonds of gold. Now, in early 1975, when the time came to choose up sides between Hoffa, out of power, and Fitzsimmons, in power, it was not difficult to guess which way the brotherhood of greed would go.

Consider an early defector to Fitzsimmons, Big Bill Presser, the jukebox racketeer who rose to boss Ohio's Teamsters and, while serving as Teamster vice-president, pleaded guilty to extortion. (He served no time, successfully arguing ill health.)

According to Labor Department reports from 1975, Presser drew salaries, expenses, and allowances from five Teamster jobs:

As International vice-president and as general organizer:	$ 38,484
As president of the Ohio Conference of Teamsters:	45,296
As president of Cleveland Joint Council 41:	72,659
As president of Cleveland Local 555:	10,800
Total:	$167,239[1]

1. In the prior year, 1974, Bill Presser also received $28,930 for three months as trustee of the Central States pension fund. The Pension Reform Act of 1974 forced Presser to relinquish this job. He handed it over to his son, Jackie. He returned to it later, only to be forced out in 1976 under Labor Department pressure.

Yet, even the whopping total of $167,239 doesn't tell the whole story. To it must be added the incredible travel expenses allowed him, in just one of his jobs, that of president of Cleveland Joint Council 41. A provision in its constitution—taken almost verbatim from the International constitution governing travel expenses for the Teamster president—permitted Presser to travel anywhere in the world for "periodic rests" and to take his wife as well as secretaries and any aides he chose. The travel expense provision took special notice of Presser's sojourns in Florida by permitting "travel to and from any of the fifty states, *including Florida . . . apartment or hotel-motel accommodations, utilities,* gas and car expenses, entertainment, and miscellaneous expenses." (Italics added.)

Bill Presser's son, Jackie, a corpulent 260-pounder, did his father proud by feeding even more greedily at the Teamster trough. Jackie's five Teamster jobs yielded him $193,749 in 1975. On this, Jackie somehow managed to pile another $31,000 from two non-Teamster union jobs. *Total take: $224,700!*[2] How Big Bill and his son could possibly pay attention to all the jobs they held, no one knows.

All in the Presser family union business, too, was the $233,000 yearly haul by Bill Presser's brother-in-law, Harold Friedman, an ex-convict. As president of Teamster Local 507, Friedman drew $117,432 in 1975, plus $115,982 from another Presser preserve, a Bakery Workers local.

Counting Teamster jobs only, Bill and Jackie Presser took down some $360,900 yearly. Bestriding this golden pile, which they owed to Hoffa, Big Bill and Jackie told reporters at a dinner in Presser's honor that they agreed with Fitzsimmons' description of Hoffa: "Just a bum not worth writing about."

When the twenty-man Teamsters' executive board, headed

---

2. Finances of the Culinary Workers Union from which Jack Presser drew a salary were under investigation by the Labor Department in 1977.

by Fitzsimmons, marched to the dais at the 1976 Teamster convention in Las Vegas, a band struck up "When the Saints Go Marching In." These "saints"—the Teamster president, secretary-treasurer, fifteen vice-presidents, and three trustees— live somewhat less than austere lives. Fitzsimmons, enjoying a $155,300 yearly wage, lives in three homes, one of them a $250,000 spread adjoining the La Costa Spa in southern California, built with Teamster loans and frequented by gangsters. Ray Schoessling, the secretary-treasurer, could live equally well, for his $110,000 salary is supplemented by two others, which bring him a yearly total of $165,000.

Every Teamster vice-president—except Harold Gibbons, who was stripped of extra jobs because of loyalty to Hoffa—is also a general organizer and holds two or three other paying union jobs besides. Joseph Morgan, who gets $79,660 as vice-president and general organizer, for example, draws another fat $54,930 as president of the Southern Conference. Total: $134,590 yearly.

Nor is the affluence limited to national officers. For his labors as secretary-treasurer of Chicago Local 710, William D. Joyce drew down a cool $134,500 in 1975. Not far behind is Frank J. Matula, who was once temporarily let out of jail—where he was serving a six-month stretch for perjury—so that he could attend a Teamster executive board meeting in his capacity as a trustee. For his labors as secretary-treasurer of Los Angeles Local 396, Matula collects $85,898. With his trustee's salary and allowances of $16,988, Matula takes down $102,886 yearly.

Along with the payroll bonanzas at the disposal of a Teamster president, there is the rich Teamster treasury. Some $51,000,000 of per capita dues pour into the Teamsters headquarters yearly, plus returns on investments. Of the Teamsters' yearly income, $5,800,000 is spent for "organizing"— a ready source of gravy with which to win friends for the Teamster president.

Consider the case of Rolland McMaster, an outsized man whose outsized fists and skill with a dynamite stick were at Hoffa's disposal in Hoffa's early organizing drives. Hoffa rewarded McMaster with a job as business agent of Detroit Local 299 at a salary of $32,000 yearly—plus whatever he could shake down from employers. The McClellan Committee revealed that McMaster had accepted fifty-five head of cattle from a trucking company employer, plus cash rake-offs from others. In 1966, the law caught up with McMaster and he served five months for extortion.

Putting McMaster in charge of organizing, as one Teamster vice-president put it, was to set a fox to watch over chickens. Yet McMaster could help Fitzsimmons wrest control of Local 299 from Hoffa loyalists. So in 1971 Fitzsimmons named McMaster a general organizer at $39,000 a year, then assigned him to organize an estimated 150,000 steel-hauling drivers in the Midwest. Into extortionist McMaster's hands—to finance the job—Fitzsimmons put $1,300,000 over a period of two years.

When secretary-treasurer Murray "Dusty" Miller cut McMaster off this campaign in 1974, it was generally known inside the Teamsters that the $1,300,000 had gone down the drain with only a handful of new Teamster card holders to show for it. But it wasn't until mid-1976 that the full story of McMaster's operation became known. The Detroit *Free Press* revealed that McMaster and his thirty-man task force had waged a campaign of terror employing dynamite, truck destruction, and brutality. Hapless employers, facing ruin, paid off through a middleman to obtain "labor peace."

Organizing money that was ladled out lavishly to those who defected from Hoffa was withheld altogether from those who remained loyal to him.

Consider Travis Dumas, an honest union man who risked his life to run for the presidency of Miami Local 390 against opponents backed by regional Teamster officials. As president, Dumas didn't play the game. Instead of accepting employers' bribes to permit sweetheart deals, Dumas turned these offers over to the feds. Instead of hanging Fitzsimmons' picture in the union hall, Dumas hung that of Jimmy Hoffa. So he received not a penny of organizing money during his three-year regime. His successor, elected with campaign money from above—the Southern Conference—promptly received an International organizing grant of $10,000.

If all else failed to force defections from Hoffa, Fitzsimmons had another method, inherited from Hoffa, with which to apply the final turn of the screw. This is the Teamster procedure for settling members' grievances—rare among other unions. Usually, when a union member has a grievance—a claim, say, that he was fired without cause—he goes to his business agent, who takes up the matter with a foreman or other low-level management man. If there's no agreement here, the grievance works its way up to top-level union leaders and management and, if unresolved, ends up in arbitration.

But in the Teamsters, at about the time Hoffa was fashioning his constitutional dictatorship, he also won an important concession from employers. Members' grievances were to be settled by an "open end procedure." Translated, this meant there would be no arbitration at the top. Unless the employer saw things as Hoffa did, he faced a terrifying prospect—a Teamster strike. With this "open end procedure" Hoffa not only won an important club over employers, but over his own people as well. A local leader who was in Hoffa's bad books would get no favorable grievance decisions from him. And a local leader who couldn't settle his members' grievances didn't last long as a local leader. And what went for Hoffa's enemies when he was in power, went for Fitzsimmons' enemies when he achieved power.

Travis Dumas, the Hoffa loyalist-president of Miami Local 390, provides a dramatic example. Dumas could survive the withholding of organizing subsidies from Fitzsimmons. But he could not survive his failure to win favorable grievance decisions for his members from a hostile Fitzsimmons. The successful campaign to unseat Dumas was largely based on the opposition's slogan: "Elect a local president who can work with the International."

As the spring of 1975 turned into summer, lines had formed and forces had crystallized in the subterranean Hoffa-Fitzsimmons struggle for power. Hoffa and his charisma had been no match for Fitzsimmons and the monster created by Hoffa.

The regional Teamster barons—the Pressers, the Provenzanos, and others—were now solidly in Fitzsimmons' camp. And with them were the regional Mafia families, much of whose power and income derived from their alliances with the regional Teamster bosses.

To persist in his comeback effort, Hoffa would now have to challenge not only the Teamster powers who had deserted him, but also the gangsters behind them. Being Hoffa, he was not deterred.

Chapter Nineteen

HOFFA AGAINST THE UNDERWORLD

FROM THE MOMENT the regional Teamster barons chose up sides against him, Hoffa's life was in danger, for war against the Teamster turncoats would mean war against their underworld sponsors.

To Hoffa, the loss of underworld support was unsettling, for here men who owed Hoffa much betrayed him. And he could brood that the earliest and most damaging defections came from those with whom he had the closest ties—both of friendship and of business.

Anthony Giacalone had been a lifelong friend and neighbor of Hoffa's. Their children had grown up together. Giacalone owed his wealth and position as one of Detroit's most powerful men to Hoffa—able to call Hoffa and put in the fix, he could head off a threatened strike, block unionization, or perform a hundred-and-one salable favors to businessmen. When Hoffa flourished, Giacalone courted him.

When Hoffa was in purgatory, just out of prison, Tony Jack remained friendly with Hoffa, but kept himself flexible. He visited Hoffa at his place on Lake Orion. But he began to cast about for another Teamster power source in case Hoffa faltered.

To Giacalone, this potential power source was Tony Provenzano. Because of his extortion stretch, Provenzano had been barred from union activity for five years. But by 1975, he was again secretary-treasurer of Local 560 and boss of northern New Jersey Teamsters. Inside the Teamsters, some believed, the eastern mobs were grooming him as a successor to Fitzsimmons.

When I asked an underworld source about Tony Pro's future, he replied: "Mr. Provenzano is capable of filling any post in the Teamsters, even that of president."

Tony Giacalone of Detroit began to court Tony Provenzano of New Jersey. The two Tonys played golf together at the Doral Country Club outside Miami, frequented the same Florida health spa, and dined with each other at their Hallandale and Bal Harbour condominiums.

Meanwhile, Tony Pro, who owed his very life to Hoffa, began to court Fitzsimmons. And Fitzsimmons, needing eastern underworld support, was willing. He let Provenzano into his innermost circle and invited him to a golf tournament—in which ex-President Nixon was a fellow guest. Ex-felon Tony Pro didn't get into the fivesome that played with Nixon, but he did get into the group picture with the ex-President.

Fitzsimmons also hosted a testimonial dinner for Tony Pro several months later. He hinted strongly that he would soon restore Tony to the national offices he had held on going to jail, those of general organizer and vice-president.[1]

For Hoffa, Tony Pro's defection had chilling implications. If Hoffa returned to power, Tony Pro and his brother, Salvatore, would have to go. But Tony Pro was a violent man. His

---

1. Two indictments against Tony Provenzano—one for pension fraud, another for the Anthony Castellito murder—blocked these appointments, at least until Provenzano cleared up his legal problems.

hold on his labor and rackets empire was refreshed periodically with spilled blood. The roll call of Teamsters—rank and filers as well as officers—killed or maimed in action fighting Tony Pro, read like a war casualty report:

Anthony Castellito, Local 560 secretary-treasurer: missing in action and presumed dead. He had announced in 1961 that he planned to run against Tony Pro for president. (Tony Pro was indicted for his murder in mid-1976.)

Walter Glockner, Teamster rank and filer: killed in action in 1963. He had campaigned for an anti-Tony Pro ticket. He had also planned to testify in the extortion trial that sent Tony Pro to prison.

George Phillips, wounded in action (beaten around the head with a claw hammer) while running against Tony Pro in 1962.

One employer, who had bribed Tony with the gift of a house, committed suicide rather than testify against Tony.

Another time, Tony foisted a loanshark, Armand Faugno, on a trucker's payroll. Faugno proceeded to ruin the trucker with forged company checks. Faugno disappeared, never to be heard from again.

Looking back on Hoffa's disappearance, one has to wonder whether this disquieting thought ever crossed Hoffa's mind: If war comes with Tony, can my own disappearance be far behind?

Hoffa could have other disquieting thoughts about Tony Pro. Tony had formidable allies. Behind him stood the northern New Jersey mob, bossed by Jerry Catena. Behind Tony, too, was the southern New Jersey Mafia, headed by Angelo Bruno. And across the Hudson in New York City, Tony Pro could call on the heirs of Lucky Luciano—Carmine Galente, Carlo Gambino (who has since died), and Anthony "Tony Ducks" Corallo.

Tony Pro showed his clout with these New York gangsters when a fellow Teamster from New York invaded Tony's New

Jersey territory in 1975. The invader was Mark Davidoff, son of New York labor racketeer Harry Davidoff. Young Mark had prepared himself for his inheritance—the family's union business, Local 295—with a degree in criminology from New York University. But perhaps he should have studied prudence instead. Already in control of the freight moving in and out of John F. Kennedy Airport, young Mark rushed in where he should have feared to tread. He tried to organize employees at Newark Airport, which lies in Tony Pro's preserve.

Tony Pro promptly took out a contract on young Mark's life. Because the elder Davidoff, Harry, had enjoyed lifelong connections with the New York Mafia, the contract required the New York mob's approval. Tony got it. To save his son's life, Harry Davidoff hurried up from Florida and engaged the mediating services of New York gangster Johnny Dio. Tony Pro called off his disappearance-act artists—but only after the Davidoffs promised to stay out of New Jersey.

Naturally, as in New Jersey, violence is a handmaiden of union politics in Ohio. As Hoffa knew, nowhere in all this country was a Mafia crime family's hold on the Teamsters stronger than in that state. Here, the Mafia dictated who should hold what offices in the Teamsters.

Big Bill Presser, the Ohio Teamster boss, provides the best example. Presser's first boost up the Teamster ladder came in 1952. The reigning chief of Cleveland's Mafia, Anthony Milano, tapped him for the presidency of Joint Council 41, which rules Cleveland's Teamsters.

When Milano was nearing ninety and had become known as "the old man on the hill," he still showed who was the real boss of the state's Teamsters. Presser, pleading ill health, announced in 1974 that he would resign his presidency of Joint Council 41 and name his son, Jackie, as his successor. But "the old man on the hill" sent down a veto. John Scalish, born John Scalise, now the acting head of the Cleveland Mafia, passed the word to Presser. At a luncheon in a restaurant owned by Jackie Presser, John Scalish's brother-in-law told Bill Presser that he had to continue in office until it pleased "the boys" to retire him. Meanwhile, Presser was to give up the notion that his son, Jackie, would succeed him. The post was being reserved for the son-in-law of Louis "Babe" Triscaro, Cleveland Mafia and Teamster power. This was a minor Teamster official named Sam Busaca.

"The mob didn't want Jackie," Presser told friends the next day. Dutifully, as ordered by the mob, Presser stood for reelection to the Cleveland Joint Council.

In the mid-1960s, an audacious Teamster by the name of Walter Bryant formed a slate and ousted the mob-connected Babe Triscaro and his associate, Skip Felice, from the leadership of Teamster Local 73. The ousting didn't last for more than several hours. For, while celebrating his victory, Bryant got word that the mob didn't approve. Bryant promptly rejected his newly won presidency. On thinking things over, Bryant told the U.S. Department of Justice that he had been forced to resign. Then, seemingly on additional word from the mob, Bryant changed his mind again. When the feds began to investigate, Bryant pleaded with them to drop it.

Tony Giacalone of Detroit, Jerry Catena of New Jersey, Tony Corallo of New York, and Tony Milano and John Scalish of Cleveland turned against Hoffa because under Fitzsimmons the mobs had never had it so good.

For one thing, Fitzsimmons had something Hoffa never had, nor ever could have: access to the White House. And through the White House, for a time, the mobs had a veto over investigations and prosecutions by the Department of Justice.

The New York Times brought to light a major instance of such interference in 1973, with a story obviously leaked by frustrated FBI agents. According to the *Times,* "Two ranking officials of the Department of Justice" had halted court-approved wiretaps "that had begun to penetrate Teamster connections with the Mafia."

While listening in on West Coast gangsters suspected of labor racketeering, FBI agents learned of a Mafia plan to rip off millions from the Teamsters, via a prepaid medical plan to be financed by Teamster welfare funds.

In an affidavit submitted to the Justice Department, the FBI disclosed that Fitzsimmons had taken time out from the Bob Hope Golf Classic tournament at Palm Springs, California, to meet with three representatives of the Mafia. One of these was Peter Milano, son of Cleveland's Mafia chief, Tony Milano, indicating the Ohio mob's interest in the medical plan. The Chicago Capone gang was interested, too. For, according to *The New York Times* article, Fitzsimmons met also with Lou Rosanova, an emissary from the Chicago Capone gang. Fitzsimmons approved the plan, according to the FBI, and sent the gangsters to work out the details with Allen Dorfman, who serviced the Teamster welfare insurance fund. Dorman, convicted of extorting a bribe from a Teamster pension-fund borrower, was preparing at the time to leave for prison.

When all this was put before the then Attorney General Kleindienst and Assistant Attorney General Henry Peterson, in an FBI request for permission to continue the wiretaps, they said no. The investigation had "failed to show probable cause . . ." to continue the eavesdropping.

Young lawyers in organized crime strike task forces around the country suffered agonies of frustration as they made cases against Teamster-Mafia malefactors, only to have them gather dust on Justice Department desks in Washington, or to get turndowns to requests for permission to indict.

For example, when Travis Dumas, then president of Miami Local 390, was offered a bribe to accept a sweetheart deal, he took pains to have his conversations with the bribe giver recorded by the Dade County sheriff's office. The seducer was a self-styled "labor relations consultant," Harry Shulman, acting for his client, a Food Fair supermarket. With the knowledge of the Organized Crime Task Force in Miami, Dumas met with Shulman and accepted the $5,000 bribe, which he promptly turned over to the Miami Organized Crime Task Force. Its lawyers just as promptly sent the case along to the Justice Department in Washington. This was in 1974. But problems with the tape-recorded evidence held up an indictment against Shulman until 1976, and then only on a technical violation. He was subsequently acquitted.

It did not escape the underworld that the Labor Department, too, had a hands-off-the-Teamsters policy. Although the Pension Reform Act of 1974 gave the Labor Department a mandate—and money—to investigate the Teamsters' scandal-ridden pension fund, nothing was done in time to help Hoffa.

Along with the Fitzsimmons White House connection, the underworld could gather other benefits from his regime. Unlike granite-hard Hoffa, the putty-soft Fitzsimmons rarely said no to the ripoffs that were forever being proposed to him by racketeers.

Consider the get-rich-quick insurance scheme of Louis Ostrer, a mob-connected confessed swindler. Ostrer conceived a severance-pay scheme and promptly sold it to New York Local 295, dominated by labor racketeer Harry Davidoff. Employers paid $40 per week per employee to buy individual insurance policies for union members and build a severance-pay fund. Actually, as the New York State Insurance Department found, the employers' contributions were largely drained away by excessively costly insurance that yielded Ostrer $337,000 in yearly commissions from one local alone. Straight life insurance, which cost the severance fund $1,238,274, could have cost but $52,546 in term insurance. This depleted the fund by $1,185,000.

Eager to go national, Ostrer hired Fitzsimmons' son, Don, who was selling vending machines for a company owned by a Detroit hoodlum. As "consultant and public relations man," Don introduced Ostrer to the elder Fitzsimmons. As Ostrer told me later, "Mr. Fitzsimmons quickly saw the value of my plan as a fringe benefit." Ostrer's scheme rapidly spread to eight states and some sixty to seventy Teamster locals.[2]

While Fitzsimmons was good for underworld business generally, he was especially good to the Ohio gang. When Allen Dorfman, the "man to see" for Teamster pension-fund loans, went to prison in 1973, Bill Presser, then a trustee of the Central States pension fund, took Dorfman's place as chief dispenser of loans. With Presser as the gateway, the Ohio mob became the clearinghouse for millions of dollars in loans, with all the opportunities for finder's fees, commissions, bribes, and diversion of pension money to unclean hands that this afforded.

The Pressers and, through them, the Ohio mob also became dispensers of important Teamster business patronage.

For a picture of the Teamsters' corruption cesspool at its malodorous worst, let's follow the adventures of a Teamster public relations contract.

When Fitzsimmons looked about for a public relations firm in 1972 to polish the Teamsters' image, he went to Bill Presser. Big Bill, in turn, went to Tony Liberatori, who had served a twenty-year prison term in connection with the slaying of two Cleveland policemen. This seemed no bar to Liberatori's holding the job of business manager of a laborers' local—nor, apparently, to his subsequent employment as a Teamsters "public relations consultant."

---

2. For further details of this adventure, see "The Mafia Tightens Its Hold on the Teamsters," by Lester Velie, *Reader's Digest*, August 1974. Also, "Staff Study of the Severance Pay-Life Insurance Plan of Teamsters Local 295," published by the U.S. Senate Committee on Government Operations, June 11, 1976.

Liberatori got in touch with a Harry Haler of Los Angeles, also known as Harry Helfgot, who had served fifty-five months for three nonviolent crimes—among them, the use of stolen securities as collateral for a bank loan.

Harry Haler described himself as a "double agent" who supplied tips to the IRS. At the same time, he said, he "helped people in trouble with the law," because of his "connections in government."

Given the job of finding a public relations firm, no difficult task in Los Angeles, Haler went instead to Las Vegas. There he enlisted a former disc jockey, Duke Hoover, for the job. Hoover obtained a contract calling for the yearly expenditure of some $1,300,000. It wasn't until eight days after receiving this contract that Hoover formed a firm, Hoover-Gorin, to fulfill it.

Why the circuitous Cleveland-to-Los Angeles-to-Las Vegas search for just the right image-improver? The search, it seems, was for somebody willing and eager to share the gravy.

From Hoover-Gorin, in the form of "commissions and consultant fees" flowed no less than $539,000 to Harry Haler in the twenty-month period beginning in late 1972 and continuing through 1974. Income tax and other records, examined by this writer, supplied the proof.

What service did Haler provide for payments averaging $20,000 a month? He provided the services of a conduit. The gravy did not remain with him. Big ladles of it were sluiced by courier to an unidentified recipient connected with the Teamsters, who picked up the cash at Las Vegas and at Palm Springs.

Meanwhile, back in Cleveland, convicted killer Liberatori was receiving $2,000 a month as a public relations consultant. That he divvied this up with others—as Haler divvied up his share—is suspected, but not known for sure.

Finally, the power that Hoffa had centralized in his strong hands had, under Fitzsimmons, reverted to the regional Teamster leaders, a state of affairs that was just fine with their Mafia sponsors. Hoffa, at the top, permitted the sale of sweetheart deals, on a selective basis; under Fitzsimmons they ran wild.

The trucking industry was plunged into chaos as honest truckers, meeting standard wages and conditions, were driven to the wall by the unfair competition of truckers who paid off underworld "labor consultants" for a sweetheart deal.

From the chaos, big-city crime families extracted a new and vast source of loot and influence.

Woe to anyone, even a Hoffa, who threatened this state of affairs.

Chapter Twenty

WHOM THE GODS WOULD DESTROY

THE LAST DAYS of Jimmy Hoffa were days of frustration, obsession, and desperation. Hoffa was a bound giant, tied down, like Gulliver, by the restraints against union activity. Powerless to stop his empire, everything he had built, from sliding away from him, Hoffa began to act out of character, to do "flaky things," as Mafia characters described it.

Hoffa dreamed of instant rehabilitation via a miraculous court or White House move that would permit him to resume union activity. He toyed with the idea of running for the U.S. Senate on the Republican ticket. This, he thought, would bring instant pressure on a Republican President, who would then call him off with the bribe of a full pardon. Hoffa chased instant public acclaim with a proposed peace-making mission to North Vietnam. He hunted instant millions with strange business schemes. And he threatened instant revenge against those who had feasted at his table and then turned against him—inside the Mafia as well as the Teamsters.

Realistically, the chances were slim of lifting the ban against union activity before the 1980 date set in his commutation. A lower federal court summarily turned down Hoffa's constitutional plea. A circuit court of appeals had let Hoffa's appeal gather dust for more than a year.[1]

On Capitol Hill, influential politicians who once lobbied in Hoffa's behalf now drew back. Fitzsimmons' agents had been busy. As one congressman put it: "Buck the Teamsters? Do you think I'm crazy?"

And with Fitzsimmons visiting the White House and traveling occasionally in Air Force One, help from that quarter seemed remote.

Yet Hoffa became obsessed with the idea that some move in his behalf was imminent. "He talked about the lifting of restraints twenty hours a day," his prison-reform associate, C. Edward Lawrenson, recalls.

Like a man lost in a desert, Hoffa began to see mirages.

On a July Sunday, three days before he disappeared, Hoffa telephoned his oldest friend and advisor, seventy-two-year-old Nick Morrissey of Boston, who, until Fitzsimmons fired him, had been a general organizer since the ancient days of Teamster president Dan Tobin.

"Where are you?" asked Morrissey.

"Up at the lake."

"Who's with you?"

"Nobody. I'm alone."

"Where's Chuckie O'Brien?"

"Who knows where that fellow is."

"You shouldn't be alone," Morrissey scolded.

"I can take care of myself," Hoffa said.

These preliminaries out of the way, Hoffa—in a voice charged with excitement—got down to the main business of the call.

---

1. The circuit court of appeals never did hand down a decision, declaring—after Hoffa's disappearance—that the issue was moot.

"I've got it made! It's in the bag," Hoffa said. "There's been a White House meeting. A full pardon is on the pardon attorney's desk at the Justice Department. I've got a new lawyer going over there tomorrow to pick it up."

"You've been spinning your wheels for so long, Jimmy," said Morrissey, "this may be all bullshit."

"I know this is the real McCoy this time," Hoffa said.

There was, of course, no pardon waiting. And, as later inquiry revealed, there had been no meeting at the White House.

At about the same time, Hoffa told reporter Ralph Orr, of the Detroit *Free Press,* that he expected a full pardon in a matter of days.

"Assign someone competent to handle the story," Hoffa urged. Orr himself was about to leave for vacation. "Not just some kid, Ralph, not just some kid," he kept saying.

Then there was Hoffa's financial plunge down a coal hole. Its zanier aspects emerged only after Hoffa's disappearance. As noted earlier, Hoffa, in 1973, had invested an unstated sum in a company that owned anthracite properties in Pennsylvania—Great American. Its principal owner was a James Durkin, who had borrowed frequently from the Teamsters' Central States pension fund. Where Hoffa got the money to invest—a rumored $600,000—is not known. It did not come out of his $1,700,000 pension settlement, for the first $640,000 installment was not made available to him until July 1974. It must be presumed that Hoffa tapped the cash he had hoarded in secret caches here and abroad.

In any case, Durkin—with whom Hoffa invested—turned Great American over to a Hyman Green, who, like Durkin, was also a friend. Hoffa had often favored him with Teamster loans.

When Hoffa disappeared and his family tried to salvage Hoffa's coal investment, they were in for a surprise. Green blandly told Hoffa's widow and son that Hoffa's investment in Great American was news to him. As far as he knew, Hoffa had never put in any cash.

When the family threatened to haul Green into court, they faced a practical difficulty. They had no evidence of Hoffa's ownership. Since Hoffa had done all his business in cash—even deals involving hundreds of thousands of dollars—there was no canceled check to prove he had lent money to the coal venture. Nor, search as they might, could the family find a receipt, a document, a scrap of paper to support a claim. Hoffa had done one of three things, all irrational. He had either told his family that he had put money into Great American when, in fact, he had not. Or, he had turned over a substantial amount of cash to promoter Durkin without obtaining a receipt. Or, he had obtained a written confirmation of ownership, but tucked it away without telling his family where it was hidden. Neither the family nor its lawyer would answer any questions about the affair.

From coal to concerts was just one easy jump for entrepreneur Hoffa during his final days. Of his adventure in coal, he had exulted, "There's a billion in it!"

Now, there was gold in Western-style country music. And a place to dig it in—the 80,000-seat stadium of the Detroit Lions at Pontiac, Michigan. And Hoffa knew where to get country music talent. One of his trials—that for taking bribes from an employer—had taken place in Nashville. So Hoffa said he had connections there. Hoffa discussed the concerts with Pontiac's mayor and with the stadium's management. Typically, a potential Hoffa partner in the venture was a man with dubious financial credentials. For with Hoffa at the early negotiations was convicted union embezzler Louis C. Linteau, in whose limousine business Hoffa had a secret part-ownership. But the world never found out if it had another Sol Hurok in Jim Hoffa. Murder intervened.

In happier days, Hoffa had always kept his cool in public. True, in the privacy of Teamster headquarters or in a hotel room, he could throw a wild tantrum or even use his fists against a subordinate. But in dealing with the press or testifying before a congressional committee or while being taken in shackles to prison, Hoffa was the unperturbed, self-controlled leader. Now, in his last days, none could predict where or when Hoffa would explode.

One time, a grand jury questioned Hoffa about his ex-convict brother, Billy Hoffa. The grand jury was investigating the charge that Billy Hoffa and an associate had robbed Pontiac Local 614 of some $37,000 by drawing pay for which they did no work.

Back in 1957, the McClellan Committee questioned Hoffa about his brother, too. The senators wanted to know whether Hoffa had asked a union aide to hide out Billy, who was wanted for armed robbery. Abjuring the protection of the Fifth Amendment, yet skirting perjury, Hoffa came up calmly with an answer that has become a classic:

"I'm saying that, to the best of my recollection, I have no disremembrance of discussing with Scott [the union aide] any such question."

But now before the grand jury, Hoffa—uncharacteristically—resorted to the Fifth Amendment. Then, equally out of character, he "ranted and raved," as a federal attorney recalled, charging the grand jury with leaking derogatory information. U.S. marshals virtually had to carry Hoffa from the room. (Brother Billy, indicted on eight counts of fraud, died of a heart attack while awaiting trial.)

A lawyer who was at Hoffa's side during some of his darkest courtroom hours once observed that "Hoffa could not abide being alone with his thoughts. He had to lose himself in work." This was possible when Hoffa was Teamster president and even when he was in prison, where he filled his time with a prison job and voracious reading. But out of prison and out of a union job, Hoffa brooded during long stretches of idle time. The consequent bitterness would bubble over in intemperate outbursts before television audiences. Interviewed by Detroit television reporter Ven Marshall, Hoffa once burst out that Fitzsimmons "is crazy and goes to see a psychiatrist." Hoffa could provide no evidence of this, for there was none.

His autobiography, which he finished dictating several weeks before his disappearance, provided evidence that he himself was somewhat less than balanced toward the end.

Hoffa, The Real Story is described on the front of the dust jacket as "The only authorized book of Hoffa's life." On the back of the dust jacket is an affidavit signed by Hoffa's widow, Josephine, his son, Jim, and daughter, Barbara, and duly notarized. It attests that "The book contains the thoughts, views and hopes of James R. Hoffa, expressed in language we have often heard him use to convey [them]."

The book contains a series of charges against Fitzsimmons. These had been dictated by Hoffa, according to his writing collaborator, Oscar Fraley, and the transcribed tapes were in the hands of the publisher.

In his opening chapter, Hoffa wrote:

"I charge him [Fitzsimmons] with *selling out to mobsters* [italics added] and letting known racketeers in the Teamsters.

"I charge him with making vast loans from the billion-dollar Teamster pension fund to *known mobsters.*

"I charge him with permitting the *underworld establishment* of a union insurance scheme..."

The insurance-schemes promoter, says the book, "was convicted on a federal stock swindling charge in company with Johnny Dio Dioguardi" whom Hoffa describes as "linked to the New York Mafia."

When those who knew Hoffa best read these charges, they shook their heads in disbelief. In the underworld, as one informant indicated to me, there was rage as well as disbelief. From the grave, Hoffa was saying things they had never heard him say in life. Hoffa's attack on Fitzsimmons for letting ''known mobsters into the Teamsters'' was curious enough, in view of Hoffa's lifelong working partnership with gangsters. Even more curious was Hoffa's tacit acceptance of the existence of an underworld and of a Mafia.

This Hoffa had pooh-poohed almost until the day he disappeared. Here is an excerpt from an interview granted in June 1975 to radio reporter Jerry Stanecki, and later published in *Playboy* magazine.

PLAYBOY: Then you don't think that he [Meyer Lansky] is a member of organized crime?

HOFFA: I don't think there is any organized crime, period. Don't believe it. Never believed it. I've said it for the last forty years.

And a little farther on in the interview:

PLAYBOY: What about Johnny Dio?

HOFFA: Friend of mine, no question about that.

PLAYBOY: Member of organized crime?

HOFFA: Like you are.

PLAYBOY: Member of the Mafia?

HOFFA: Like you are.

PLAYBOY: What about Tony Giacalone [Detroit Mafia figure]?

HOFFA: Giacalone! Giacalone! Giacalone's a businessman.

If the authenticity of his autobiography is to be believed, why then did Hoffa acknowledge the unacknowledgeable— i.e., the existence of organized crime? And why did he put at least one of his close friends, Johnny Dio, into the book? Why did he break the underworld code of silence in the light of what he knew about the Mafia treatment of turncoats?

Let's listen to Morris Shenker, long a Hoffa lawyer, who believes he knew Hoffa better than most men did.

"Jimmy did a lot of talking during the last months of his life. As for the book, he had to do something radically strong to get attention, as a means to his aim of getting back to power."

Shenker shook his head.

"Jimmy had lost his finesse. He was telegraphing his punches. He was a desperate man."

But Hoffa's wasn't a quiet desperation. Hoffa was putting his desperation in Gimbels' window for all the world to see.

Chapter Twenty-One

DEATH AND CONSEQUENCES

FROM THE GRAVE, Jim Hoffa turned more heat on his enemies in the underworld and the Teamsters than he could have generated had he lived.

As we have seen, Hoffa's abductors or killers had expected local police to take charge of the case. And, as in other underworld disappearances, they had expected the investigation to be limited to the killing alone. But what they had *not* expected was a public outcry against the seeming impunity with which the mobs could decree and carry off the abduction of a major public figure. Nor had the abductors or killers anticipated that such an outcry would turn the full might of federal law enforcement into a renewed interest in the underworld and the much investigated Teamsters as well.

Breathing down the necks of the mobs and the Teamsters were the FBI, the Justice Department's Division of Organized Crime, eighteen organized crime task forces around the country, plus Internal Revenue Service and Labor Department sleuths. In Detroit, in Newark, in New York City, Chicago, Los Angeles, and Cleveland, scores of witnesses, some granted immunity from prosecution, were telling what they knew about those suspected of murdering Hoffa, and about Mafia and Teamsters affairs.

Chief federal investigative effort involved a pincers movement against Hoffa suspects. If these could be indicted and convicted of crimes unrelated to the Hoffa murder, sentences of heavy time might induce one of them to tell what he knew about the Hoffa killing—in return for a lesser sentence. So Tony Giacalone, Chuckie O'Brien, Tony Provenzano, and Sal Briguglio found themselves struggling in a tangle of legal difficulties.

Against Tony Giacalone, the Detroit Organized Crime Task Force obtained a tax evasion conviction carrying a ten-year sentence (which he was appealing in early 1977). Giacalone had been prosecuted unsuccessfully on tax evasion charges twice before but for this third try, the government had prepared with special diligence. The prosecution called two hundred-odd witnesses and presented such a mountain of evidence against Giacalone that the trial lasted one hundred and two days. Assistant U.S. Attorney Jeff Anderson, who prosecuted the case successfully, was promoted to head the Detroit task force against organized crime.

Tony Provenzano, at sixty-three, faced the prospect of ending the rest of his days in prison—unless he talked. Not only had the ghost of the fifteen-year-old murder of Anthony Castellito come back to haunt Provenzano, but other prosecutions loomed as well. A new indictment charged Tony Pro with conspiracy to defraud a local union's pension fund.

Sal Briguglio, indicted with Provenzano in the Castellito murder case, faced other prosecutions too. A federal grand jury in Newark, New Jersey, was hearing evidence in late 1976 that could lead to loanshark indictments against Briguglio and two others.

Grand juries, impaneled to sift evidence in the Hoffa investigation, cast their nets farther afield. Looking into the doings at Detroit Local 299, the Organized Crime Strike Force at Detroit dredged up evidence for an indictment against no less a fish than Richard Fitzsimmons, eldest son of Teamster president Frank E. Fitzsimmons. Local 299 is the home base from which both Jim Hoffa and his successor, Fitzsimmons, rose to power. The elder Fitzsimmons had groomed his son, Richard, to take over the local, but pro-Hoffa forces there had frustrated the attempt. However, Richard Fitzsimmons had retained the vice-presidency of the local, and, while serving in this job, so the indictment charged, had embezzled the union's severance pay funds in order to buy personal insurance policies for himself and other associates in Local 299. Conviction could carry up to ten years in prison and up to $20,000 in fines.

Probing with fresh diligence into Chuckie O'Brien's conduct as a business agent, the Detroit Organized Crime Task Force obtained an indictment charging Chuckie with accepting a bribe from an employer he was seeking to organize. The bribe was an automobile. Chuckie was convicted and sentenced to a year. He appealed. If the appeal was denied, Chuckie, behind bars, would have time to reflect on whether he would spend additional years dodging other indictments or tell what he knew, if anything.

Hoffa's disappearance also brought to life the first serious effort by federal investigators to find out what was happening to the millions that employers were pouring in as contributions to Teamster pension funds.

Although a pension reform law had become effective January 1, 1975, little was done to implement it until after the uproar over Hoffa's disappearance, seven months later. A joint Labor-Justice Department task force was deployed to look into the Teamsters Central States Fund. One quick result was the resignation of the most notorious of the Central States' trustees, Big Bill Presser, Teamster boss of Ohio. Called before the Labor-Justice task force to answer questions about his role in some of the fund's lending, Presser sought refuge in the Fifth Amendment against self-incrimination. Soon after, he quit the board of trustees. So did Fitzsimmons and others.

Although the federal investigation into pension funds commands somewhat limited forces, some of the more egregious looting was being uncovered. Federal investigators told a federal court, for instance, that since July 1974, George Snyder, the secretary-treasurer of Teamster Local 806, headquartered at Melville, L.I., had taken some $1,000,000 in fees from the local's pension fund. During the fiscal 1976 year, fully 80 percent of the local's pension-fund contributions had gone to Secretary-treasurer Snyder as fees. He had also taken 33 percent of employers' contributions to the local's health and welfare fund.

By mid-1977, pressure on the Hoffa abduction suspects had yielded nothing, and a federal law enforcement official told me: "The Hoffa investigation is dead in the water." Soon after, however, it was revived with a nation-wide series of FBI investigations aimed at putting new pressure on Hoffa suspects.

"No one is talking," an FBI source told the Detroit *News*. "These (the suspects) are stand-up guys. We've got to put on enough pressure to open somebody up. If we apply enough pressure, someone is going to want to make a deal."

Another FBI source said: "We've covered a lot of ground in two years. And some of that ground was literally skipped over. Now, it's time to go back over some of it and walk a bit more slowly, looking at the trees instead of the forest."

PART IV

AFTER HOFFA

CHANCES ARE THAT no streets or airports will be named after Jim Hoffa, nor will any monuments be erected to him. But Hoffa left his own monuments behind him. One is the underworld bank that he fashioned from the Teamsters' biggest pension fund. Another is the underworld's pervasive—but invisible—presence in Las Vegas. Still another is the union dictatorship, now ruled by a junta that draws its power from the constitution Hoffa wrote to perpetuate himself in office. And finally, there is an empire-building union that knows no jurisdictional boundaries. It signs up new members among professionals, technicians, wage earners—white, blue, and gray collars—and grows explosively, and at a faster pace than any other union.

Curiously, the last two monuments—the union dictatorship and the empire-building union—contain fuses inside them that may yet shatter the evils that lived after Hoffa.

Chapter Twenty-Two

THE HOUSE OF JACK THAT JIM BUILT

IN HIS WILDEST syphilitic deathbed delirium, Al Capone, the architect of modern organized crime, could not have fantasized a bank whose millions could be heisted without guns, face masks, or getaway cars. Yet Jim Hoffa not only created such a bank but successfully defended it against reporters who exposed it, prosecutors who tried to put it out of business, and union members who sued to regain money the bank dissipated.

The House of Jack that Jim Hoffa built for the underworld is the Teamsters' Central States, Southeast and Southwest Areas Pension Fund. Into it yearly employers of some 500,000 Teamsters pour $400,000,000 of pension contributions. By 1977, reserves had piled up to equal those of a major bank—$1,400,000,000. From it, gangsters had taken hundreds of millions.

When he became Teamster president in 1957, Hoffa realized that the Central States fund, then four years old, could be mined to line one's own pockets and to repay the big-city mobs that had helped him up the union ladder. The fund had been born, along with others, when the U.S. Supreme Court ruled that unions could negotiate fringe benefits—pension, health, and welfare contributions—in lieu of wage increases barred by wartime wage ceilings. Although the Central States fund was to be run jointly by eight union trustees and eight employer trustees, Hoffa took over as tsar. Union trustees, appointed by Hoffa, could not challenge him. Neither could employer trustees who feared "labor trouble." While most pension funds employ professional investment counselors to place reserves in safe securities, Hoffa converted his pension fund into a lending institution—a private bank for the Mafia—and took a personal hand in the lending.

Any resemblance between the loans that Hoffa made and those of a straight banker would be hard to detect.

References? A criminal record wasn't necessary, but it helped. For assisting Hoffa with the lending as "loan finders" or "arrangers" was a curious crew whose chief credentials were their mob connections. In Detroit, the man to see to arrange a Central States loan was Tony Jack Giacalone. In Ohio, it was Big Bill Presser, the Teamster boss who takes orders from the Cleveland mob. In Florida, two mob mouthpieces convicted of tax fraud made the deals: Ben Cohen of Miami and Frank Ragano of Tampa. In Chicago, it was Allen Dorfman, the Capone gang's conduit to the Teamsters.

To Irwin Weiner, Chicago Capone gang bail bondsman, and five Capone gangsters—including an expert in taking over businesses to loot them—went $1,400,000. With it, the borrowers were to rehabilitate a toy company into which the Central States fund had already plowed $4,200,000. The rehabilitators, as an indictment charged, diverted the loan to other enterprises, to household expenses, and even to defense lawyers. The fund was left with a bankrupt company and some plastics-fabricating machinery. (Tried, the gangsters were acquitted when a key prosecution witness was murdered.)

Collateral? Central States' money managers put up millions

on properties already in hock, taking back second and even third mortgages. Or in lieu of collateral, a 10 percent to 20 percent kickback would do—or a bribe. One borrower, already in default on $3,800,000 of borrowings from the fund and under a stock-swindling indictment, came looking for a further $1,400,000. Instead of collateral, as he testified at a criminal trial, he put up a $55,000 bribe to the then-consultant to the Teamster fund, the mob-connected Dorfman. The loan sailed through.

With juicy pickings like these under Hoffa, mob quarrels erupted over the division of the borrowing loot, or over territorial rights to lush loan finder's fees. Once, Allen Dorfman was ambushed at his Chicago home by gunmen who, police theorized, had come from the East to warn Dorfman against neglecting eastern mob interests. Once, too, the Detroit Mafia got into so bitter a quarrel with New York gangsters over the right to a kickback on a loan that a Mafia court was convened in neutral territory in Pennsylvania to settle it.

Repayment? As the secrecy that long shrouded the Central States fund was pierced, it emerged that many of the borrowers treated the loans as gifts.

A suit against the fund revealed that, as of 1972, more than one-third of its loans were in default. When Labor Department auditors began to examine the Central States accounts in 1976, they found themselves looking into a hole the size of a skyscraper excavation. Some $179,000,000 in loans had disappeared and had to be written off. One Labor Department investigator said, "Loans have been out for ten years or more, and neither principal nor interest has been paid."

With loans like these, mobsters and associates built spas in California and Florida, acquired land, office buildings, and a wide range of businesses in thirty-odd states, thereby increasing underworld affluence, power, and potential for mischief against the rest of us.

As banker to the underworld, Hoffa tied up so much cash in nonliquid mortgages and speculative land deals—and lost so much in defaulted loans—that he was hard-pressed to meet pension claims. So Hoffa, the lavish dispenser of cash to the underworld, became a tight-fisted miser at pension-payout time. He hedged his payouts with so many restrictions and interpreted them so stringently that they became booby traps to blow teamsters' pension hopes sky-high. Here are some of them:

Catch No. 1: To win a pension, a Central States teamster had to put in twenty years of continuous service with contributing employers—no mean feat in a trade in which a teamster might work for more than a dozen employers during his lifetime, some of whom made contributions to other pension funds, or were nonunion, or were organized by another union. Jesse Noe, a truck-repair mechanic in an Illinois town, had seventeen and a half years of service with the Central States when his employer moved to a neighboring town and signed Noe and others into the International Association of Machinists. Too bad for Noe. When he applied for his Central States pension later, he was told he was two and a half years short of the requirement.

Catch No. 2: This one was called "break in service." When Chicago teamster Edward B. Goss applied for a pension after thirty-four years of truck driving, he was told he had only three and a half years of credits toward a pension. Why? Because he had interrupted his driving (and his employers' contributions to Central States) from 1965 to 1971 to take a supervisory job—a "break in service." None of the twenty-nine years Goss had put in before the break counted. He had to start all over again after the break.

Catch No. 3: This was the "you-can't-take-it-with-you" catch. Elmer A. Petersen had already logged thirty-six years of truck driving in 1963 when he changed employers and transferred from one Chicago Teamsters local to another. When Petersen applied for his pension seven years later, he learned that all those years with his old local didn't count for a Central States pension. His old local had its own independent pension fund, and Petersen could not take his credits with him into the Central States fund. Despite forty-three years as a Teamster dues-payer, Petersen failed to qualify for a pension.

Catch No. 4: This was the "try-and-prove-it" catch. When Cleveland teamster Stanley Flowers applied for a Central States pension in 1970, he heard nothing from the fund for almost a year. Then he learned that the fund could not find records covering his employment—and employer contributions—from 1939 through 1949. No wonder. The fund's records, as we found out later, were in chaotic disorder.

For years, as the fund's own executive director, Daniel Shannon, told us, records consisted of scribbled notations on filing cards. Later, when records were reduced to microfilm, many of the tapes were undecipherable. Flowers spent three months tracking down prior employers who dug up old records to supply him with affidavits. These, Flowers forwarded to the fund—but received no acknowledgment.

"They could have been lost in the mail," executive director Shannon told a reporter, "or they could have landed in the circular file [a waste basket]." After six years of battling in the courts, Flowers finally won his pension in 1977.

Catch No. 5: This one is known as "Loser Loses All." If other catches deprived you of a pension, none of the money that had been contributed for you was yours.

A teamster might protest, "But that money my bosses put into the fund is mine. It was paid for me in lieu of wages."

"Wrong," the teamster would be told. "That's not what it says here in the plan."

And there was little that the despairing pension claimant, facing old-age penury, could do about it. Pension funds were virtually unregulated. Lawsuits? Where would a retired truck driver muster up the lawyer's fee? And if some courageous lawyer took the case on a contingent-fee basis—or as a crusade—he would be confronted by the Teamster bar association, which would drown him in a sea of technical objections.

"Millions for defense against lawsuits, but pennies for paying claims!" seemed to be the fund's motto. For legal services to the Central States in 1972, the Washington, D.C., law firm of Rhyne & Rhyne received $462,104! In 1974, when Rhyne & Rhyne received $264,633, the fund's legal costs for the year were $1,419,000.

The outraged cries of frustrated pension claimants, plus the clamor raised by reporters, eventually reached Congress. So Hoffa achieved a dubious distinction. He became the only public figure in recent history to have two major pieces of federal legislation passed to cope with problems he'd raised.

In 1959, the McClellan Committee's airing of Teamster racketeering had resulted in a new labor relations act, known at the time as the "Jim Hoffa Law." In 1974, Congress passed a pension reform act (the Employee Retirement Income Security Act). As Mike Gordon, ex-counsel to the Senate Labor Committee, told us, "The fundamental purpose of the pension reform act was to put an end to the abuses in the Central States fund." A law that could do this could also correct abuses in pension payments to some 35,000,000 Americans in 500,000 other pension plans.

The pension reform law provided the feds with a new high-powered weapon: broad subpoena powers. They could now knock on any pension-fund door, just as national bank examiners do with national banks, to search records and question managers. For the first time, too, law enforcers could hold pension-fund trustees responsible, as fiduciaries, for the way they handled other people's money.

"Fiduciaries," says the new law, "must act with the prudence and diligence that a prudent man would use.'' If they did not, they could be sued for damages, not by some impecunious pension claimant, but by a battery of government lawyers. Damage verdicts could strip trustees of everything they owned.

But the underworld was not about to give up its bank—and mob brains began to whir on how to circumvent the reform law.

Almost two months after the effective date of the pension reform act, the trustees approved a $15,000,000 loan to a partnership whose principal figures were associates of Meyer Lansky, long the chief financial advisor to the mobs. In revealing the deal, *The New York Times* stated: ''Despite a new federal law and government controls... Teamster pension fund money was lent to known associates of organized crime figures... to finance business operations that are still funneling millions of dollars into the underworld treasury.''

To put an end to underworld use of Central States cash, law enforcers declared a moratorium on all loans from the fund. To show they meant business, the two agencies delegated to the pension-fund-cleanup job—the Labor and Justice departments—deployed a task force of twenty auditors and lawyers inside the headquarters of the fund in Chicago. These watchdogs would not only sniff out past heists but protect the fund against new ones.

When federal law enforcers took over the Central States cleanup job, they faced a dilemma. What should they do with the material that their task force—armed with subpoena powers—dug out of the Central States files and from questions to trustees?

Should the feds go the old route—convene federal grand juries and try to send fund mismanagers and loan misusers to jail? Criminal prosecution had failed woefully to interfere with the plundering of the Central States fund. In all of its scandal-ridden years, no trustee other than Hoffa had been convicted of a fund-connected crime. And in Hoffa's case, the conviction resulted from a three-year search by a special get-Hoffa unit in Robert F. Kennedy's Justice Department for some crime—any crime—with which to jail Hoffa. In the end, it was mail fraud: the use of the mails to further the payment of loan kickbacks to Hoffa.

Even when the government seemed to have an open-and-shut case, as in the Capone gang's boodling of a $1,400,000 plastics factory loan, the feds could get no conviction. The U.S. attorney's office in Chicago spent several million dollars and several hundred thousand man-hours toward the effort. The government hoped not only to jail the gangsters but to put the fund into trusteeship and end its services to the under-world. The Capone gang, rising to the challenge, rubbed out a chief government witness. The gangsters did not take the stand, so the prosecution could not reveal their criminal back-grounds through cross-examination. "Not guilty," said the jury, "on all counts."

A Justice Department lawyer, James Hutchinson, called to the Labor Department to head up the pension reform effort, brought a new idea with him.

Since criminal-law remedies had failed, why not use civil remedies for the Central States cleanup job? The pension re-form law provided such remedies.

The section on fiduciary responsibility, for instance, could be used to pressure the trustees into a true cleanup. If Frank E. Fitzsimmons and other trustees failed to go along, they could be sued for everything they owned.

With this threat, in 1977 the feds finally purged the Central States board of trustees, forcing all to resign, including Team-ster president Frank E. Fitzsimmons. The Labor Department also forced Central States to turn the investment of its cash over to an insurance company, thus slamming the door shut against the underworld. The looting that had begun with Hoffa—and had lasted for two decades—was over.

The biggest Teamster pension fund had been cleansed. But as subsequent scandals in the Central States Health and Welfare Fund (not to be confused with the pension fund) and in the handling of local funds indicated, the Hoffa legacy of pension- and welfare-fund looting lived on.

Chapter Twenty-Three

THE GOLDEN GODFATHER OF LAS VEGAS

Yearly, LAS VEGAS and other Nevada gambling towns take about $1,000,000,000 from the pockets of the American people—some of it from housewives who will drop a month's grocery money at the slots or keno, and some from "high rollers" who may leave $100,000 of "markers" behind them after a night's play.

A portion of this river of gold will flow to corporate casino owners who arrived relatively late in Nevada: MGM, Hilton Hotels, Inc., the (Howard) Hughes Tool Company. But a considerable stream—nobody knows how large—will flow to overlords of organized crime in our big cities. These overlords will recycle their secret Las Vegas profits, pouring them into further penetration of legitimate business, into the bankrolling of loanshark rackets, and perhaps even into dope distribution.

This flow of Las Vegas suckers' losses to unclean hands is one of Jim Hoffa's most mischievous legacies to the rest of us. For, more than any other man, Hoffa made the underworld invasion of Las Vegas possible by opening up the coffers of the Teamsters' biggest pension fund—that of the Central

States, Southeast and Southwest Areas—to gangsters hidden behind fronts.

The Teamsters' role in the growth of Las Vegas gambling is often acknowledged, although the secret role of the underworld is not.

When the Teamsters held their presidential convention at Las Vegas in June 1976, the town's mayor gave President Frank E. Fitzsimmons the key to the city and a book: *Las Vegas, As It Began, and As It Grew*. Much of the gambling town's growth, Hizzoner made clear, was due to the "very large Teamster investment in Las Vegas"—i.e., the union's financing of gambling-hotel construction with loans from its Central States pension fund.

Since "the Teamsters had started such investments," said the mayor, air travel to Las Vegas had tripled and gross revenues (from the gambling business, presumably) had climbed steadily, each year's revenues exceeding those of the prior year.

Prudently, the mayor neglected to say anything about the ultimate destination of much of these revenues, or about Hoffa's role as the golden godfather of Las Vegas.

Yet when Hoffa was Teamster president, he spent much of his crowded time and limitless energy on bankrolling the underworld's schemes to expand its Las Vegas jackpot. Hoffa was so involved that he knew more of the town's secrets than anyone else.

Hoffa knew who the hidden owners were and how the big-city mobs cut up the Las Vegas "territory." He knew about the respectable bankers who helped hide some of the "hidden interests." Hoffa knew who cheated on taxes by "skimming" gambling profits, and how much. He knew who had made millions in kickbacks from the Las Vegas loans, because he had given approval for such kickbacks, including handsome ones to himself.

Indeed, Hoffa knew so much about Las Vegas—including the inside on gangster killings over subterranean disputes there—that a knowledgeable lawyer once told this writer: "If Jimmy Hoffa talked, a dozen of the town's best-known people would be destroyed overnight."

A man who could do this was obviously in danger. And there are some in Las Vegas who are convinced that Hoffa's disappearance had its roots in his extensive Las Vegas involvement.

How was Hoffa able to get involved? More specifically, how was he able to let the gangsters in via Teamster loans? Doesn't the State of Nevada maintain a Gaming Control Board whose function it is to keep undesirables out? It does. All casino owners must be licensed. The Gaming Control Board maintains a staff of fifteen investigators who check the source of casino-license applicants' money. If it can't be explained or is misrepresented, it is presumed to be underworld cash, and the license is denied.

Gangster penetration of Las Vegas requires a legitimate money source. It also requires a front—an ostensibly straight person with no criminal record and no visible underworld ties, who applies for a casino license with legitimate cash.

Hoffa was able to produce both legitimate cash and fronts. The legitimate cash source, odd as it may seem, was the Teamsters Central States fund. True, the fund was notorious for bankrolling underworld schemes all over the country. But the cash itself is untainted because it comes from the contributions of trucking-company employers—some $200,000,000 yearly. It is not "hot money." The Central States fund, at the turn of 1977, had more than $1,400,000,000 in reserves. From these have come a staggering $300,000,000 of loans to Nevada gambling enterprises to provide the mobs with a golden back door to Las Vegas.

Hoffa's first front, as I found on looking into Las Vegas in

1959, was not a person but a holding company. Hidden in it were assorted gangsters from the big-city mobs. The most important of these was the vinegary Moe Dalitz, a graduate of the old Cleveland gang who once, according to Senate testimony, was an intermediary in bribing Hoffa to fix a laundry workers' strike. The mobsters' holding company owned the Las Vegas Desert Inn, a gambling hotel, so hiding the true ownership by Dalitz and his pals.

As a first step toward building Nevada's biggest gambling empire, Hoffa lent the Dalitz-controlled company $8,000,000 to buy the Stardust Hotel.

In company with Minneapolis mobsters, then hidden in the ownership of the Fremont Hotel, Dalitz next tried to buy the Riviera Hotel, and so make the underworld the biggest factor in Las Vegas gambling. But the state's Gaming Control Board interceded to block the deal.

When Moe Dalitz' hidden role was exposed, he left Las Vegas—at least physically—for southern California, where, with further cash supplied by Hoffa from the pension fund, Dalitz built La Costa, a spa favored by Teamster and underworld brass.

Hoffa's next big loan in Las Vegas was entrusted to a pudgy promoter named Jay Sarno, given to loud talk and loud clothes. Sarno was one of those frequent Teamster fund borrowers whose fast and loose handling of other people's money did not diminish his credit rating in Hoffa's eyes. Hoffa turned over $28,000,000 of Teamster cash to Sarno to build Caesar's Palace Hotel in 1965, a time when Sarno was already in the process of bankrupting three Teamster-financed motels in Atlanta, Dallas, and Palo Alto, California.

In the Atlanta misadventure, Sarno admitted in a lawsuit that he and an associate had diverted some $500,000 of the hotel's money to their own use. The suit was brought by movie star Doris Day, a limited partner. She and other investors got their money back when the court put the motel into receivership—uncontested by Sarno—and ordered it sold to raise the cash.

Yet, as events proved later, Sarno had offsetting values to Hoffa; behind him could be hidden certain characters who could not obtain casino licenses on their own, including Hoffa himself. In Las Vegas, wherever Sarno went, the underworld was sure to go.

Even before Caesar's Palace opened in 1966—with Sarno as chief owner of record—the Los Angeles *Times* reported a summit meeting at Palm Springs, California, to cut up the underworld's hidden ownership of the hotel. Cited as a chief conferee was Anthony "Fats" Salerno, the New York Mafia figure reputed to operate a loanshark ring with some $75,000,000 of loans on the street on any given day. Another conferee was Jerry Zarowitz, a Salerno partner, listed by the Miami, Florida, police as a top-echelon hoodlum. As a book-maker, Zarowitz had the inordinate brass to try to fix the New York Giants–Chicago Bears National Football League cham-pionship game of 1946. He served a twenty-month jail term for his pains.

Banker Hoffa did not attend the underworld meeting that involved his Caesar's Palace investment. But seemingly he knew and approved of whatever arrangements were made there.

These became apparent as Caesar's Palace opened in 1966. Who should be its executive vice-president and casino boss but Tony Salerno's partner, Jerry Zarowitz?

Yet more soon came to light on the gangsters hidden behind Sarno. When Sarno and his associates sold Caesar's Palace to Lum's, Inc., in 1969, that corporation, publicly traded on the New York Stock Exchange, had to disclose all to its stockhol-ders and to the Securities and Exchange Commission.

But, as the SEC spelled it out in a subsequent court action

against Lum's and against Sarno, Zarowitz, and others, the corporation had omitted certain juicy details. Juiciest omission of all was the fact that hoodlum Zarowitz, although no owner of record, had received $3,500,000 of the $58,000,000 sales price. This, said the SEC, was "de facto proof of [Zarowitz'] part-ownership in Caesar's Palace"—i.e., that Zarowitz had a "hidden interest."

Indeed, it appeared that gangster Zarowitz, not license-holder Sarno, was the boss of the place. As the SEC charged, Zarowitz controlled the casino cash. This fell so precipitously during the last five months of Zarowitz' and Sarno's owner-ship that the SEC charged that the profits were being skimmed in advance of the hotel's sale.

The sale of Caesar's Palace did not end Sarno's usefulness to banker Hoffa. With loans from Hoffa, Sarno obtained Gaming Control Board clearance to build and operate another hotel, the gaudy Circus Circus. Again, federal investigators suspected "hidden interests" behind Sarno. For one thing, Paul Dorfman, a lifelong friend of Jim Hoffa's with criminal connections, spent almost all of his time there.

What was Dorfman doing at Circus Circus—and for whom? And what was Sarno's true role? Federal authorities believed they were on the threshold of getting the answers from Sarno himself, when he got into financial and legal difficulties.

First, an investor in Circus Circus sued Sarno, charging that he had diverted casino cash. As a defendant in such a suit, Sarno had to answer questions about the hotel, some of which could lift the veil on the suspected "hidden interests" there. But in pretrial hearings, Sarno refused to answer questions on the ground that his answers might incriminate him. Next, Sarno ended the suit altogether, and possible exposure, by settling out of court—paying the suing shareholder $500,000. This large sum was a small price to pay for the right to keep his secrets.

Sarno ran the risk again of having to spill the beans about suspected underworld involvement in his hotel when the Justice Department Organized Crime Strike Force at Los Angeles obtained an indictment charging Sarno with offering a $64,000 bribe to an IRS agent. The feds believed that a conviction on this charge and the prospect of serving heavy time might induce Sarno to talk in return for a lesser sentence. One of the things the feds dearly wanted to know was whether Hoffa himself was a hidden owner of Sarno's hotel. They never found out, for Sarno was acquitted. Again, his secrets remained with him—and with his backer, Hoffa.

When Tony Provenzano, a fellow Lewisburg Prison inmate of Hoffa's, wanted a pension-fund loan to finance a restaurant in New Jersey, he didn't send word outside to the pension-fund trustees. He went to Hoffa in prison, who turned him down and so started a blood feud that persisted after both Tony Pro and Hoffa were freed.

By the time Hoffa left prison in 1971, his feud with Frank E. Fitzsimmons had shut Hoffa out from any influence he had had over Teamster pension-fund lending. But Hoffa's legacy—the underworld's hammerlock on Las Vegas—did not diminish. Thanks to the pattern, employed by Hoffa, of using fronts, it grew. Only the faces of the frontmen changed. And this brings us to one, Allen Glick, a financial *wunderkind* who, when little more than thirty—with scant experience in real estate and no experience in gambling-hotel management— suddenly emerged as the mysterious recipient of $160,000,000 in Teamster loans. Part of this—$62,700,000—went to buy the majority shares of Recrion Corp., which owned the Stardust and Fremont hotels—the very gambling hotels that figured in Moe Dalitz' frustrated effort to dominate Las Vegas gambling back in 1962. Part of Glick's Teamster-fund borrowings—$13,000,000—went to buy the casino at the Las Vegas Marina Hotel & Casino. Add to these holdings the Hacienda

Hotel, which Glick had acquired earlier, and the young wiz-
ard—at least nominally—was one of the biggest men on the
Las Vegas gambling scene.

Nor was Glick's access to Teamster pension-fund loans limited to gambling enterprises. When the Teamsters fund fore-
closed on a Santa Monica real estate venture that was in default
to the tune of $13,000,000, it sold the foreclosed property to
Glick for $7,000,000—or about half of the defaulted loans.
The interest rate to Glick, further, was 4 percent at a time
when the prime interest rate was 11 percent.

Who was Allen Glick? And why did the Teamsters pension
fund—and others—do such nice things for him?

Here the same questions swirled about Glick that had been
raised earlier about Sarno.

Soon after Glick—a law school graduate—left the army in
1969, he was the recipient of substantial loans, and suspicions
were raised about whom the money was actually going to. For
example, Glick had been working as a salesman for a San
Diego real estate development company, Saratoga Development Corp., for only a short time when the company's foun-
der, Dennis Wittman, gave Glick a 45 percent share of the
company. Although this was worth an estimated $2,000,000,
all Glick gave back for the stock was a $2,500 promissory
note. Why the virtual gift of almost half the company to Glick?
And was he the real recipient—or merely a front for gangsters?

At about the same time, Tamara Rand, a neighbor of
Glick's and the wife of a San Diego gynecologist, lent Glick
$560,000. Subsequently, in late 1975, Mrs. Rand was found
shot to death in her home. San Diego police described the
murder as a "syndicate hit."

The police found $435,000 in $100 bills in one of Mrs.
Rand's safe-deposit boxes. Police discovered, too, according
to Jim Drinkhall of *Overdrive* (a Los Angeles-based truckers'
magazine), that Mrs. Rand was "making frequent trips to Las

Vegas, and to the Bahamas, Switzerland, Italy and Holland,'' leading to the suspicion that she was ''a courier of money from Glick's operations.'' Police did not connect Glick with the Rand murder, nor was there any indication that he was involved. As in other gangland slayings, the investigation came to a dead end. But the murder did draw attention to Mrs. Rand's $560,000 loan to Glick and raised questions about Glick's possible connections with the underworld.

Further questions were raised when Glick turned control of gambling operations in his hotel over to an underworld figure, Frank (Lefty) Rosenthal. A big-time bookmaker, Rosenthal had long been known to federal authorities as a confederate of organized crime figures.

Rosenthal took over as chairman of the executive committee of Glick's gambling-hotel enterprises, with total control of day-to-day gambling operations. His salary was an astounding $500,000 yearly. The Nevada Gaming Control Board promptly ordered Rosenthal ousted from his job as an undesirable. A state court upset the Gaming Board's action, and Rosenthal was reinstated—at a $250,000 salary—pending further action by higher courts, if any.

Question: For whom was Rosenthal a watchdog? Was it for Glick? Or was it for hidden interests behind Glick?

THE LAS VEGAS VISITOR does not sense the underworld's presence. Outsized, deputized police are everywhere. Gang violence is rare, for discipline is enforced away from Las Vegas. Gangsters' meetings involving Las Vegas interests are held out of the state, either in nearby Palm Springs, California, or at La Costa, the Teamster-funded spa already described. Notorious Mafia figures seldom come to Las Vegas. If they tried, the sheriff's men would pick them up at the airport.

Yet the underworld's influence, thanks in large part to

Hoffa, is there in ways that not only affect the sheep who flock to be shorn there but federal taxpayers as well.

First, there is the Las Vegas pattern of greed, of never-give-the-sucker-a-break. A legalized gambling casino is as solid a business as the Bank of England—and more profitable. With mathematical certainty, the casino keeps 22 cents of every dollar the customer pays, providing there's enough volume to make the odds work.

So the Las Vegas casinos never close. And as if that were not enough to kick up the volume (and so take more from the player), the pace of the play at Las Vegas is the fastest anywhere. In contrast to the fifteen twists of the roulette wheel per hour at Monte Carlo, at Las Vegas there are forty-five.

But the greed doesn't end there. Not satisfied with "beating the customer," gangsters hidden behind the Las Vegas fronts are forever trying to "beat Uncle" as well. This the mobsters do by "skimming"—i.e., by knocking off a chunk of the casino's winnings to understate their earnings for tax purposes. Once the skimmer simply pocketed bundles of bills in the counting room. Today's skimming is harder to detect. "Markers" left behind by players are collected later by the casinos—with the help of mob collectors back home—but are written off on the books as bad debts. The Internal Revenue Service maintains agents in Las Vegas. Yet, over the years, the mobs—as occasional tax-evasion indictments at Las Vegas indicate—have cheated the government—and the taxpayers—of millions; nobody knows how many, for sure.

To round out the picture of greed, there is the underworld invention known as the "free gambling junket," which uses the sucker's own greed—the illusion of something for nothing—as bait to lure him to the gaming tables—and the cleaners.

When gangster Meyer Lansky ran the casinos in London and Athens in the 1950s (a business so big that Lansky operated his own gambling-equipment factory at Liverpool), his pals back home would load bulging planes with "high rollers" and fly them free to the gaming tables.

Today, few of the big Las Vegas hotels are without junket arrangements, many of which, federal investigators say, pay commissions to the mobs. The Nevada Gaming Control Board registers (but doesn't license) no fewer than six hundred junket operators—called "junketeers." What they contribute to Las Vegas gambling profits can be judged by the single contribution of the biggest junketeer of them all, "Big Julie" Weintraub, who is six feet four inches tall and sports a broken nose and two broken knees, which, he says, resulted from a mugging. But months before the "mugging" the New York underworld grapevine hummed with the report that Big Julie was "going to be taught a lesson" for failing to cut in the mobs.

On a Memorial Day weekend, Big Julie, who calls himself the Pied Piper of Las Vegas, is likely to load up a Boeing 747 jet, a DC-8 Stretch, and other airplane space with some six hundred VIPs (very important players) from New York, Connecticut, and New Jersey. These can fill half the Teamster-financed Dunes Hotel, for which Big Julie does his pied piping. Over a four-day Memorial holiday, according to Big Julie, the junketeers he lures to Las Vegas lose a cool million to Big Julie's employers. By his own account, Big Julie's junketeers have dropped $10,000,000 to $15,000,000 yearly to the Dunes.

It's all very businesslike. If you apply for a free junket trip—all travel, room and board, and liquor paid—Big Julie checks you out at your bank to determine whether you can lose big. On the plane, Las Vegas-bound, Big Julie will hand you a questionnaire inquiring how much credit you will require at the casino cashier's cage. Should you ask for less than $5,000 of credit, Big Julie will make a note to keep an eye on you at the casino.

If you start out playing $1 chips, Big Julie's spies, called
"evaluators," will grade you "poor." Big Julie may wait a day
to see if you've mended your ways and moved up to the $100-
chip class. If not, your name goes on a list associated with a four-
letter word. A message from the front desk invites you to pay
for the room and board—and liquor—you thought were free.

In his New York office, Big Julie maintains a list of six
thousand "qualified" players—including a special list of VIPs
who are capable of dropping thousands in an evening's play.

"We run this like a legitimate business," Big Julie once
told me in a relaxed moment at his poolside suite at the Dunes
Hotel, which pays him a six-figure salary. "Of course, it's not
legitimate," Big Julie added. "We give them nothing."

Actually, less than nothing, if Big Julie's figures of his
customers' losses are to be believed.

It costs a Las Vegas gambling hotel some $800 to fly a
player in (from the East Coast) and to house, feed, and provide
him with liquor. But the take is so big that one hotel, Caesar's
Palace (also financed with Teamster loans), hosts junkets from
as far away as Hawaii, Hong Kong, and Tokyo, and in a recent
year spent $10,500,000 on the players' free travel, room, and
board.

With the Pension Reform Act of 1975 as a club, the Labor
Department beat the Teamster pension fund's policymakers
into promising to make no further new loans and to emphasize
investment in securities instead. However, loans could still be
made to borrowers who needed additional funds for expansion
or to protect the original loan. This left a loophole for some
additional lending for Las Vegas projects. Criminal lawyer
Morris Shenker, chief owner of the Las Vegas Dunes Hotel,
for instance, was able to get a commitment for an additional
$40,000,000 after the Reform Act went into effect. (The
Nevada Gaming Control Board blocked the loan on a techni-
cality, and the matter is in the courts.)

Chapter Twenty-Four

CAN THE RANK AND FILERS DRIVE THE RASCALS OUT?

WHEN HOFFA FLOURISHED, chances were remote that rank-and-file rebels would upset him and end the dictatorship he had cemented into the Teamster constitution.

Hoffa kept the channels of communication open to his members. He was available to them on the telephone and during visits to their locals. He spent a good deal of time at truck terminals, listening to members' beefs. The men felt he was one of them and would take care of their interests.

Although sweetheart contracts existed in Hoffa's day and employers chiseled on the men with the connivance of Teamster officials, Hoffa tried to keep this evil at a minimum.

But with Hoffa gone there was no other charismatic leader to keep the sweetheart-contract evil in check. In contrast with Hoffa, his successor Fitzsimmons was a remote figure who seemed as busy playing golf with Hollywood and Washington bigwigs as he was minding the Teamster store. Employers were ripping off the Teamster members, but Fitzsimmons and company were doing little to prevent them.

In Ohio, long-suffering Teamster rank and filers formed a

rebel group called Teamsters for a Democratic Union and
began rallying Teamsters in Detroit and elsewhere to rebel.

Yet at the Teamsters' 1976 convention at Las Vegas, a
successful revolt by the Teamsters for a Democratic Union and
other dissident groups seemed remote. There was the familiar
convention juggernaut that steamrolled 25 percent pay hikes
for the already obscenely affluent Teamster top command;
there was the return to power—by acclamation—of men who
were as familiar with the inside of a grand jury room as they
were with the inside of a union hall. But thanks to an incredible gaff by Fitzsimmons, aggravated by Teamster brutality,
the dissident rebels got a much-needed assist. The possibility
arose that, for the first time, the little men at the bottom of the
Teamster pile could topple those at the top and do what Senate
investigators, crime busters, and courts had failed to do: make
the Teamsters go straight.

This brings us to the saga of Pete Camarata, a rank-and-file
Daniel who confronted the lions at Las Vegas and came away
bloodied but unbowed to ignite the local fires of rank-and-file
rebellion into a national movement of Teamster rank-and-file
liberation.

Among the 2,200-odd delegates, Pete Camarata was a
strange one. He loaded trucks for a living, and he had been
elected to his role as delegate. Most of the delegates could
claim neither. They were officeholders—porkchoppers in
union lingo—who, under an article in the Teamster constitution dictated by Hoffa, served as delegates by virtue of their
office. If a local is big enough, an election is held to provide
additional delegates. Pete Camarata was one of these.

At thirty, Pete was one of the new breed of young, educated
Teamsters around whom others can rally. He had worked his
way through Wayne State University as a loader on a warehouse dock—represented by the Teamsters—and left after
two years because he had found a cause. No one seemed

to be minding the Teamster store. Fellow workers' grievances against the boss went untended. The men didn't have a voice over the conditions of their work. Pete had plunged into union-reform activity with such enthusiasm that his wife of a year—alone during the day while Pete worked, and alone at night while Pete fomented union revolution—left him. Pete had moved into his old college fraternity and, unimpeded by family ties, gave himself up to building a local and national rank-and-file rebel movement.

Now, as a delegate, Pete had come to Las Vegas with a quixotic mission: He meant to try to return the vast union to its members. Pete, a former football tackle, is a 250-pounder with height and muscle to match. The top of Pete's skull is beginning to push through thinning black hair. A luxuriant Fu Manchu moustache gives him a somewhat fierce look but actually, he is quite gentle-voiced and likes to end a conversation with God Bless You. Abhorring violence, Pete thought it prudent to bring with him a fellow Teamster who had once been a professional wrestler. This precaution protected neither the protected nor the protector.

Pete got a hint of things to come on the night of his arrival at Las Vegas. Walking through the convention hotel's gambling casino on his way to his room, Pete bumped into a son of Teamster president Fitzsimmons. Thanks to his father, Richard Fitzsimmons was vice-president of Pete's local and held three other Teamster payroll jobs besides—yielding him over $100,000 yearly. Young Fitzsimmons had been drinking heavily and losing heavily at the gambling tables.

"What you doing here?" young Fitzsimmons demanded. "You here to cause trouble?"

Pete reminded Fitzsimmons that he was a duly elected delegate from Local 299.

"Well, don't you cause trouble now," young Fitzsimmons warned, and staggered off.

But, as the convention opened the next morning, "trouble"—i.e., demand for change—was just what was needed.

As President Fitzsimmons led his fifteen vice-presidents and other top officials to the dais, the band, seemingly oblivious of the irony, struck up "When the Saints Go Marching In"!

As successor to Jim Hoffa, "Saint Fitz" had opened new vistas of labor racketeering opportunity for the Mafia. And marching with him were some of those who had been exposed by the McClellan Senate Rackets Committee twenty years before. Under Saint Fitz they were prospering more than ever. In step with the company were Big Bill Presser, Salvatore Provenzano, and Frank Matula.

There had been rank-and-file rumblings about their leaders excesses and about crooked deals between Teamster officials and employers that shortchanged the union member. Now, secure in his wealth and with the knowledge that the delegates' own salaries and perquisites as officers depended on him, Fitzsimmons showed his contempt for Pete Camarata in the audience and fellow dissidents back home.

Usually a genial fellow who rarely raises his voice in anger, Fitzsimmons, opening the convention, made a blunder Hoffa never would have made. He blurted: "To those who say it is time to reform this organization, and it's time officers stopped selling out the members, I say to them, 'Go to Hell!' "

It was a gesture of arrogance and contempt for the dues-paying rank and filer that Fitzsimmons would try to explain away for some time to come. The contempt and arrogance were further reflected in Pete's reception on the convention floor.

Pete had hoped to propose and discuss constitutional amendments dealing with rank-and-file voting rights and with official corruption. In line with Teamster rules, he had submitted his proposals to Teamster headquarters in advance of the convention, for inclusion in the printed convention agenda. But they had been excluded. Seemingly, someone at Teamster headquarters had simply thrown them away. So Pete got up on the convention floor to press his amendments in person.

One amendment called for the expulsion of any officer who took an employer's bribe. Before Pete could finish reading it, a delegate bellowed from a floor microphone: "I wish he [Camarata] would stop wasting the convention's time!"

When Pete offered his second proposal—to reduce Teamster officers' salaries—a storm of catcalls and boos drowned him out.

As a gesture of rank-and-file dissent, Pete had also intended to vote against the reelection of Fitzsimmons and his slate. Election is by voice vote, so that it is a brave man, indeed, who stands up to be counted against a convention juggernaut. But Pete didn't even get a chance to do that.

"Everyone was so psyched up, marching and shouting, that I didn't know whether I'd get out of there alive if I voted," Pete said later.

As it was, Pete almost "didn't get out of there alive" anyway. As the convention ended, Pete dropped in at a "victory cocktail party" hosted by the reelected Fitzsimmons. With him was his ex-wrestler friend, Don Combs. Pete and Combs had become well-known and well-harassed figures at the convention; when Combs, no delegate, took a seat in the gallery, goons sat behind him, taunting him and kicking the back of his seat with their heavy boots. Now, at the Fitzsimmons party, when some of the heavies began to glare at Camarata and his friend, Pete told Combs that it was time to leave and asked a security guard to accompany them out of the hotel. Instead, the guard called several Teamster sergeants-at-arms.

These escorted the two rank and filers to the street. As Pete turned to thank them, one escorter felled Pete with a round-house blow to the face. Then, as Pete lay stunned on the sidewalk, the jackbooted sergeant-at-arms kicked him heavily in the head. Pete's friend, too, had been knocked down in the meanwhile.

"We were about to be ripped wide open," Pete's friend recalled, "when a big black guy wearing a delegate's badge knocked the kicker down." The knockdown saved Pete's skull and probably his life.

A Las Vegas policeman had come up. Instead of taking the sergeants-at-arms to the stationhouse, he told the dazed Camarata: "Get out of town, buddy, and get out fast."

When Pete asked for police protection to the airport, the policeman turned and walked away. Pete's head was throbbing. His right eye was closed, and when he went back to his room to pack, he could see in his bathroom mirror that the right side of his face was a grotesque and swollen purple. Pete and his friend hurried to their rented car. But they didn't head for the airport. "We were afraid they would be laying for us there," Pete said later. Instead, they turned southwest and headed for Los Angeles, 285 miles away. Pete had come to the convention with high hopes of getting a hearing for rank-and-file dissatisfaction. He fled the convention in fear of his life.

At Los Angeles, Pete drove directly to a meeting of dissidents from Teamster locals in the area. They had come to discuss changes in their locals' by-laws to permit the rank-and-file election of business agents. Instead, they listened, first with disbelief then with rising anger, as Pete recounted his Las Vegas ordeal.

"We all knew it was bad," Pete told his fellow rank and filers. "But we didn't know how really bad it was. After all, I was an elected delegate and I expected to have some credibility at the convention. Here is what I got instead." Pete pointed to his right eye. Then, pulling up his shirt, Pete showed them his bruised ribs.

"Looking back," Pete said later, "that Las Vegas convention was a turning point. When Fitz gaveled down every one of our proposals and told us to go to hell besides, he dramatized our helplessness and moved a lot of Teamsters who were on the fence.''

Soon, Pete's fellow Teamsters in Los Angeles were on the telephone to Seattle, Cleveland, Denver, and to other cities of organized rank-and-file dissidents. A flourishing underground Teamster press already existed. In Seattle, it was *The Fifth Wheel*, in Cleveland it was *The National Convoy*. Pete had his own newspaper which he financed out of his wages. Through this underground press, thousands of Teamsters had a worm's-eye view of the Teamster convention—from the bottom up—as Pete had experienced it.

Riding the wave of rank-and-file indignation, Pete and his fellow rebels called a Teamster convention of their own—for rank and filers only. To Kent, Ohio, in September of 1976 came 250 delegates from forty-two locals in fourteen states. Unlike the porkchopper delegates to the Las Vegas convention, these delegates were clad in jeans instead of tailored, hand-stitched outfits. They paid their own way, some coming from California by bus; they slept two and three in a room. Instead of a gambling town, their meeting site was a college campus, that of Kent State University.

In a borrowed lecture hall, Pete and his grim-faced friends came to grips with the underlying irony of their predicament. In a free society, a union is a civil-rights instrument, empowered by law to use the collective strength of the members to exert a voice over the conditions of their work. Yet, although Pete and his friends belonged to the most powerful of all unions, they had no more voice over their pay and working conditions than if they belonged to no union at all.

Wages, hours, and benefits were negotiated for them at the top by their president, Fitzsimmons, and a committee of aides meeting with a national committee of employers. These terms, embodied in a national agreement, were supposed to be ratified by the members whose lives they affected. But ratification was a farce, and Teamster officialdom seemed to regard the contract as secret, classified material.

In Pete's local, at meetings to ratify the agreement, the local's president would rattle off the contract—some forty typed pages—in a monotone and at such speed that members could not remember it, let alone comprehend it, as a prelude to a vote. When members brought recorders to tape the contract, goons smashed the equipment and threw the offending rank and filers out of the hall. Nor were officials in a hurry to make printed copies of the contract available.

"It ain't ready yet," Pete was told at his union hall in September—five months after the contract was negotiated.

During the preceding summer (1976), frustrated Teamsters who haul cars away from Detroit auto plants went on strike—not against their employers, the car-hauling companies, but against their own union. They contended the International union didn't give them a fair shake in voting on their contract.

With the denial of a voice over their wages and benefits went another evil that affected the members' livelihoods: sweetheart deals, in which an employer paid off a crooked Teamster official to permit him to pay substandard wages. Sweetheart deals were rampant. In Pete's own local, officers turned their backs as one company hired "part-timers" and paid them $2.60 *less* per hour than going Teamster wages—a loss to the driver of $106 a week!

At first, to cope with the contract problem, some of the rebel rank and filers meeting at the Kent, Ohio, convention had formed a dissident movement called Teamsters for a Decent Contract (TDC). But when they realized there could be no decent contract without union democracy, they had renamed their rebellion Teamsters for a Democratic Union (TDU).

The question before the convention, then, was how to

achieve union democracy inside the Teamsters, how to give the union back to its members.

The obvious answer was to win a voice at the national convention, for it was the convention that elected the officers who negotiated the wages. It was the convention that amended the constitution. It was the convention that served as a supreme court in settling members' grievances, whether against their own officials or against employers.

But winning a rank-and-file voice at the convention would be difficult. For the Teamster constitution limited convention attendance almost wholly to Teamster officeholders. To have a voice at the convention, Teamster rebels would have to elect new slates of officers from their ranks. This, in turn, posed problems, since local incumbents had many weapons with which to knock down heads raised in opposition.

First, there was the threat to the dissidents' livelihood. Although Pete had held his job for six years, he was summarily fired in April of 1976. Behind the firing, as fellow workers saw it, was union pressure on the employer. When Pete's fellow members threatened to strike and shut down the warehouse, Pete was restored to his job.[1] But some of Pete's followers didn't fare as well. Four of the most able of them lost their jobs and have been out of work for months.

Curiously, employers who would benefit from honest unionism, conspire with corrupt union officials to harass dissidents. Some do it under union pressure, but others do it willingly to protect cozy deals with union leaders.

"If the union and the company want to get you, they can get you," Pete told me. And his ex-wrestler friend, who had accompanied Pete to the Las Vegas convention, added: "My terminal manager kept waving his finger in my face the other

---

1. In March 1977 Camarata was expelled from Local 299 because of "conduct unbecoming a union member," but reinstated by court order.

day, cussing me out and just trying to get me to punch him. I
would have, too, if Pete here hadn't gotten me out of there.''

To the threat against one's livelihood is added the threat
against one's life. Pete lost a key TDU member when threatening telephone calls panicked the man's wife. The man, white-
faced, told Pete he couldn't come to TDU meetings anymore.
In Cleveland, Teamster rebels, aware of their local's ties with
the Mafia, greet each other on the street with: ''What! Are you
still alive?''

At the union hall, local leaders don't have to rely on intimi-
dation alone to silence opposition. When Pete tried to intro-
duce motions to reform election procedures, the local's president would rule him out of order. Then, when Pete and his
followers persisted in pressing their motions, the local's leader
would summarily adjourn the meeting and stamp out of the
hall.

''*They* won't let me let you make those kinds of motions,''
his local's president explained to Pete privately. The ''they''
were the top officers at Teamster headquarters.

When Pete and his followers continued to ''make those
motions,'' local meetings were discontinued altogether. As of
September 1976, Local 299 had not held a regular meeting for
ten months.

In union dictatorships as in political ones, when all else fails
to discourage opposition, martial law is declared. In unions,
martial law—the suspension of all members' rights—takes the
form of trusteeship under a ''trustee'' named by the national
president. Pete's local staved off trusteeship shortly after the
Las Vegas convention only by threatening to take such a move
to court.

Fellow delegates to the rank-and-file convention could
match Pete's account of the difficulties involved in mounting
an opposition. Yet convention delegates felt that successful
local opposition and a take-over of local offices were possible if

rank and filers organized and had a battle plan. As a first step, the rank-and-file convention mapped an election strategy. Delegates would return to their union halls and seek changes in local by-laws that would permit mail-referendum elections and other balloting reforms. With this would go recruiting drives to build Teamsters for a Democratic Union to a size that would give rank and filers a feeling of "safety in numbers." As the meeting broke up, delegates vowed to elect at least half of the delegates to the next Teamster convention, four years away, from their own ranks.

Many Teamster rebellions have flared and died. Whether the current one, flying the banner of Teamsters for a Democratic Union, will succeed remains to be seen. Since TDU has already absorbed a half-dozen competing rebel movements, there is reason to believe it has better prospects of success than its predecessors.

Chapter Twenty-Five

THE CHANGING TEAMSTERS

EVEN WITH HOFFA gone, the International Brotherhood of Teamsters kept growing explosively, adding during each year as many members as are contained in some sizeable unions. And with growth went diversity. A great wave of white collar workers, nurses, pharmacists, teachers were flooding into the Teamsters—bringing hope of eventual change in the character of the union's leadership.

Already, in mid-1977 the image of the Teamsters as a union of physically durable, big-fisted and tough-talking truck drivers was out of date. Of the union's 2,000,000-odd members, only 700,000—about 30 percent—drive trucks. The other Teamsters administer schools, teach classes, sport masters degrees in social work, and care for the troubled. Teamsters tend kidney (dialysis) machines, man fire and police departments, write and broadcast news. They make coffins and clothes, can food, tune pianos, repair telephone lines, bake hamburger buns, sell in stores. Teamsters strap you in on airplanes and take dictation in business offices. There are

few occupations in which the Teamsters can't claim card hold-
ers. And in some, they are rapidly becoming the dominant
force. The Teamsters represent almost as many office and
store clerks as the 700,000-member Retail Clerks Union, and
are battling the 750,000-member Association of Federal, State
and Municipal Employes Union (AFL-CIO) for the number-
one position in the biggest remaining field for unionization—
that of public employment.

Already the biggest union, accounting for 10 percent of all
the 20,000,000 union members in the United States, the
Teamsters are also the fastest growing. They win most National Labor Relations Board elections and, in recent years,
have accounted for 20 percent of all new union members in the
country.

For this vast and diversified growth, Hoffa was largely responsible. Indeed, he laid the foundation for it when he was
but a local Teamster official in Detroit, still in his twenties.

Back in 1934, Hoffa watched, fascinated, as a union idea
fought for its life. The idea, improved and expanded by
Hoffa—and in part by his predecessor, Dave Beck—was to
change the Teamsters.

The idea belonged to a band of men who controlled Teamster Local 574 in Minneapolis. In the midst of the Great Depression, which had the unions gasping for their lives, the
brothers Vincent, Grant, and Miles Dunne and Farrell Dobbs
had a vision.

As trucks replaced railroads, these men felt that the
Teamsters were destined to dominate the labor scene. They
already controlled the truck terminals and the unloading in
Minneapolis. By insisting that Minneapolis union men would
not unload incoming trucks unless Teamsters were driving
them, they forced truck owners outside of Minneapolis to sign
their drivers into the Teamsters. These newly organized union

drivers could then organize other terminals, and this leapfrogging process could go on and on—corralling members into the Teamsters by the thousands.

Hoffa perceived that the Minneapolis Teamsters had fashioned an economic fist against which few employers could stand up. Inside this fist were the wheels that move goods in and out of virtually every business and industry in the country.

This control-of-the-wheels concept of Hoffa's lived after him as a chief driving force in shoveling new members into the Teamsters.

Paul Meyer, a pharmacist for twenty-three years and now a member of Las Vegas Teamster Local 995, tells why.

"About five years ago," Meyer recalls, "the drug chain for which eleven of us pharmacists worked doubled its prescription business but wouldn't put on additional pharmacists. When we formed a guild to demand additional help, the management wouldn't even talk to us. So we went to Las Vegas Teamster Local 995, which has three thousand members and represents hotel employees as well as truck drivers. We had heard the Teamsters had clout, but didn't really appreciate how much. Within two weeks, the management put on another pharmacist and raised our pay. That was in 1972, when we were earning $6 an hour. Now we're up to $10.50 an hour—a 75 percent increase—which brings our yearly pay and fringes up to $21,840."

Whence the Teamster clout?

"They can stop deliveries, and without deliveries where would the drugstore be?" pharmacist-Teamster Meyer asked.

When two hundred pharmacists employed by a southeast Texas chain left the Retail Clerks Union recently to join the Teamsters, a local Teamster leader explained: "There's not a helluva lot the Retail Clerks could do to stop the switchover. For one thing, the pharmacists voted to do so in an NLRB election. For another, we control the truck drivers and the warehousemen at the drug wholesalers'. If the Retail Clerks or management act up, we can stop deliveries to drugstores any time we want, and there's not a damn thing they can do about it.''

In the early sixties, Hoffa, ever sensitive to further growth possibilities, sensed some nationwide trends that in time further expanded Teamster membership and brought some strange bedfellows into the Teamsters.

Hoffa noticed that the composition of the American labor force was changing dramatically. For the first time, in the early 1960s, those who provide services—teaching, carrying the mail, fixing teeth, writing magazine articles— outnumbered those who produce things: baking bread, building homes, harvesting crops, digging coal out of the ground. This shift toward white-collar and professional-service providers and away from blue-collar producers was to move so swiftly that in time fully two-thirds of the work force would provide services, and only one-third would do the producing.

Within this shift toward the white-collar pursuits, Hoffa noted another—the swift growth of public employment. Federal, state, and local employment was on its way toward tripling the pre-World War II figure. Unionization in this field was gaining rapidly, aided in part by growing restiveness by public employees who felt they were being underpaid and aided, too, by growing public acceptance of public-employee unions.

So, in 1965 Hoffa asked one of his protégés, a thirty-five-year organizer in Hoffa's Detroit Local 299 by the name of Joe Valenti, to "take a look at Detroit's public employees" as a possible new source of union members.

Valenti brought back so radiant a vision of prospects in the public-service field that Hoffa chartered a Teamster public-employees union—Local 214—and turned it over to Valenti with the words: "Go get 'em, Joe."

The first group Joe "got" were the 1,300 drivers of municipal street department equipment—traditional Teamster jobs.
But Valenti soon moved out into employment areas not so
traditional for the Teamsters. He became the sparkplug of
organizing drives that helped turn the Teamsters into the leading rival of the top union in the public-employment field: the
Federal, State and Municipal Employees Association (AFL-
CIO)—750,000 members strong. And among those that Valenti organized were the police.

For curious reasons of his own, Hoffa had long wanted to
get the country's police under the Teamsters' wing. Perhaps it
was an idea conceived by puckish underworld cronies who
relished the idea of their pal, Jimmy, winning economic benefits for cops—or giving orders to them. Perhaps it was Hoffa's
own dead-end-kid gesture of spitting in the eye of the Establishment.

In any case, back in 1958 Hoffa tried his hand at organizing
the country's biggest police force—that of New York City.
This was as curious an undertaking at the time as it was
foolhardy. For one thing, the police-organizing effort coincided with Hoffa's appearance before Senator McClellan's
Senate Rackets Committee and the exposure of his gangster ties. For another thing, public fear of and hostility to
police unionization—an aftermath of the Boston police strike—
still lingered. The then New York City Police Commissioner Stephen P. Kennedy expressed both fear and hostility
when he warned: "If the police are unionized [by Hoffa],
I advise the people not to waste their money paying a police commissioner a salary. Hoffa would be police commissioner."

Hoffa thought it the better part of valor to back away, and
the Teamsters didn't get the New York City police.

The goblin of hoodlum domination conjured up in the late
1950s has persisted into the late 1970s. But curiously, it

seemed to scare everybody except a growing number of police themselves.

The man whom Hoffa had exhorted to "go get 'em, Joe," was largely responsible.

By 1977, Valenti had become a central figure in organizing police around the country. Thanks largely to him, the Teamsters—still exiled from the AFL-CIO as corrupt—was a major spokesman for policemen's economic needs by representing some two hundred police departments of varying size around the country.

Every policeman in Alaska is a Teamster. So is every lieutenant and captain in Michigan's state police. The Teamsters bargain for the police of San Diego, California, and Flint, Michigan; they are strong and growing stronger in Ohio, Illinois, California, Pennsylvania, and Iowa, and have active organizing drives going in Cleveland and Toledo.

Indeed, to some Teamsters and police-association executives, the country's police constitute a ripe plum ready to fall to the Teamsters, largely for lack of competition.

There are some 450,000 to 500,000 police in the United States, according to Edward J. Kiernan, president of the International Conference of Police Associations, an umbrella organization that embraces 279 individual police associations, most of them called police benevolent associations.

Only 170,000 work under collective bargaining agreements. Local chapters of the Fraternal Order of Police negotiate for some 138,000 of these in thirty-eight states. The Teamsters represent an estimated 20,000, and the American Federation of Federal, State and Municipal Employees (AFL-CIO) another 10,000.

Since none of the Teamsters' rivals command the financial, professional, and political resources of the Teamsters, even the rivals' leaders admit that the Teamsters have the edge in organizing the 300,000 police that still remain nonunion.

"The Fraternal Order of Police (FOP) can't compete with the Teamsters as a police union," the FOP's national secretary, William Bannister, a retired captain of the Flint, Michigan, police department said. "The FOP doesn't have the financial muscle," says Sergeant Bannister. "Most FOP lodges charge their members $3 and $4 a month and have trouble collecting even this little. On the other hand, Valenti's Local 214 of Detroit charges its 3,000 police members $17 a month and gets it—because of the solid gains in police income the local has already provided. In addition, Local 214 gets $1,800 monthly from the Teamsters International for organizing purposes. And it also gets legal services from the International worth an estimated $100,000 yearly. The Teamsters bring in their high-powered lawyers and they tie the politicians into knots." Not only is Sergeant Bannister secretary of FOP, but he is also a member of a police department that is affiliated with the Teamsters.

The Teamsters' ability to provide professional negotiators is particularly attractive to police.

A Michigan state police sergeant explained: "The police are a quasi-military organization. So it's never possible for a subordinate in a police or military situation to be effective in negotiations. But an outsider can negotiate as an equal, and say what he wants without fear of retaliation."

The Teamsters got their foot in the door of police unionization in 1967, two years after Hoffa chartered Local 214. Michigan's state legislature had passed a law permitting binding arbitration to settle police and fireman's disputes with local governments. The command unit of Ann Arbor's police department, consisting of sergeants up through deputy chief, promptly knocked on Joe Valenti's door.

"We were being used," Joe Valenti recalls. "The cops were telling Ann Arbor's city fathers, 'If you don't give us what we want, we're going to the Teamsters.'"

Local 214 took on the cops anyway, and carried them through arbitration and to a $2,000-a-year raise. Next, the Teamsters won an even more impressive $4,200-a-year wage and benefit raise for Flint's city police. The Fraternal Order of Police, which had been doing the bargaining for the Flint police, had been settling for $500 to $700 yearly increases without going to arbitration, because of legal and other costs. So the rush was on from the FOP to the Teamsters.

While the professional police associations seemed resigned at first to let the Teamsters take over the bargaining, some have changed their minds and are establishing statewide collective-bargaining services to challenge the Teamster drive for police members. Whether the police benevolent associations and the Fraternal Order of Police chapters will succeed in slowing the Teamsters remains to be seen. But with a foothold in Michigan—three thousand members in 131 police departments—the Teamsters are moving out into other states. As news of Valenti's success in winning substantial gains for his police members gets around, emissaries trek to Detroit to seek his organizing help. With it, sheriffs and police departments in Virginia, Indiana, Illinois, California, Florida, Minnesota, and Pennsylvania have affiliated with the Teamsters. And under Valenti's guidance, campaigns are under way to organize the police of Cleveland and Toledo, Ohio.

Both towns are Teamster strongholds. They are dominated by Ohio Teamster boss William Presser, who, in turn, is dominated by and takes orders from the Cleveland Mafia. And this raises the kind of question that former New York Police Commissioner Kennedy raised when Hoffa tried to organize the big city's police: "If Cleveland and Toledo police join the Teamsters, will Big Bill Presser become the police commissioner of the two cities?"

Valenti and the police he bargains for have several answers to questions like these.

"We tell our police members," says Valenti, " 'You're a law enforcement officer first and a Teamster second.' "

As for the Teamsters' reputation for corruption and ties to organized crime, Sergeant Bays of the Michigan state police observed: "We're connected with Local 214, and nobody can tell me any of their officers has done anything wrong. We have checked Valenti and his people out from every possible angle. They're clean."

Yet, to make it easier for some state police to swallow the idea that they're connected with the notorious union, their leaders have resorted to a conscience-salving device.

They say they are affiliated with—but have not joined—the Teamsters. The Michigan state police, for instance, benefit from Teamster services, such as contract negotiations, grievance settlement, and legal representation. But the state police don't vote in Local 214 elections, and don't get involved in the local's operations. The police of San Diego, California, have chosen the same affiliation device. They can therefore say, "We aren't Teamsters; they just do our bargaining for us." But Joe Valenti says that many police organizations choose the affiliation method as a cautious first step but change to full membership because they want a voice in the conduct of union affairs.

If the Teamsters and the police make an odd couple, what about Teamsters and nurses? New York Teamster Local 803 has printed up stationery that bears in its upper lefthand corner a postage-stamp-size picture of a black-haired beauty of a nurse in pert cap and immaculate uniform. The stationery is for the use of the local's "nurses' division," which embraces 225 registered nurses employed by a private hospital. Other divisions of the local represent security guards, off-track-betting managers, racetrack undercover agents, and truck drivers.

How did nurses get to become fellow Teamsters of undercover agents and off-track-betting managers? Charlene Doak, a registered nurse specializing in pediatrics, explains: "The nurses at our hospital were underpaid, and received no extra pay for working weekends and holidays."

How do the nurses feel about the Teamsters' reputation for corruption? Here the answer was both innocent and cynical. "When our committee approached the Teamster local's leaders," Charlene Doak recalls, "they all came nicely dressed, not packing any guns—and we didn't see any evidence of crookedness."

The hoodlums in the union?

"That's at a much higher, more complex level," Charlene Doak said. "Sure, we know about it, but we feel disassociated from it. We're not affected directly." Here the note of cynicism entered that we heard from other professionals who had joined the Teamsters. "In every profession, every walk of life, there's some corruption, somebody getting paid off," Mrs. Doak said. "What can you do? Our local is clean, and that's all we care about."

Our early unions began life by representing workers in a single craft. Sam Gompers, the father of the American labor movement, belonged to a union for cigarmakers only. George Meany, the eighty-three-year-old president of the AFL-CIO, came out of a union for plumbers only. The Teamsters, too, started out with one craft, the drivers of horse teams. But a curious union philosophy, peculiar to the Teamsters—and tailored to the empire-building visions of Jim Hoffa—changed all that. To protect truck drivers' jobs, as the Teamster philosophy went, you must organize related fields. For example, the truck driver who hauls fruits and vegetables to a cannery may be idled by a cannery workers' strike. So, to protect the truck driver's job, you organize and control the cannery workers. Next, to protect the cannery workers, you organize the farm laborer in the fields, because if *they* strike, the cannery workers will be idle, and that, in turn, will idle the truck driver. The Teamsters' organizing vistas, then, have no horizons. And this is reflected in the Teamsters' constitution:

"This organization has jurisdiction over all teamsters, chauffeurs, warehousemen and helpers; all who are employed on or around horses, harness, carriages, automobiles, trucks, trailers, and all other vehicles hauling, carrying, or conveying freight, merchandise or materials; automotive sales, service and maintenance employes . . . persons engaged in loading or unloading freight . . . to and from any type of vehicle; all classes of dairy employes, inside and outside, including salesmen; brewery and soft drink workers; workers in ice cream plants; all other workers . . . in the manufacture, processing, sale and distribution of food . . .; all truck terminal employes; cannery workers; *and all other workers where the security of the bargaining positions of the above classifications requires the organization of such other workers.*" (Italics added.)

To this elastic jurisdiction, Hoffa added incentives for organizing and lubricated them with cash.

Each of the Teamsters' nine hundred-odd locals is headed by a full-time official—a president or secretary-treasurer who is, in effect, in business for himself, providing bargaining and other services to members. If his service-buying membership is small, the leader's income will be small. If the local is big, so is the leader's income. Don Peters, president of Chicago Local 743, the Teamsters biggest, with twenty thousand members, pays himself $80,000 yearly. The incentive to build the union is obvious. And Teamster headquarters encourages such expansion with cash. Of the monthly $1.65 per member that each local sends up to the Teamster International, 10 cents comes back to a regional Teamster conference for distribution to locals to finance organizing campaigns.

From such dimes, the locals of the Central States Conference have $600,000 yearly to spend on acquiring new members, plus their own funds, and special grants from the International.

To the organizing cash, Hoffa added political clout. In this, he had the help of numbers. In St. Louis, where the Teamsters claim fifty-five thousand members, the union has long been a political force with a voice in community affairs. In Chicago, Ray Schoessling, the union's secretary-treasurer, was long regarded as second in influence only to his close friend, the late Mayor Richard Daley. In Detroit, where the Teamsters claim 60,000 members, Hoffa was long a force in municipal and state politics. By putting political power together with cash and incentives and boundless jurisdiction, Hoffa developed a self-propelling, perpetual-motion organizing machine.

A wag once observed of another aggressive union, "They organize everything that begins with an *A—a* pickle factory, *a* pants factory, *a* camera manufacturing plant." So do the Teamsters. Indeed, every salaried and hourly-wage employee in the country who doesn't already belong to a union is fair game for the Teamster organizer.

Even school administrators.

Duncan Hill Hodel, a San Francisco school principal, was on the school board when the city's school superintendent ordered 126 other fellow school administrators fired in 1971.

"None of us had ever been members of a union, but we knew we needed someone to represent us," Hodel recalls. "We turned first to a union of municipal workers, which didn't seem to be able to help us. Then we went to a Teamster local that represents public-service employees and automobile salesmen. We just signed cards showing that we wanted the Teamsters to go to bat for us, and they did. Within a matter of weeks, the Teamsters blocked the school superintendent's order to fire us. And they showed they had clout at the state level, too. When the legislature passed two bills to remove tenure [lifetime job security] from school administrators, the Teamsters convinced the then Governor Ronald Reagan to veto the bills.

"Since we've had the Teamsters represent us," says Hodel, "we've never been transferred, demoted, or pushed around."

The influx of police, nurses, school principals, poses a central question. As the Teamsters absorb ever-greater numbers of professionals, technicians, and educated public servants, can the present minority of truck drivers remain in the driver's seat? And can the underworld retain its grip on the union?

The answer lies with such new members as registered nurse Charlene Doak. Charlene, having wetted her feet in the union movement, has become an ardent unionist with prospects of becoming a professional labor leader. Although she is in line for the job of head nurse at her hospital, Charlene has decided against accepting a promotion. Being head nurse—a managerial job—would bar her from union activity, and "right now," she says, "my union work is important to me."

When Bill Hagner, the president of Charlene's local, makes organizing trips to out-of-state hospitals, Charlene occupies a speaker's platform with him, as she recently did at conferences on organizing nurses in North Carolina and Virginia. She is also a trustee of a special pension fund set up for the nurses in her local. When Charlene Doak is eligible to run for office in the general local—two years of membership are required—Bill Hagner expects her to do so, and with other white-collar persons, eventually move into higher positions of leadership in the Teamsters.

Joe Valenti of Detroit Local 214 also believes that white-collars and professionals are destined for a role in running the Teamsters. "It'll happen," says Valenti, "as more public employees, professionals, and other nontrucking occupations join the union and start to move up through the ranks and make their needs known."

But don't look for the change overnight. The take-over from the present high command of hard-bitten ex-truck drivers may not become visible for at least a decade, perhaps more. Yet, if the Teamsters continue to acquire such strange bedfellows as nurses, school principals, police, teachers, can the birth of a new union be long delayed?

ACKNOWLEDGMENTS I CAN MAKE
AND SOME I CANNOT

REGRETTABLY, SOME OF those who contributed the most revealing insights and information about Jim Hoffa cannot be acknowledged or credited here. To do so would endanger their lives.

Since prior work had made me *persona non grata* at Teamster headquarters, and the current work would depict further evils, truck drivers, employers, Teamster officeholders who talked feared union reprisals. Others feared an even stronger force than the Teamsters—one that could decree a man's disappearance.

Yet, some talked out of love for Hoffa; he had been a trusted and respected friend. Others talked out of hate for him; he had been an infuriating taskmaster, rewarding twelve-hour workdays and almost continuous travel away from families with violent and demeaning tongue-lashings. Both admirers and haters would talk only in out-of-the-way hotel rooms, in automobiles—safe from electronic and human ears—and in one instance, only in the privacy of a steam bath—just as in a grade B movie.

"Remember, you never saw me," was the word.

Of those courageous ones who talked for the record, I owe a special debt to rank and file Teamster members such as Pete Camarata of Detroit, who suffered a cruel beating at the Teamster convention of 1976 and risked his Teamster member's card for fighting for a democratic union; to Bob Smith and John Markarian also of Detroit; to Steve Kindred and Stanley Flowers of Cleveland; to Lloyd Barrentine of Little Rock, Arkansas; to

Travis Dumas of Miami; and to Vincent "Jim" Refino of Yonkers, New York—to name only a few.

Of the "stand-up guys" among Teamster officeholders, I am indebted to Nick Morrissey, a Boston Teamster leader and confidant of Hoffa's, and to Ed Partin who, with two 300-pound bodyguards hovering nearby, told of his problems of running an honest Teamster local in Baton Rouge and of mob and union ties that reach all the way from New Jersey to his Baton Rouge local's territory.

II

A book seldom is the work of only one mind and one pair of hands—or, as in this case, of one pair of legs. And as in the theatre, it needs an angel, someone to watch over it and sustain the writer and the work until publication. The angel for *Desperate Bargain,* as in the case of some distinguished predecessors—Cornelius Ryan's *The Longest Day,* Alex Haley's *Roots,* James Michener's *Centennial*—was the *Reader's Digest.* At the suggestion of my present editor, Fulton Oursler, Jr., I had embarked in the summer of 1975 on an article with the working title "The Last Days of Jimmy Hoffa." But with the backing of Tony Oursler and Edward T. Thompson, now the *Digest*'s editor-in-chief, the article grew into a book. This brought into play the invaluable and considerable research resources of the *Digest.*

For instance, my then investigative assistant, Jennifer Bolch, was in the air constantly for some eighteen months, turning up pieces of the Hoffa jigsaw puzzle in Detroit, Chicago, Miami, New York City, Los Angeles, Atlanta, Newark, New Jersey—and in Yonkers, New York, Little Rock, Arkansas—and wherever else the trail led.

For editing backup, my chief debt is to my "in-house editor," my wife, Frances Rockmore Velie, a writer in her own right. When her ear for the rhythm of written words rebels at what I submit to her, I have learned over the years not to argue, but to return to the typewriter to reorganize, rewrite, and to tighten and brighten. To my "outside" editor, Susanne W. Howard of Reader's Digest Press, I am indebted for additional editorial backstopping, and particularly for the excision of repetitious material. Three heads, it seems, are better than two.

Chris Kirby of the *Reader's Digest* research department, who keeps writers honest by checking their sources, tracked down factual errors with the devotion of a bloodhound, and so, hopefully, kept to a minimum the errors in dates, places, figures, that inevitably creep into a manuscript.

The title, *Desperate Bargain,* I proudly admit, is not my invention, but that of my elder son, Alan R. Velie, an associate professor of English literature at the University of Oklahoma. He created the phrase in his doctoral thesis to describe the Faustian bargains with evil that recur in literature.

III

As a journalist, the author relied as much as possible on interviews. These ranged from a two-hour conversation with Jim Hoffa about a year before he disappeared, to continuous conversations with high Justice Department officials in charge of the Hoffa investigation, to conversations with informants—about two hundred in all—who, besides federal, state and local law enforcers, included those who knew Hoffa best: his lawyers and his colleagues (that is, those who would talk), and one member of the Hoffa family. To some of the interviewees, Jennifer Bolch and I returned as often as a dozen or more times.

Special mention must go to a group of lawyers: To Edward Bennett Williams of Washington, D.C., who served as Teamster general counsel for fourteen years and so could shed important light on "life with Hoffa"; to Jacob Kossman, the Philadelphia trial lawyer whose capacious memory dug up memorable scenes from Hoffa's final two trials; to Morris Shenker of Las Vegas, who handled Hoffa's attempt to curtail his prison sentence; to Leonard Boudin, the New York constitutional lawyer, who appealed to the federal courts to remove the restraints against Hoffa's return to union work, and to Leonard Wilson of Las Vegas, whose eyes and ears escape little of importance that "goes down" there.

As for the million-odd written words about Hoffa, perhaps the most valuable were those of Walter Sheridan, an old friend and companion-in-arms, in his book, *The Fall and Rise of Jim Hoffa*. As the head of Bob Kennedy's "Hoffa Unit," Walter Sheridan could do what few other writers could do: compile an encyclopedic blow-by-blow account—from his own insider's vantage point—into the legal tracking-down and destruction of Hoffa.

Clark R. Mollenhoff's *Game Plan for Disaster* provided missing pieces of the story concerning Richard Nixon's pardon of Hoffa—and of the Nixon-Fitzsimmons conspiracy to prevent Hoffa from ever returning to Teamster power. Victor Navasky's *Kennedy Justice* provided a dramatic narrative of the epic Hoffa-Bob Kennedy struggle.

The reporting of A. H. Raskin in *The New York Times*, of Harry Bernstein in the Los Angeles *Times*, of Ralph Orr in the Detroit *Free Press*, and of reporters in *The Wall Street Journal* were indispensable for background. In addition, Ralph Orr generously shared his on-the-spot Detroit knowledge about Hoffa with our Jennifer Bolch. So did Mairye Jayne Wogge, of the Cleveland *Plain Dealer*. Although I had looked into the Teamsters Central States pension fund as early as 1962, I had turned to other journalistic concerns later. So Jim Drinkhall's articles on the Teamsters' biggest pension fund, published in the Los Angeles-based magazine *Overdrive* from 1970 through 1976, provided valuable leads for our own investigations.

With the work of fellow reporters went generous help from their newspaper libraries. Librarians at the Los Angeles *Times,* the *Newark-Star Ledger,* the Las Vegas *Sun,* the Detroit *News* were generous with their time and their facilities.

A word about documents. Senate Investigating Committee testimony, transcripts of Hoffa's three major trials and civil suits, as well as those of some of his colleagues, corporate financial reports filed with the SEC, and union financial reports to the Labor Department contained nuggets of information that could not have been readily available in any other form. Without the affidavits of former Attorney General John Mitchell and former White House counsel John Dean—as contained in one Hoffa suit, for instance—it would not have been possible to reconstruct the story told in Chapter Sixteen, how The Watergate White House Helps Steal a Union.

A word of gratitude to Barney McHenry, general counsel for the *Reader's Digest,* who scrutinizes my manuscripts with a legal—yet friendly—eye, eager to preserve as well as protect.

And to my typist, Sherley A. Raices, whose devotion is above and beyond the call of duty.

Lester Velie
June 1977

INDEX